How to play the piano despite years of lessons

What music is and how to make it at home

By Ward Cannel
and Fred Marx

A Crown & Bridge Book

Library of Congress Catalogue Card No. 76-4037
ISBN (Hard cover): 0-385-14262-5
ISBN (Paperbound): 0-385-14263-3

Set in phototype by John Romano Inc.
Elmwood Park, N.J.
Printed in the United States of America

Painting, *The Kreutzer Sonata*, Rene Prinet, 1898
Courtesy of Dana Perfumes Corp.

despite years of lessons

What music is and how to make it at home

An original work created and produced by
Crown & Bridge, Publishers
P.O.Box 1604
New York, N.Y. 10159

Book and cover design
Mary Coyne Aiken

Art and illustration
Ingrid Allex

INTRO

Norman Lloyd is an
accomplished composer
and arranger.
He has also been
Director of Education
of the Juilliard School,
Dean of the
Oberlin Conservatory
and Director for
Arts and Humanities of
the Rockefeller Foundation.

This is an honest book. It is a book about many things, not the least of which is music.

In part, it is a book by someone who, naively, tried to find out about music from those who, ostensibly teachers, tried to put up pedantic barriers. In part, it is a book by a true trouvere —someone who is a finder. In part, it is a "how-to" book which pretends to teach you about a *small* area of music: popular "standards" of the 20s, 30s, 40s, 50s, etc.

It is true that this book could teach you how to harmonize most of the best-known, best-loved tunes. It can tell you how to make accompaniments, how to make simple variations, how to inject a bit of countermelody, how to fool around and make new, save the mark, harmonizations of tunes that everyone knows how to harmonize.

But don't be fooled. *This is a subversive book.* It is a book of discovery. It is "every man a king" —or, at least, everyone his own judge of good and bad.

The result is not a true textbook, in the "educationist" sense. It is not built on what other writers of textbooks have written. And yet it is a textbook, in the true amateur tradition of that great mid-nineteenth century theorist, General Virues y Spinola, who "discovered" the theory of "Amphibophony," or the secret harmonic progression of the masters. And as the good General found a truth, so has this book. It has found one of the fundamental truths about music: *as ye fool around, so shall ye find.*

Within a consciously prescribed area, this book is an approach to music which is honest. One can extrapolate from it— but its basic reason for being is its simplified demonstration of how to use a few basic musical tools so that one can, if he follows the suggestions, learn how to sit down at the piano and have fun.

Maybe the book needs to add more drills, more technical work. A professional musician might fault it a thousand ways from up. But this book has managed to create its own little world of musical theory —which could very well be a microcosm of the larger world of music.

Musicians might be infuriated by this book. Lovers of music —the true amateurs— could very well learn much from it. Musically, the territory is circumscribed. But, to paraphrase the First of the Aeneids: *Hic ego metas rerum, tempora pone* (Bounds *are* to be set and limited).

But anyone who plays this book through to the end will know more than just what he thinks he has accomplished. He will have come close to the true meaning of music.

NORMAN LLOYD

Contents

Who is allowed
to read this book

THIS IS NOT A BOOK FOR EVERYBODY.

It is certainly not for people who want to play *The Minute Waltz* in a minute (or even two). That is to say, this is not a book for people whose aim is only to *play* music. In order to play exactly what the composer has written, you have to hit the proper note in the proper manner with the proper finger at the proper moment, properly soft or loud.

If that is what you want, then you have come to the wrong place. What you need is a teacher and a lot of scales and exercises to practice until you become skilled at that sort of super touch-typing at the keyboard.

But if you want to *make* music, then this book is for you —*whether you've had piano lessons or not*. If you want to make music at the piano with show tunes, popular songs, Christmas carols, hymns and the like, this book is for you. It will tell you how to take a tune, a melody, and turn it into a whole lot of music by knowing what you are doing and why you are doing it.

That's not a great deal to know. Just about all our music —from our symphonies and our operas to our folk songs— is made from a few simple ideas and a few almost child-like facts. And as you will see, you know most of these elementary ideas and facts already. (And you've known them since you were a child.) It remains only to see how they apply to the piano keyboard.

Consequently, the only exercise —if you can call it that— is an occasional sample or fragment of a number to try on your own piano, no matter now haltingly or tentatively you play it. This is, after all, a book of knowledge about music. And music does not really exist unless you can hear it.

THE CONTENTS OF THIS BOOK are served up in ten parts. Each part provides enough knowledge to make *some* music at the piano. But, of course, the more parts of the book you know, the more music you can make.

But you can stop anywhere along the way —even for weeks at a time— and come back again without having lost any ground. That is because you are acquiring *knowledge and ideas* —things you cannot forget once you understand them.

However, to use this book to its greatest advantage, you ought to bring some knowledge to it. So, this book is for you if you know two rudimentary facts at the outset.

1. You should know where middle C is.

The answer to that question is, middle C is in the middle of the keyboard. And if you don't like that answer, then this book is not for you because it is out to de-mystify music and bring its components down to eye level.

2. You should know the names of the lines and spaces of the treble clef so that you can pick out a single-note, one-finger tune —no matter how badly.

If you've forgotten everything you ever knew about that matter —or if you never knew anything about it at all— take a look at the back of any music paper notebook. It's all said right there. Or, if you would prefer to take a lesson from a teacher on this subject, one lesson ought to do it.

But if it seems like too much work to refresh your memory or to learn the names of five lines and four spaces, then this book is not for you. But don't take it to heart. This book is not for everybody.

And it's a good thing, too. A book for everybody is a book for nobody.

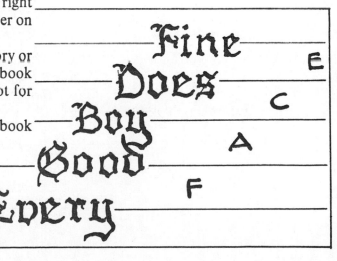

 BURTHEN

THIS BOOK OWES ITS BEING TO a grant from the Rockefeller Foundation and to the help and guidance of many individuals. Unfortunately, there is room to thank only a few of them by name:

Richard T. Baker, Madeleine Beakhurst, Richard Benda, John Berkenfield, William Bradley, Lo Buecheler-Gerfin, Gerald E. Burns, Jacques Chabrier, Donald Craig, Libbis C. Eilenberg, Elke Elmont-Elton, John R. Everett, John Firrincieli, Harriet Goldschmidt, P.K. Jakobsen, Howard Klein, Norman Lloyd, Ruth Lloyd, Janet O'Morrison, Rudolph Schramm, Artie Shaw, Paul Taff, Laura Weber and Alec Wilder.

This book also shines by the reflected light of a lot of great music and the people who wrote it:

All Through The Day	by Jerome Kern and Oscar Hammerstein II
Begin The Beguine	by Cole Porter
Blueberry Hill	by Al Lewis, Larry Stock and Vincent Rose
Close As Pages In A Book	by Sigmund Romberg and Dorothy Fields
A Cottage For Sale	by Willard Robison and Larry Conley
Eleanora	by Lawrence Kluger
Everything's Coming Up Roses	by Jule Styne and Stephen Sondheim
Fanny	by Harold Rome
Gigi	by Frederick Loewe and Alan Jay Lerner
Harbor Lights	by Jimmy Kennedy and Hugh Williams
Haunted Heart	by Arthur Schwartz and Howard Dietz
How High The Moon	by Morgan Lewis and Nancy Hamilton
I Could Write A Book	by Richard Rodgers and Lorenz Hart
I Can Dream Can't I?	by Sammy Fain and Irving Kahal
I Love Paris	by Cole Porter
If Ever I would Leave You	by Frederick Loewe and Alan Jay Lerner
I'll Follow My Secret Heart	by Noel Coward
Look To The Rainbow	by Burton Lane and E.Y. Harburg
Love Is Here To Stay	by George Gershwin and Ira Gershwin
Nevertheless (I'm In Love With You)	by Bert Kalmar and Harry Ruby
September Song	by Kurt Weill and Maxwell Anderson
Show Me	by Frederick Loewe and Alan Jay Lerner
Some Enchanted Evening	by Richard Rodgers and Oscar Hammerstein II
Someday I'll Find You	by Noel Coward
Spellbound Concerto	by Richard Addinsel
The Entertainer	by Scott Joplin
This Can't Be Love	by Richard Rodgers and Lorenz Hart
This Nearly Was Mine	by Richard Rodgers and Oscar Hammerstein II
There's A Small Hotel	by Richard Rodgers and Lorenz Hart
True Love	by Cole Porter
Try To Remember	by Harvey Schmidt and Tom Jones
Where Or When	by Richard Rodgers and Lorenz Hart

How to play the piano despite years of lessons

THE MYTH: There is music. And then there Is something else called "music theory."

THE FACT: Music *is* theory. We share an idea —and a very simple idea at that— which makes music.

Part one

How not to play the plano (whether or not you've had lessons), including the 10 best-loved myths, half-truths and obsolete beliefs which keep people away from pianos. How much you really know about making music, probably without knowing that you know it. After all, you're making music just by listening to it.

How not to play the piano

1

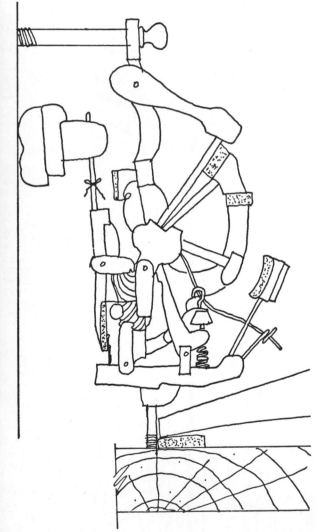

NOW THAT THEY'VE TAUGHT PIGEONS to play table tennis and chimpanzees to play word games and computers to play chess, it's becoming quite difficult to distinguish humans from the rest of the landscape. So, if you set out to ask what makes people people rather than animals or machines, by and by you have to look into the subject of music. It appears that the ability to make music is a characteristic of human nature only.

True, birds sing. But their repertoire is very limited, fixed for each species by its habits and family background. Take the starling. Its familiar song of "cheap, cheap, cheap" bespeaks its natural habitat: city halls and bank buildings. Or listen to the melody of the dove —"plop-plop, plop-plop." That is clearly a genetic message, as the original names of the dove reveal. In old English, this bird is called the *pigeon,* a word clearly derived from *pig* (meaning pig) + *eon* (meaning eternal). In Spanish, of course, the bird is called *plopaloma*.

Properly speaking, then, birds cannot really be said to make music even though they can do a number on you.

On the other hand, every human society under the sun has a variety of musical compositions and instruments. And furthermore, people from one part of the planet can learn to sing and play the music from another part. So the ability to *make* music is part of human nature.

Well, with just about everybody able to make music, an inquiry into how they do it ought to be a simple matter of asking the question and getting the answer. But that is not the case at all. The people who ought to have the answer at the ready —people who have taken music lessons and people who have given music lessons —are vastly reluctant to discuss the subject. Most of those who have had music lessons tell you that it was a long time ago and by now they have forgotten everything they ever knew about it (including how to play anything). Those who give the lessons often respond by explaining that music is another language, and with that they run through a few scales to prove it. And the people who teach those teachers in professional schools often reply with a sad, understanding smile, a copy of the current catalogue of courses, and the suggestion that you enroll now before the rush.

Oh no, it is not easy to find out how music is made. And, in fact, you are in constant jeopardy of forgetting the question itself. It is quite a bit like asking Psychology —the study of the human mind— how the human mind works. What you learn instead is that the question is not allowed, at least not that way. You must ask first how the rat's mind works. And then, while your attention is directed to the exercises in the maze, it is very easy for someone to walk off with your hat and lunchbox. And so, before you are even aware of it, your original inquiry has been detoured into the Lost & Found Office — which is hardly the place to ask about how people make music.

All in all, it seems to be human to make music, but absolutely unnatural to ask how it is done. Quite the contrary, in fact, it is much easier to find out how it is that people *do not* make music, even those who have had years of lessons. Most especially piano lessons.

There are a number of reasons for this condition: popularly-held superstitions, obsolete beliefs and half-true principles —monkey wrenches in the machinery— which prevent people from understanding the few simple facts of how music is made and thus keep them from making music at the piano. When you look at some of these items of misunderstanding, you can see how they got to be that way and, most important, how to clear things up and get the show on the road.

1. When it comes to music, either you have it or you don't. If you have it, then you can make music. If you don't, then you can't. But either way, there are no questions you can ask about how to do it because music, like grace and second sight, is an ordained and inborn knowledge.

But the truth of the matter is that there are very real and specific question to be asked of music. That is because music is made of a few simple, basic facts. How people make music —or don't make music— depends on how they understand the facts, or misunderstand them. For instance, many people think they are making beautiful music when they are merely making love. Many people think that they have had years of music lessons when they have really had instrument lessons.

Such people have not forgotten all they ever knew about music because it is impossible to forget something if you never knew it to begin with.

2. Music is a hallowed realm, an almost superhuman body of knowledge. Only a gifted person can compose real music. Only musicians can make music. At best, music is a very complicated subject with its lines and spaces and stems and ties and key signatures and other hieroglyphics. It may not take a superhuman to understand it, but it certainly requires a genius.

Clearly, those notions call the question of *talent* —what it is, who says so, how to prove it, what is a lot of talent and what is a little, and whether being paid for what you do is the same as being talented at it. . . .As you can see, the question of talent opens a lot of difficulties.

But it has to be asked. Otherwise, people who cannot carry a tune will be labeled "No Musical Ability" and deprived of hope that they will ever make music —when, in fact, singing is only *one way* to make music. Similarly, people who took years of

lessons and now cannot play a note will continue to be intimidated by the belief that they are somehow incompetent and inept deep down.

3. In order to make music, you have to know your scales and do your exercises fluently. It takes a year at the least, and closer to two, before your study pays off and you are prepared to play actual music. There are no short cuts to playing the piano.

How familiar and reasonable that sounds. And how discouraging. And as a result of that popular belief, nobody bothers to ask any further questions, such as : why do you have to know scales; and why do you have to do a half-hour of exercises daily; and if exercises, why not ten minutes of calisthenics as well?

Nobody notices that this obsolete belief talks about "making music" and "playing music" as though they were the same enterprise. The implication is clear: a good grasp of the subject means that you can play the *Minute Waltz* in a minute; a better grasp means that you can play it in 59 seconds. In other words, the aim of that kind of piano playing is a professional career in Carnegie Hall (or, at the very least, in the Stardust Cocktail Lounge).

Once upon a time, that was a plausible way to learn to play the piano. That was in the days before the phonograph, tape deck, radio and easy transportation. If you wanted to hear good music played well in those days, you had to perform it yourself. But today, master performers are available at the touch of a button —brilliant renditions made even more perfect by technology in recording and editing. So, the need to play that kind of music at home has just about disappeared. Today, there is a real difference between following somebody else's blueprint to the letter and making your own.

True, there are no short cuts to making music. But scales and exercises do not make music. Only a knowledge of the subject —an understanding of the basic facts— makes music. And making music makes for fluency and competence at the piano. But that isn't difficult. In fact, it's quite easy to know what you're doing and why. So, really, you don't need any short cut. And as for the old fashioned, tedious long cut —that leaves in its wake people who can't play a note after years and years of lessons.

4. There is real music. . .and then there is popular music. Real music, naturally, is classical music —music created by the great composers. To be able to play what they wrote is to make more music than to play what Tin Pan Alley turns out.

Well, yes and no.

No, there is no "real" music vs. "popular" music. There is only music. Both classical and popular music are made exactly the same way —by the same few facts, the same idea. That is why you can tell when the orchestra is playing *Smoke Gets In Your Eyes,* and when the number is finished and the orchestra begins to play Beethoven's *Fifth Symphony.* But popular music is more elementary than the classical. The basic facts are much more evident in popular music, so you see the raw material of music there. Consequently, it is easier to understand popular music and thus approach an understanding of classical music in a reasonable way.

On the other hand, yes —you are producing more music if you play what a great composer has written rather than what a sheet of tin pan alley music prescribes. That is because tin pan alley keeps its music simple in order not to discourage the people who buy it. A frustrated customer will not come back for another piece of sheet music.

But on the first hand again, you don't have to play what the sheet music prescribes. You can take a popular melody and *make* music with it. But you can only *play* a classical piece composed for the piano.

5. Playing by ear is inferior to playing what is written.

On the contrary, the human ear is the first musical instrument of all. The ear and mind make music by organizing oncoming tones. If you can recognize or remember a piece of music, that's because it was composed by someone whose ear and mind organize tones with the same idea you use. But if the music sounds like gibberish to you, then the composer is probably working with a different organizing idea and a different set of basic facts. In other words, *listeners make music.* But few "listeners" were told that as youngsters. They were simply asked to be silent while the rest of the class sang.

6. There is music. And then there is something else called "music theory."

Now, there is a very effective road block to throw in the path of somebody who wants to know *why* —why those needless hours of scales? why do chords change? etc. You have only to reply, "Don't think about it! Just do it!" and catastrophe has been averted. You have only to say, "People aren't interested in theory; they just want to know how to play." And with that, you have done your part to keep that know-how out of their reach.

The true fact is that music *is* theory. We share an agreement, a contract —*an idea*— which pulls a few simple facts together and makes what we call music. Once you grasp that elementary idea, making music becomes quite simple. In other words, *your fingers are connected to your mind.*

Just as important, once you grasp the idea which organizes the facts, you have knowledge which you cannot forget. Only information learned by rote, such as exercises and memorized set pieces, are easily forgotten because they contain no idea to understand.

7. Music is another language.

Certainly. And so are painting, sculpture and architecture other languages. But if you come at those topics that way, you'll have a hard time speaking them.

It's a lot easier to look on music as a motion picture in sound. That way you can stop the reel, freeze the frame, and take a calm look at what is going on in the scene without having to read the bass clef or the ledger lines or the note-by-note lines for each instrument or finger. Looked at as a snapshot of frozen action, a bar or two of music becomes readily understandable as to its intention —an explanation about how, when and where to interrupt the silence.

8. Music is written in this key or that key. And this key is harder than that key. But you have to master them all. Otherwise you can't make real music or understand harmony.

No key is harder than any other. In fact, there is no real need for the notion of keys in order to make music or understand how harmony works and moves. The key signatures can be looked on as merely pre-set accidentals which tell you which notes to sharp or flat throughout the melody (unless the pre-setting is cancelled here or there for a note or a bar at a time).

9. Harmony is very mathematical.

Yes, that public belief is true. In order to understand harmony, you must be able to count to twelve. You can perform a scientific experiment at home to determine whether you have the necessary mathematical ability. Just look at a clock or a wrist watch. Can you tell what time it is? If so, you will be able to understand harmony. If not, then wait for the sequel to this book: *How To Tell Time From A Clock and Wrist Watch*.

10. There are a lot of rules and regulations in music.

No, there is only one rule in making music, and that is: *if it sounds good, then it is good*.

What sounds good is what follows from our agreement with each other about what makes sense, or nonsense, of oncoming tones. That agreement, that idea, has evolved and grown slowly in the past 400 years, and it continues to evolve and grow. So there is no rule, regulation or law at work. There are only a few historical principles of growth which can be observed with a backward look. If you want to make your own music, these few principles become starting places and options only. In the end, *your idea* makes music that sounds good to you.

IN A NUTSHELL, THEN: People know how to pull oncoming tones together and say whether it is music or gibberish. And they do so all the time simply by listening. That is because people have an idea in mind which organizes those oncoming tones. If people can't organize those tones into music, it is usually because the composer has a

different idea in mind. Making music with an instrument
—a piano for example —is merely expressing the idea out
loud.

The fact remains, however, that people know how to
make music because they are people —creatures who use
ideas in order to organize the world and all the things in it.
But whether people are aware of the ideas they use all the
time is another matter.

What everybody knows about music (without knowing it)

TAKE AN EXAMPLE OF AN IDEA at work in everyday life. A man
is getting dressed on a typical Monday morning. All of a
sudden he feels choked and hears a buzzing in his ears. He calls
out to his wife: "Darling, what the hell have you done to my
shirts this time? The collar is three sizes too small."

"Sweetheart," his wife calls back without looking up from
her newspaper, "are you sure you don't have your head
through the buttonhole again?"

Well, you can see at once how ideas go to work, organizing
the world into understandable patterns such as *everyday* life
and *typical* Monday mornings when it is time to put on a clean
shirt *again.* You need an organizing idea in mind in order to see
two angry strangers as a *happily married couple.* Similarly, it
requires an idea to transform a bunch of black lines and dots on
a page into *a newspaper* of meaningful *words* and *pictures.*

In the same way, you must have an idea in mind before you
can even hear music. You must have an idea of a musical pitch
in order to distinguish tones from the other noises in the world.
And then you need a further idea of music so as to organize oncoming single tones into an understandable pattern known as a
melody.

Obviously, it's not a very complicated idea. After all, babies
recognize and respond to songs long before they make understandable sense of words and sentences. And as most of us
in this part of the world began as babies, most of us in this part
of the world are agreed to the same organizing idea for making
music from oncoming tones. So, everybody knows what that
idea is. At least, everybody knows two of the three elements of
that organizing idea.

ABOUT 400 YEARS AGO, composers and piano tuners agreed on the idea of dividing the octave into twelve tones —just as earlier architects and carpenters had agreed on the idea of dividing the foot into twelve inches. So, if you look at the piano keyboard and count the keys from one C to the next C above it or below it —or from one C#/D♭ to the next C#/D♭ —you will find twelve. (C# is the same key as D♭. It is called C# when you go up the keyboard. It is called D♭ when you go down.) Those twelve notes which make our music are (to begin counting from C up to the next C for convenience):

The complete set of 12 notes we use to make our music. Counting upward the black notes are called sharps.

Counting downward, they're called flats.

Without any doubt, that ruler is in just about everybody's mind, measuring the heights of notes as they come along —telling you that this note is higher or lower than that note, or letting you know that the distance between notes is not what it should be and thus advising you to get the piano tuned or to get the vocalist off the stage as quickly as possible.

Obviously, you don't need to use all twelve notes to make a melody, just as you don't need all twelve inches on a ruler to make a line. Take one note only —E, say— of the possible twelve. And there you have two bars of *Jingle Bells.*

With four tones of the possible twelve —C D E G— you have the oncoming single notes which our common organizing idea says is the opening pattern of Cole Porter's familiar *Begin The Beguine.*

One note can make lots of melody.

These 4 notes start a Cole Porter tune.*

Naturally, you can reorganize and re-reorganize those four notes in other ways. You can spell them backwards — turning C D E G around to G E D C — and thus make the opening pattern of Tchaikowsky's *Piano Concerto No. 1.*

Or you can turn the order inside out, to make the pattern of

---

highs and lows which Jerome Kern used to begin his *All Through The Day.*

Obviously these very same high-and-low patterns can be made with other notes of the twelve, just as the opening bars of the chorus of *Jingle Bells* could be made of any note of the twelve. And, in fact, Tchaikowsky used the four notes A♭ F E♭ D♭; and Kern used A G F C. The moral of that story is that the musical ruler we have in our mind —like any ruler— measures distance of height, regardless of which note you decide to put at the bottom. The distance from B to C is exactly the same as from E to F. In other words, an inch is an inch whether you measure it at the seashore or on top of Mt. Everest.

In any case, rearranging and re-rearranging the order of four notes is not the end of the reorganizing possibilities. You can make hundreds and hundreds of patterns —melodies— of those four simply using one or more of them more than once. Take C D E G again, this time using C and E twice. There you have the opening of *Red River Valley.*

The possibilities, of course, multiply toward infinity as you increase the number of different notes in your pattern of highs-and-lows. It is hardly astonishing that millions of tunes have been composed with this vocabulary of only twelve tones. And millions more are possible. (Actually, the difficulty is not composing new patterns; the hard work is finding out whether your melody has already been composed by someone else.)

Well, there is no need to go on and on about this. Everybody knows this part of the organizing idea which we use to make music —namely that we have agreed to divide the octave into twelve parts, with each tone a specific height above or below the others. Everybody knows that a melody is a pattern, in part a pattern of higher and lower notes. And because of this clause in our contract with each other, we can make sense of the notes most of our composers send at us.

But if you can't make sense of a shipment —if a composer's assortment of oncoming notes sounds like gibberish —that doesn't mean he has put his head through the buttonhole by mistake. It only means that he has a different organizing idea in mind. There is no eternal law which says the octave must be divided into twelve tones. Conceivably it could be divided into sixteen or twenty or more or less and make very understandable patterns of highs and lows for people who agreed to *that* idea.

IN PART, THEN, A MELODY is an understandable organization of *heights* —a pattern of notes which are exactly as high as others, or lower or higher. But like any understandable pattern of sound such as an SOS in Morse Code, a melody has another dimension. And everybody knows what it is: notes of different *widths.*

The same 4 notes upside down make a Tchaikowsky tune.

Inside out, the very same 4 notes begin a Kern melody.

RED RIVER VALLEY

The same notes with 2 used twice.

So, in part, a melody is a pattern of notes which last exactly as long as others, or are shorter or longer in duration. Consequently, it is only partially true to say that the first six notes of *Red River Valley* are G C E E D C. Each of those notes also lasts a specific amount of time. In reality, they look more like this:

What that river valley REALLY looks like.

As you can see, the first two notes are exactly equal in width —in duration— and the third note lasts exactly twice as long. And that pattern of widths is repeated exactly in the next three notes.

That is certainly a much more apparent and understandable pattern than "everyday life" or "typical Monday mornings." And it explains why so many people have trouble getting dressed for work at the beginning of the week. They are yearning for the Red River valley —or some equally simple-minded way to organize their time.

The plain fact is that it takes a simple and well-organized idea of time in order to organize oncoming notes according to their duration. It takes a regular and steady clock tick-tocking in your mind in order to make an understandable pattern of tones according to their widths (just as it takes a firm ruler to make an understandable pattern of their heights). And that built-in clock, assorting oncoming tones and saying that this one is a quarter-tick long, and that one a tick in duration and the one beyond a whole tick-tock in width —that regularly-beating clock is part of the idea we share with each other about making music.

With that idea of regular time sorting out notes into patterns of widths, it is a breeze to reorganize and re-reorganize different but still very understandable melodies without changing the pattern of highs and lows. For example, look at what you can do with the duration pattern of *Red River Valley* merely by changing the widths of those very same high and low notes:

Same notes, same order. But re-timed, they make two tunes by Mozart.

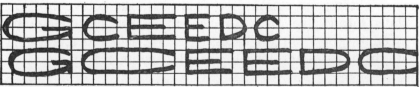

Both were organized by Mozart. The top one is from his *Serenade in D* (The *Haffner,* Orchestra, 8th Movement). The bottom one is from his *Concerto for Clarinet and Orchestra* (2nd Movement).

But why stop there? With a commonly-shared idea of organizing notes into patterns of widths-in-time, you can go on

18

and on, composing melody after melody by altering durations without disturbing the pattern of highs and lows. Here are several examples of what re-timing can do. (All have been transposed to the Key of C so that there can be no mistake about it. The high-and-low pattern of G C E E D C is the same in all.)

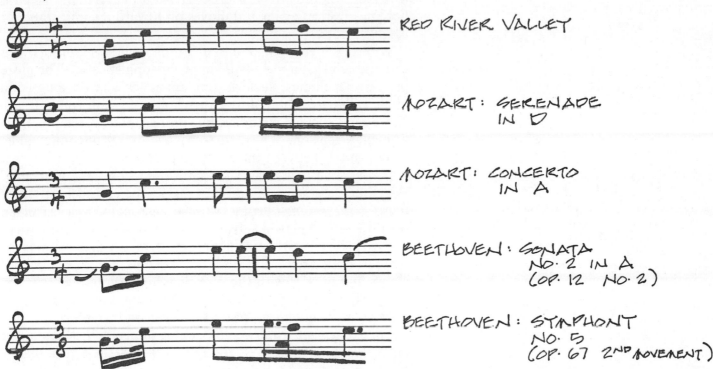

Well, there is no need to go on and on about this part of the idea, either. Everybody knows this clause in the contract, too —namely that we have agreed with each other to tell time in the same way. Consequently, we organize oncoming single tones into a pattern by sorting them out according to their exact duration in time as well as their exact height in space.

If you can't make an understandable pattern —a melody— of the single tones coming at you, it may well be that the musician is measuring time by a different clock from yours. It may be a clock which goes slowly for a while and then goes faster for a bit, thus making it impossible to make exact measurement of each note's duration as it passes by. That doesn't mean the musician is wrong. It may only mean that the musician is a novice and still learning to be fluent, concentrating on hitting notes of the proper height and not worrying about how wide they are.

THERE IS ONE FURTHER CLAUSE in the contract, one final part of the organizing idea we have in mind, one more dimension of the pattern we call music. And that is *comfort*. In addition to

The up-and-down pattern is the same in each. The difference is in the wides-and-narrows.

sorting out the oncoming single notes by heights and durations, we also organize those tones according to their comfortableness and uncomfortableness. Oh, absolutely, you can tell if this note or that in a melody is comfortable and at rest, or if it is uncomfortable, restless, and longing to come home to a comfortable note. That is how you can tell when a melody has begun, when it is moving, and when it has come to a pause. . .and when it becomes restless again and moves on toward a comfortable or resolved note.

With this idea we share about comfort and un-comfort, you can also tell that a melody is simple or sophisticated. The more primitive melodies, such as folk tunes, children's songs and bugle calls, are made mostly or wholly of comfortable tones. More sophisticated melodies, like more sophisticated life, have a higher tension. These tunes have more uncomfortable, restless notes between the comfortable resolved, settled notes.

Now, what makes a note comfortable or uncomfortable? Why, the very same thing that makes a person feel settled or tense —*the setting*. People who are perfectly at ease in an operating room may be terribly on edge in a court room setting, and vice versa. And still others (most of us, in fact) may be tense in both places. But does that keep us from watching TV shows and movies with those settings? No, quite the contrary. We seek out entertainments for the very reasons that they provide us with tension, restlessness, uncomfortableness —in a word, *excitement*. And we go back to these settings again and again for diversion, even though we know their formula by heart.

For the very same reason, we go for music with uncomfortable, unresolved tones amidst the comfortable ones. And we go for such music again and again, even though we know their formula by heart. That formula for comfort —that setting in our common mind— is the third part of the idea we share with each other hereabouts for making music. It's not called a formula or a setting in polite musical circles. Rather, it goes by the name of *chord*.

Basically, that formula for comfort pulls together a three-note chord out of the full set of twelve notes —three which are in complete comfort, complete harmony, together. That basic chord is pulled together the moment a melody begins, and it goes to work in the mind's ear scanning the oncoming single notes and sorting them out into the comfortable and the uncomfortable.

You can see easily how that works. If you have an agreed-to setting for comfort, anything that fits into it is comfortable and anything that doesn't fit is uncomfortable. So, if you have a formula which pulls together three comfortable notes out of the complete set of twelve, then out of all the possible oncoming notes of any melody there will be three resolved notes and nine unresolved. Or, to put it still another way, there are in most melodies an assortment of settled *notes-of-the-chord* as well as unsettled *notes-not-of-the-chord*. So, what we call music is in part a pattern of comfortable *chordal notes* and restless *non-chordal* notes which are longing to come to rest on a chordal note.

Now, what does our ideal setting of comfort sound like —our formula for the basic three-note chord? Well, if you begin to pull that chord together starting on C, for example, the formula will select E and G to complete the comfortable sound.

Take it home, as the old ads used to say, and try it on your own piano. Play the three notes of the basic chord as it begins on C and listen to the echo of a familiar sound in your mind. Use your left hand: pinky on C, middle finger or index on E, thumb on G. Play all the notes together. After all, it's a chord —a setting.

Obviously, you can apply that formula anywhere on the keyboard, making each note of the twelve serve as the root of the basic chord. If you apply the formula to F, say, it will add A and C to complete the three-note chord. If you use G for the root note and thus make the basic G chord, the formula will add B and D to make the three-note setting.

So, take these examples home and try them on your own piano and hear the news for yourself. The root note may change, and with it the two additional notes; but the relationship among the three always stays the same no matter on which note the chord is rooted.

As for how the basic chord sorts out comfortable chordal notes from restless non-chordal notes in an oncoming melody —well, that is quite easy to see. Take the basic chord rooted on C. That setting, made of C, E and G, makes comfortable notes out of any oncoming melody notes which are Cs, Es and Gs —and, obviously, that setting makes uncomfortable, restless notes of those which are not Cs, Es and Gs.

Here are the opening notes of *Red River Valley*. As you can see, those oncoming melody tones are mostly comfortable chordals —resolved notes-of-the-chord rooted on C. The only non-chordal notes are the two Ds. It is this preponderance of resolved, settled chordal notes which earmarks *Red River Valley* as a primitive kind of tune, like most folk songs.

In any case, try it on your piano. With your left hand play the basic chord rooted on C —the basic C chord. With one finger of your right hand, pick out the melody higher up on the keyboard. If you hit a wrong note in the melody by mistake, the chord will make it uncomfortable and pull your finger away from it.

Just as obviously, any string of oncoming melody notes

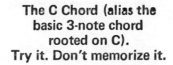

The C Chord (alias the basic 3-note chord rooted on C). Try it. Don't memorize it.

The F chord and G chord (the basic 3-note chord rooted on F and on G). Listen to their sound.

The basic C chord makes all Cs Es and Gs in the melody comfortable notes-of-the-chord

and makes any other note (x) a restless non-chordal.

Likewise, the basic G chord. It turns all Gs Bs Ds into comfortable chordals and others (x) into uneasy notes not-of-the-chord. Try it on your own piano.

which are mostly Fs, As and Cs will be made into comfortable chordal notes by the basic chord rooted on F. Similarly, the basic G chord will make comfortable chordals of Gs, Bs and Ds in the melody. And so on with the basic chord rooted on each of the twelve in the complete set.

As for the way the basic chord makes unresolved, uneasy, uncomfortable non-chordal notes of an oncoming melody —that is just as obvious. Try the opening bars of *Red River Valley* again. But this time play the basic chord rooted on G with your left hand. All of those Cs and Es in the melody are now not-of-the-chord —are now restless non-chordals. Only the G and the two Ds are comfortable chordal notes.

That ought to tell you in no uncertain terms that a change in harmony is needed —to the basic chord rooted on another note (namely on C). In other words, sometimes the chords have to change in a number because the formula works better with a different starting point. But which root to change to and exactly when to change? Don't worry. Most sheet music tells you in explicit terms above the melody whether to play the chord as a C chord or as an F chord or rooted on some other note.

ALL RIGHT, THEN, IN A NUTSHELL: The making of music *is* theory. We share an idea which selects musical pitches from world noise and then organizes those oncoming tones into patterns we call melodies. So, people who only listen are really making music, too. And that means the ear is one of the finest musical instruments.

Some parts of the idea we share for making music:

To begin with, we have agreed with each other to divide the octave into twelve specific pieces, and we use those twelve notes to make our music. Then we organize them by listening for three patterns —their high and low pattern in space; their wide and narrow pattern of duration in time; and their pattern of comfortableness and restlessness, the pattern of chordal notes and non-chordal notes. These three patterns form the skeleton which holds all of our music together.

You can make quite a bit of music at the keyboard with one finger, simply by picking out the oncoming single notes of the melody. In that way you express two-thirds of the skeleton — the pattern of high and low notes and the pattern of wide and narrow duration. But you leave it to your listeners (including your own ear) to supply the pattern of comfortable chordal and uneasy non-chordal notes. That is, you are asking your listeners to supply the basic chord in their minds while you play.

Naturally that is not guaranteed to make friends. People will not put up for very long with a music-maker who asks

them to do a third of the work. That is why vocalists, no matter how wonderful, seldom work without accompaniment. That is why a lone violinist working in a restaurant sounds charming and romantic for a little while and then becomes irritating and finally a pest. For that reason, there is usually an accordianist at the least to help the violinist by supplying the very necessary chord accompaniment.

Under the circumstances, then, you have to express more than the single notes of the melody in order to make music at the piano. You must also express the setting, the formula, which makes those oncoming melody notes chordal and non-chordal.

But don't worry. It's a very simple formula to understand, remember and apply in all sorts of ways. That formula for the basic chord is in the next chapter. And all the things you can do with it make up the rest of this book.

The chords transform the melody into notes-of-the- chord & notes-not-of-the chord (x).

JINGLE BELLS

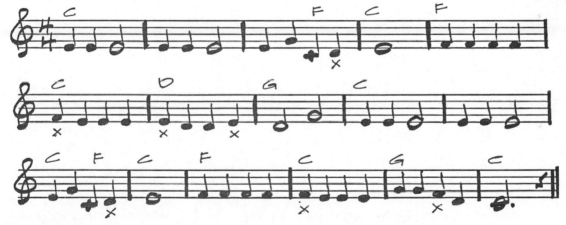

$$C = \begin{matrix} G \\ E \\ C \end{matrix} \quad F = \begin{matrix} C \\ A \\ F \end{matrix} \quad G = \begin{matrix} D \\ B \\ G \end{matrix} \quad D = \begin{matrix} A \\ F\# \\ D \end{matrix}$$

RED RIVER VALLEY

How to play the piano despite years of lessons

THE MYTH: To make music, you must know your scales by heart backwards and forwards.

THE FACT: Scales don't make music. Chords make music— by bestowing on oncoming melody notes comfort or tension.

Part two

A look into your mind's ear. The formula you use to make the basic chord when you listen to music. How to apply that formula to any root note and express the basic chord on the piano. A handy chart for finding any basic chord in a hurry. Some numbers to try with the basic chord. And, finally, how to alter the basic chord in three ways to make the *minor* chord, the *diminished* chord and the *augmented* chord.

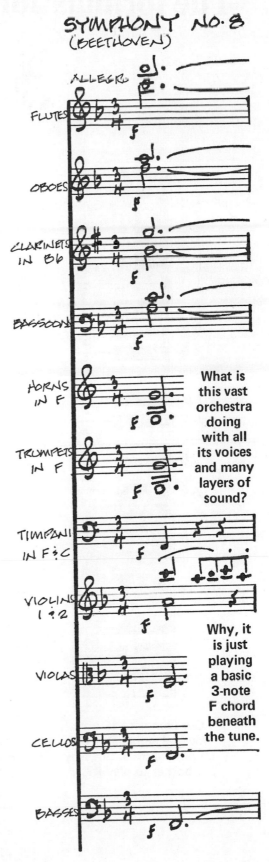

What is this vast orchestra doing with all its voices and many layers of sound?

Why, it is just playing a basic 3-note F chord beneath the tune.

The formula for the basic chord

3

IT IS A LITTLE EMBARRASSING to admit this. But the plain fact is, this book is not allowed to move forward one inch until something has been said about scales. Not that you have to know about it in order to make music at the piano. Oh no, you can do very nicely without. But there are certain kinds of people who will not let you do so. "Making music at the keyboard?" these certain people will say in hurt surprise. "But where are the scales? Where are the scales and exercises?"

Well, there is very little you can do for people like that. They are the same people who always applaud in the theater when the curtain goes *up*, before the show begins, as though to congratulate the star for having bothered to come to the performance at all. It never occurs to these certain people to reserve their congratulations until after they find out whether the star knows her part. "Knows her part?" they will say in hurt surprise. "Why, of course she knows her part. She's a star, isn't she?"

All right, then, if it has to be, so be it. A scale is an arbitrary selection of notes used to divide the octave. There are two important parts of that definition. One is that the scale, any scale, divides the octave —from any C to the next C, say, or from any Ab to the next Ab —up or down. The other important part of the definition is that scales are man-made: some are held by general agreement among us; some are selected and used by a few composers and agreed to by a few listeners. To be specific, take a couple of these arbitrary octave-dividers agreed to by most of us:

As reported earlier, composers and piano tuners decided about 400 years ago to divide the octave into twelve specific parts. We still use that scale, that man-made division of the octave. It is our complete set of notes, our complete scale, or —in pure music language— it is our chromatic scale.

You can play it if you want to simply by starting with any note (an Ab, say) and striking every note up or down the keyboard, black and white, until you come to the note an octave away (the next Ab above or below). But why you would want to play this complete scale is a mystery, unless you are tuning the piano. Why you would want to play this complete scale fluently is even more mysterious inasmuch as it does not make any music. It makes only the complete scale.

There is another scale which divides the octave and is generally agreed to by most of us. Like the complete scale, you can start it anywhere on the keyboard and finish it an octave above or below. But unlike the complete scale, this one has only seven notes in it. You can play this seven-tone scale beginning

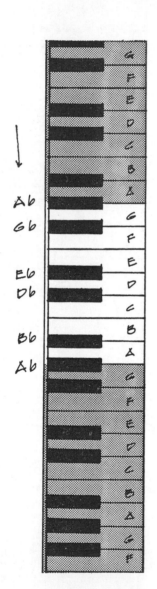

Our complete 12-note musical alphabet — the chromatic scale. But why bother to play it?

on C merely by running your fingernail up or down the keyboard on all the white notes —from any C to the next C above or below.

It is a bit risky to begin this seven-tone scale anywhere but on C if you are going to play it with your fingernail. Starting from any other root note, the formula for this scale will pull out one or more black keys. So there is always the chance that you will break your finger in the attempt.

In any case, that seven-tone scale will sound very familiar to you. It is our traditional, agreed-upon *do re mi* scale, our basic scale, or —in pure music language— our diatonic major scale. But why you would want to play it or, even worse, practice it, is hard to understand. Like the complete scale of twelve notes, this basic seven-tone scale does not make music. It only makes the basic seven-tone scale. And the same is true of other scales.

Now, it is also possible to say that the basic three-note chord is a scale, too. After all, it fulfills most of the requirements of a scale. It divides the octave (into three parts). Moreover, it divides the octave into three comfortable chordal notes and nine uneasy non-chordals. Like any scale, too, the basic chord is really a formula for selecting specific parts of the octave.

So, you can start anywhere on the keyboard —you can use any note as the root. And, depending on the formula you apply, you can pull out the complete twelve-tone scale, or the basic seven-tone scale, or some other scale altogether, or the basic chord.

ALL OF THAT TALK ABOUT SCALES was not really necessary. It was set down here only because a number of people prefer not to look at the basic three-note chord as a formula just like any scale's formula. Instead, these people see the chord only as a subdivision of the basic seven-tone scale —namely, the *root* (or starting note) plus the *3rd* note plus the *5th* note of that basic scale.

These people will tell you, therefore, that if you want to make the basic three-note chord on every note in the keyboard, then you must know every basic scale as it begins on every note. If you want the basic chord built on F, you must know the basic scale built on F. If you want the basic three-note G chord, you must first learn the basic seven-note G scale. If you want to use the Ab chord, you must know the Ab scale and so on and on through all twelve.

As already noted, there is very little you can do for people who prefer to go through all of that work, learning and practicing all of the basic scales just so they can pull out the basic chord from each. About all you can hope for them is that they will grant you a chance to explain the basic chord as a formula —a simple recipe— which pulls out the three necessary notes

Our basic 7-tone, do-re-mi scale (starting on C here). But why learn it when . . .

. . . what you really want is its basic 3-note chord —its root, 3rd and 5th notes.

The basic 7-tone, do-re-mi scale (rooted on F) with its basic chord notes circled. But you don't need to know the scales to find their chords.

from the complete set of twelve tones. (And in doing so, of course, the formula is pulling out the root, 3rd and 5th notes of the basic scale at the same time.)

All right, then. Here's how the formula for the basic three-note chord emerges from the complete scale.

THERE IS A FORMULA (agreed to by composers and piano tuners since the days of Johann Sebastian Bach more than three centuries ago) which divides the octave into twelve notes. Or, to be more accurate about it, we use a formula for the complete scale which says that the octave shall be divided into twelve notes *with each note separated from the next by a crack* —or, in more polite language, by an *interval* of silence.

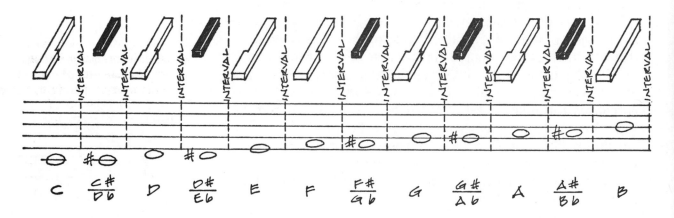

The recipe for dividing the octave on the keyboard. Everybody knows there are 12 keys. But it's very easy to forget that there are also 12 cracks.

That illustration also reveals in no uncertain terms that the black keys are no different from the white keys as subdivisions of the octave. The black keys are shorter and higher only to save space and put the entire keyboard within easy reach. If all the keys were as wide as the white keys, the keyboard would be almost twice as long as it is and you would have to wear roller skates to play the piano.

In any case, you can see what the formula for the complete twelve-tone scale is: any note to begin with, plus one interval plus one note, plus another interval. . .and so on through all twelve notes and twelve cracks.

THERE IS ANOTHER FORMULA, also agreed to by most of us, which selects from the complete set of twelve notes a basic scale of seven notes. Everybody knows this basic, seven-tone, *do re mi* scale when it begins on C. The formula selects the seven notes C D E F G A B. In fact, you can apply this formula to the root note C with your fingernail. Run your nail up or down the keyboard from one C to the next and you have selected the basic C scale from the complete set of twelve:

Obviously your fingernail can't apply that formula to the other eleven root notes because all the rest of the basic seven-tone scales, such as the F scale and the G scale, contain one or more black keys. So if, for some strange reason, you want the formula for that basic scale in order to apply it to other root notes, you will find it in a footnote* at the bottom of this page. But you don't need to know the formula to get the picture. And that is, the basic seven-tone C scale was selected from the complete scale by a recipe; and that recipe works the same way no matter where you start it. Once you select the root note, the rest is a fixed relationship of notes and intervals.

FINALLY, THERE IS A FORMULA (agreed to and used by all of us, even when listening) which makes the basic three-note chord. This is the three-note setting we have in mind which identifies oncoming tones of the melody as comfortable chordal notes and unsettled notes-not-of-the-chord.

If you start the basic chord on the root note C, as everybody knows by now, the formula will add E and G. Whether the formula takes the C + E + G from the complete twelve-tone scale —or whether the formula is taking the root + 3rd + 5th notes

The recipe of keys-&-cracks which pulls the basic 7-tone do-re-mi scale out of the complete set of 12. Here, the recipe begins on C to pull out the C scale.*

---

*Being a recipe or formula of keys-and-intervals ("i" for short), it can start on any note and will pull out the basic seven-tone, do-re-mi scale. But the note you start on — the root note — will give the scale its name, such as the C scale or F scale, etc. The formula for this basic scale is:

Root note + 2i + 2i + 1i + 2i +2i + 2i + 1i

Take another look at the illustration to make sure you've got the picture of how it works. But don't bother to memorize it because scales don't make music. The formula to remember is on the next page. That's the formula for the basic three-note chord.

from the basic seven-tone C scale, that is really beside the point. It all comes down to the same thing, namely a recipe of fixed relationships of notes and intervals:

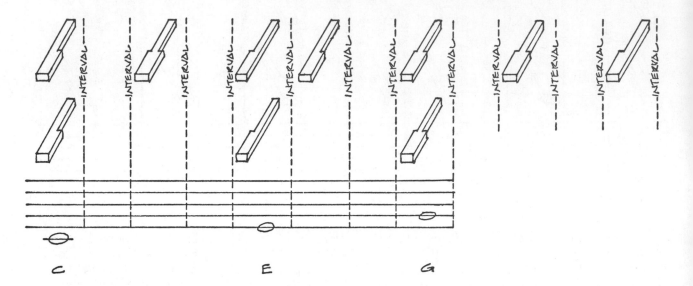

C   E   G

The one to remember. The recipe of keys-&-cracks to pull the basic chord out of both keyboard and scale. Root + 4i + 3i Begin on any note; this recipe completes the chord.

C	A	G	3 intervals
+	+	+	+
A	F#	E	4 intervals
+	+	+	+
F	D	C	Root note

Well, there it is: the formula for the basic three-note chord applied to the root note C, making the basic C chord. And the formula itself is as clear as day. It is the *root note* (C) + the note *four intervals* above it (E) + the note *three intervals* above that (G).

And as that formula made a C chord, so it will make the basic three-note chord on any root note in the complete set. Take it home and try it on your piano. Try an F chord. The root note is F, the note four intervals above it is A, and the note three intervals above that is C.

Try a G chord. For heaven's sake (gulp) try an A♭ chord. And you will find that you have made the basic chord on that root without having gone through the fuss, muss and tedium of learning the basic seven-tone A♭ scale just to get its root, 3rd and 5th notes.

Oh yes, the formula for the basic chord works on any root note you choose on the keyboard. And inasmuch as it works —and is the basis of so much music-making— you have to memorize the formula. So write it down. Put it under your pillow. Paint it on the side of your elephant. Say it out loud:

Root note + 4 intervals + 3 intervals

But above all, *try it on your piano.* Apply it to every root note of the twelve and make every basic chord.

If you make a mistake in counting intervals, don't worry. Your ear will tell you about it immediately because this formula is the echo of *the comfortable setting in your mind* which listens to oncoming melody notes and identifies them as settled chordals or restless non-chordals.

You can see, then, why some composers' work sound like gibberish rather than understandable music. Such composers are not using this basic formula for locating their comfortable, resolved chordal notes and their uneasy, unresolved non-chordals. Their basic chord may be a different recipe of tones and intervals —a different setting from the one you have in mind. You may have to reorient your thinking to find out how they are organizing their comfort pattern.

FOR THE REST OF US, IN A NUTSHELL: You can make the basic three-note chord —the root + 3rd + 5th of the basic seven-tone scale— without having to learn any scales. The formula which pulls out that root-third-fifth combination is:
Any Root Note +4i + 3i
It is the only formula you will have to memorize to make music at the piano. Everything else in the enterprise proceeds from that formula in a nice, neat, child-like manner.

The formula pulls the chord out of the keyboard and the Root + 3rd + 5th out of the scale simultaneously.

Try it on your own piano

OBVIOUSLY, THE NEXT AND urgent order of business is to put the basic chord to use and make some music with it. So, this chapter will stop talking in a moment and get on with a few bars to play.

But first, a couple of notes, comments and reminders.

To begin with the name of the basic chord itself —very commonly it is called the major triad. But that label is not nearly so descriptive or so useful as the name *basic* chord —as you will see as this book progresses.

But regardless of which name it is called, it is named in sheet music by the *root note* on which it is built. If the chord called for is C, then it is the basic chord rooted on C. This is standard notation for chord symbols, and you will find it wherever chord symbols are used. A root note with no other symbol near it calls for the basic three-note chord only.

Usually, in these numbers, there is only one chord called for per bar —and, in fact, that chord may have to serve more than one bar. So, if no chord is named above a measure, simply repeat the chord you played in the measure before. If two chords are named above a bar, the chord changes there.

Now, it would be truly amazing if you could sit right down and apply the formula immediately to each root note called for, expressing the chords with only a second's thought. Much more

Make it easy on yourself. Write down the chord notes you'll need in a number.

likely, you will have to figure out the notes which make up the chords called for. So make it easy on yourself. Go through the number before you begin to play it and figure out the chords you'll need. In fact, write the letter names —or, if you prefer, the notes— along side the chord symbol. You only have to do that once for each different chord in a number. If an F chord is called for three times, one note to yourself on the page is enough.

That done, practice each hand separately first. Use the comfortable fingers of your right hand to pick out the melody notes. And listen to what you are playing. Then, below your melody area (which is where a setting ought to be) try the chords. With your left hand, of course.

As for the fingering, use the combination most comfortable. That is usually left pinky on the first note (or root); thumb on the top note (or 5th); and either index or middle finger on the middle note (or 3rd) of the chord.

But listen carefully to this harmonic setting you are playing with your left hand. If you've made a mistake in applying the formula or in expressing it —if you have somehow put a wrong note in the chord— give your ear a chance to tell you so. That is invaluable training in *making* music, and by and by it will work wonders, even for those who always thought they couldn't carry a tune. (By far the most common mistake in using the formula is forgetting to count the cracks or intervals which set off the black keys. That is because those cracks are not visible along the front edge of keyboard.)

When you come to coordinate both hands and play the melody and chords at the same time, strike the chord only once per measure (at the beginning of each bar). After all, your purpose is to listen to the oncoming tones as they are made comfortable or uncomfortable by the setting, the chord. Naturally, if a chord change is called for in the middle of a bar, then you will be striking two chords in that measure: one basic chord on one root note, another basic chord on a different root.

And another thing: be intelligent about the speed of your playing. This is not a competition for the fastest or smoothest performance. Besides, complete mastery of these chords and these melodies is a waste of time. And anyway, speed and fluency will come with playing more, making more and more music. There is no way to stop that from happening. The aim of this chapter is to give you some first-hand experience in assembling, hearing and understanding the fundamental components with which music is made in our part of the world.

And that brings up just one more word of caution. It may come as a bit of a surprise to see seemingly disrespectful use made here of work by such eminences as Wagner, Brahms, Beethoven and the U.S. Army. Granted, it is somewhat startling to see their melodies written out as only single notes with chord symbols above. But that is because the very word itself —"chord"— is so widely misunderstood, being both disreputable and exalted at the same time. On the one hand, it is quite common to hear somebody say, "Poor Arthur, he can only play chord piano;" and, on the other hand, it is just as common to hear the same person say, "Listen to the power and glory in Brahms' closing chord!"

Well, this seeming difficulty can be resolved very easily. The plain fact of the matter is that poor Brahms, like poor Arthur, could only play chord piano. That is also true of poor Wagner and poor Beethoven. And as for the poor bugler in the army, he can play only chord bugle calls. The plain fact is that they, like almost all of us, organize oncoming notes into melody patterns in part by chords. That will become crystal clear as you try these samples on your piano.

Exactly how these eminences expressed those chords —in their minds, or divided up among a hundred instruments, or rendered by a soprano, alto and bass singing along with the tenor— that varies from composition to composition. But without any doubt they made chord music. In fact, it was the great Wagner who said: "Ich werde hier den C akkord benutzen."*

All of that explained, it is finally time to get to the music. As you will see, most of the melodies set out below are chordal —most of the oncoming single notes fit exactly the chords called for. When the chord changes, it is to make the melody notes comfortably chordal. The few unsettled, non-chordal notes in these numbers are marked with an "x" to make the matter even more tediously clear.

In the first number —the bugle call *Taps* —there are neither chord changes nor non-chordal notes. All 24 oncoming tones of the melody are settled, comfortable, resolved chordals. And, moreover, *they are chordals of one chord,* the basic chord played on the same root, throughout. That is because the bugle can play only the three notes of the basic chord. So, all bugle calls are completely comfortably chordal notes of one chord. As a result, you can easily transpose *Taps* or any other bugle call to another key —to another starting note with another root note for the chord.

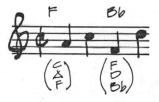

Sometimes chords change within a measure. Usually, a chord changes to keep most melody notes comfortable chordals.

---

*Auf English that means: "I'm going to use a C chord here." But whether or not he actually said it, the evidence shows irrefutably that he couldn't compose his music without the use of our basic chords.

TAPS

Try it on your piano. Play this sample of *Taps*. Then, pick another basic chord. Play it with your left hand, and use the three notes of it with a finger of your right hand to pick out *Taps* in *that* key.

TAPS

Very few tunes are made of notes-of-the-chord only. Even the simplest usually contain a few restless non-chordals.

THE BLUE DANUBE

LONG, LONG AGO

REVIVE US AGAIN

with the cello and flute. But the sound of the chord remains the same —standard, settled, comfortable together. And, as you would expect, the sound remains settled and comfortable and wholly chordal together when you invert it again by putting the bottom F# on top of the new structure. The root note, D, is now in the middle. But still the chord is that basic agreement among the three notes.

It ought to go without saying (but it's not going to) that you can do the same with any chord and with any three musical instruments —including three singers. Try a D♭ chord on your local opera company. Assign the root note to a basso, the 3rd to a soprano and the 5th to a tenor. So much for the root position. The two re-combinations work as well with the vocalists as they do with the orchestra instruments and with the keys on a piano. Whatever the combination, it leaves the chord intact.

That gives you a pretty good basic view of what arrangers arrange in the music world. They take the melody notes from the composer and assign the notes of the setting —of the chord— to the voices of different instruments and/or vocalists.

IN A NUTSHELL, THEN: The basic chord being made of three notes, it can be combined in three basic ways:
1. In root position (root at the bottom).
2. With the root at the top.
3. With the root in the middle.
And if that is clear, then you understand the most difficult concept in making music.

It should go without saying, but will not, that the formula for the basic chord (root + 4i + 3i) makes only the root position —obviously— because it pulls out the component notes of the chord beginning with the root on the bottom, the 3rd of the basic scale in the middle, and the 5th of the scale on the top.

But even when the chord is re-combined, its component notes remain the same. The root is still the root, no matter where it is in the structure. And the 3rd and 5th remain the 3rd and 5th whether they are played at the bottom, middle or top of the chord.

You have to listen to the way this works out on the keyboard. It is part of your understanding of how to make music. It is part of your ear training. So take one chord at a time and play its combinations up the keyboard two times and down again. As always, do it with your left hand; do it slowly; do it with the pinky and thumb on the outer two notes of the chord (whatever they happen to be in the combination of the moment) and the index or middle finger on the middle note.

Do it at your leisure, a chord or two per day if you want

It's still the basic
3-note A chord.

to pace it that way. You're not doing it to commit it to memory. Nor are you doing it as a finger exercise. Playing chords in their combinations over and over does not make music. But if you listen to what you are playing, your music-making ability will increase vastly —as you will see in due course. For one thing, you will know when you have introduced a new note, a wrong note, into the chord. A wrong note, as your ear will tell you (even if you can't carry a tune), is not just wrong. It also makes a new chord —a new and different setting for oncoming notes of the melody.

All of that said, the hardest part of making music has been explained. From here on it's all downhill.

Don't memorize. Just listen to what you play. A wrong note will make a new and different chord.

How to alter the basic chord— minor, diminished & augmented

7 WHEN IT COMES TO ORGANIZING and reorganizing, nobody is better at it than people. Given a few basic items such as earth, water and fire, people will alter those components this way and that and turn them into a few other basic items —a pot, say, and an aquaduct and a house.

Given a basic three-note organizing sound, people will alter those few basic notes this way and that and turn them into three additional basic organizing sounds on the same root. Those altered, basic, three-note chords are:

The Minor Chord

The Diminished Chord

The Augmented Chord

There is no telling just when people took the basic chord and first made these fundamental changes in it, any more than you can tell when people took the basic clay pot and first altered it to make a brick for building. But you can easily see *how* the basic three-note chord came to be reorganized to make the three altered forms of minor, diminished and augmented chords.

To begin with, there are only two notes of the basic three which can be moved about. Clearly, you cannot move the root note even by one interval —from C to B, say. If you did that, the chord would no longer be a C chord; it would become a B chord. So, that leaves only the remaining two notes of the chord —the 3rd and the 5th— available for alterations. Under the circumstances, then:

1. If you play the basic chord and *lower the 3rd by one interval,* you will have made a *minor* chord. That means taking the basic C chord and flatting the E, making it E♭. The resulting altered chord is the *C minor* chord.

2. On the other hand, if you take that basic three-note chord and *lower both the 3rd and 5th by one interval,* you will have made a diminished chord. That means taking the basic G chord, for instance, and flatting both the B and D —making them B♭ and D♭. The resulting altered chord is, obviously, the *G diminished* chord.

3. The third and final way to alter the basic chord is to *raise the 5th one interval* and thus make the *augmented* chord. That means taking the basic B chord, say, and sharping the F♯ to make it G. The alteration turns the basic *B* chord into the *B augmented* chord.

ALL IN ALL, THE 5TH has two possible alterations. It can be sharped to turn the basic chord into an augmented chord; and it can be flatted along with the flatted 3rd to make the diminished chord. But the 3rd has only one possible way to be altered. It can only be flatted (to make the minor chord, or —with the flatted 5th— to make the diminished chord).

In printed music, where the chords are designated by their root letter names rather than by notes on the staff, these three altered chords are clearly labeled with the root name and the alteration called for:

1. *The minor chord* is designated by the letter *m* or the abbreviation *min* or by the familiar minus (-) sign. So, when you see these symbols, you know that the sound called for is the basic chord with its 3rd lowered one interval. And inasmuch as the 3rd is always the 3rd, no matter how the chordal notes are re-combined, *the 3rd is flatted no matter where it appears,* even on the bottom (with the root played on top or in the middle).

2. *A diminished chord* is designated on sheet music by either the abbreviation *dim* or by a small circle (o). When you see one of these symbols next to the root name of the basic chord, it calls for *lowering the 3rd and 5th one interval no matter where*

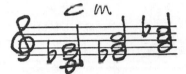

THE MINOR CHORD:
Flat the 3rd wherever it appears in the chord.

THE DIMINISHED CHORD:
Flat both the 3rd and 5th wherever they are.

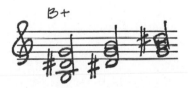

THE AUGMENTED CHORD:
Sharp the 5th, no matter where it sits in the chord.

MARCHE SLAVE (TCHAIKOWSKY)

The altered chords —the min, dim and aug— are used in the best circles.

SPANISH DANCE (MOSZKOWSKI)

they appear in the arrangement of the chord notes —above the root, below it or surrounding it.

3. *The augmented chord* is designated by either the abbreviation *Aug* or by the familiar plus (+) sign. And it calls for altering the basic chord by *raising the 5th one interval.* No matter where it appears in the combination of chord notes, you sharp the 5th.

Now, just because the original chord has been altered, that does not mean the changed sound is any the less of a fundamental, solid setting for bestowing comfort (or restlessness) on oncoming melody tones. When it comes to that work, a Db chord and a Dbm chord work in the same basic way. And just because an alteration is designated by a shorthand symbol such as C#- or Gb+, that does not mean it is some sort of jerry-built or casual organizing sound tacked together in some back room for making cheap music. Quite the contrary: these altered chords have a gilt-edge pedigree and make quite a lot of irreproachable music.

Naturally, the irreproachable composers didn't write those chords in such symbols. Instead, they assigned the notes which lie behind that shorthand to the various instruments of the orchestra —painting each component note in the tone color of the instrument playing it. But that does not change the principle. If a bassoon is playing a root note and a violin is playing the 5th and a piccolo is playing the flatted 3rd at the top, they are clearly playing a recombined version of the chord. But the chord itself is an *altered* chord, *the minor.*

WHAT THESE CHORDS MEAN or how each differs from the others in feeling is hazardous to say. For example, it is common to think that a minor chord means sadness. But that is not always so. A lot of happy music is made in part with minor chords, as you can see on a lot of popular sheet music. But even music made almost wholly of this chord with the flatted 3rd —many Russian folk songs, for instance —avoid a sad feeling by being played fast.

And the same is true for the other two altered chords. Sometimes the diminished chord imparts a forlorn and yearning feeling. And then again, sometimes it doesn't. Sometimes the augmented chord wails, and sometimes it doesn't. It all depends on how and when and where a chord is used. To quote the only rule for making music once more, if it sounds good to you, then it is a good sound.

But one thing is sure about the basic chord and its three alterations. Each has a definite shape, a personal profile, as a setting for oncoming tones. Try these chords on your piano. Play the basic chord first and an altered chord after it. Compare the sound and shape of the basic chord with each of its alterations. That way you will see that the root is never altered.

You will see that the recipes for making all of these organizing sounds always begin with the ingredients of "Any Root +" —and what changes shape and size in each chord lies on the other side of that +. *What changes is the distribution of the intervals beyond the root,* thus giving each altered chord its individuality. To wit:

The basic three-note chord is a very stable sound, as you can hear when you play it, and as you can see by looking at the distribution of intervals in its formula. The majority of its weight —four intervals— serves as a ballast to keep the remaining three intervals steady and secure. It is heavier at the bottom than at the top.

The minor chord is made by lowering the 3rd one interval. This alteration redistributes the intervals, but still makes a very stable sound, as you can see and will hear. The majority of its weight, four intervals, is now on the opposite end of the balance where it serves again as a secure ballast. Like the basic chord, the minor chord is heavier at the bottom than at the top.

I LOVE PARIS

C MIN

The remaining two altered chords, however, do not look —or sound— so bottom-heavy and stable.

The diminished chord is made by flatting both the 3rd and 5th notes. That distributes the intervals equally on both ends and makes for a perfectly balanced —and thus unstable— sound.

CLOSE AS PAGES IN A BOOK

Eb   E DIM   F M7   Bb7

Similarly, the augmented chord: It is made by sharping the 5th. Once again the intervals are equally distributed. But there are more of them in this chord —four and four. Consequently, the balance is more precarious and the sound more unstable. That is in keeping with the rule that the bigger they are, the harder they fall.

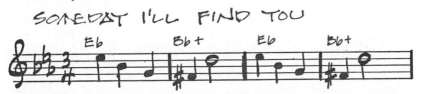

SOMEDAY I'LL FIND YOU

Eb   Bb+   Eb   Bb+

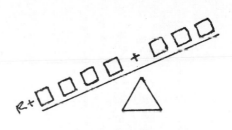

The basic chord: most intervals at one end —a stable sound.

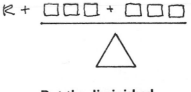

The minor, too, has a stable sound.

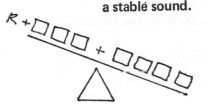

But the diminished and augmented sound more unstable. Their intervals are in even balance.

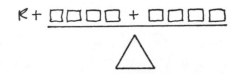

With all of that laid out for inspection, it remains only to lay it out again in a nutshell — and then to move on to PART THREE of this book, where music-making begins for real.

IN A NUTSHELL: The basic three-note chord can be altered three ways, thus making three additional fundamental settings for placing oncoming melody notes as comfortable notes-of-the-chord and restless non-chordal notes. These three alterations of the basic chord are:

1. The *minor* chord. It is made by flatting the 3rd, no matter where the 3rd appears In the configuration —top, bottom or middle.

2. The *diminished* chord is made by flatting the 3rd and the 5th —by lowering each one interval —no matter where those notes appear in the chord.

3. The *augmented* chord is made by sharping the 5th —raising the 5th of the original basic chord —wherever you happen to be playing the 5th in the chord combination.

Play those recipes. Listen to them. Remember them well enough so that you can say them immediately, even in the middle of the night if someone calls to ask. But don't bother to practice them or become fluent with them on every root note. Right now the important thing is to gain knowledge. Putting it to work will come soon enough and easily enough. That is the great breakthrough of this book, namely that the fingers are connected to the mind.

Oh, yes, one other thing about the alterations of the basic chord. Each altered chord is, of course, a three-note chord. So each can, like the basic chord, be played in three different positions on the keyboard.

The altered chords can also be played in 3 positions.

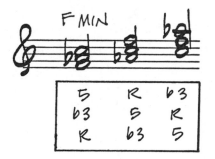

42

How to play the piano despite years of lessons

THE MYTH: Music is a very hallowed, almost super-human, body of knowledge.

THE FACT: Music is very human. Like everybody, it is held together by a skele-ton —a simple scaffolding which anyone can make at home on the keyboard.

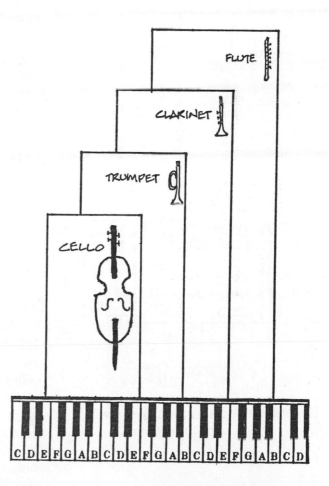

Instruments have their own layers of sound. But the piano can play in several stratums at once, making it a miniature orchestra.

Part three

The piano is a miniature orchestra. Consequently it is quite useful for building your very own skeleton. How to keep the three elements of the skeleton in their proper layers of sound so as to make easy-to-understand music. And then, some music to *make* on your piano with this elementary and fundamental arrangement.

The piano as a miniature orchestra: Stratums— layers of sound

8 AS EVERYBODY KNOWS BY NOW, most of our music is music because a skeleton holds it together —a simple scaffolding of uprights and horizontals set on a stable footing. That skeleton is available for inspection in just about every melody, classical or popular, which comes along. The uprights can be seen in the pattern of high and low notes. The horizontals are in the pattern of notes of wide and narrow duration in time. And the footing, the setting for the whole of it, is in the basic chords which make the pattern of comfortable and unresolved notes.

In other words, implicit in any single-note melody you hear (or whistle or sing or play with one finger) is the entire high, wide and chordal skeleton which holds most of our music together. But, really, who wants to listen to implicit music?* After all, a number played with just one finger gives you only the high-low and wide-narrow patterns outright. Your mind has to supply the remaining unexpressed member of the skeleton —the basic chords which bestow comfort or restlessness on those notes.

Even when two members of the skeleton are stated out loud, you are still putting out quite a bit of energy to supply the third in your mind. That is what makes a drum-and-clarinet duet hard to take for very long. You are being given the rhythmic beat and the melody line all right; but you have to fill in the chords for yourself. Similarly, there is a limit to how long you can stand the sound of free-floating melody and harmony before you long to hear an explicit beat from the rhythm instruments. And when it finally arrives, you breathe a sigh of relief.

All of that explains why the fundamental skeleton is usually stated plainly in most arrangements of music. True, it may be camouflaged and disguised with additional sounds. Moreover, one or another member may be suspended for a passage, and only the remaining two played, to keep your interest and attention by asking you to do some work. But almost always you can pick out the three members of the skeleton in the arrangement —the organizing sounds of the three patterns —the high and low melody notes, the clockwork beat of the rhythm and the

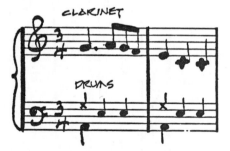

Melody and beat only. There's a limit to how long you'll put up with a missing member of the skeleton.

---

*A few people. Or, to put it another way: Heard music is sweet but Unheard music is musicology.

basic chords of the harmony.

Why you can hear and identify the three members of the skeleton is easy to see. It is because *each member is assigned to its own separate and distinct layer of sound* —or stratum of sound. So, if you can hear the three members of the skeleton, it is because you are hearing three different stratums or layers of sound at work: the *oom* stratum, the *pah* stratum and the *melody* stratum. And they are all at work simultaneously, as you can hear in any orchestra. You can identify the drums in that stratum down there, sounding their clockwork beat. You're also hearing the violins in this middle stratum of sound playing the chords. And at the very same time, you are hearing the lone flute up in that high stratum playing the single notes of the melody. And all the while, you are listening to a full, complete orchestra playing a whole composition.

LOOKED AT THAT WAY, the piano is not really an instrument at all. Actually, it is a miniature orchestra because *it can play in several stratums of sound at the same time.* It always sounds like the piano, of course. It cannot paint music with the orchestral palette of tone colors which distinguish the brasses, strings, woodwinds and percussion instruments from each other. But the piano can express the entire skeleton of music as the orchestra does by using several layers of sound simultaneously —*several separate and distinct stratums of sound.*

For that reason, the piano is not really needed in the playing of orchestral music. And so you seldom find a piano in the orchestra —except as a solo instrument in works written for piano-and-orchestra, or as a labor-saving device to keep the size of the orchestra small or to make a small one, such as a combo or band, sound larger.

Like the orchestra, the piano normally arranges the members of the skeleton as everybody knows them: melody notes in the top stratum; chords of the harmony in a stratum below that; and beat of the rhythm in the lowest or bass stratum.

The reason for that normal arrangement of the skeleton is easy to hear. *The top note of any stratum is the most penetrating in that stratum.* And naturally, the higher the stratum, the more penetrating its top note.

That is why a hundred-piece orchestra may have forty violins but only three flutes with their higher, more piercing range. Notes played up there at the top of the top stratum force themselves most insistently on your attention. So, usually the melody is played in a high stratum. And for the same reason, the clockwork beat of the rhythm is played in the lowest, bass stratum where it is least penetrating —where it can be felt rather than heard outright. And the chords of the harmony are normally played in the middle stratum where they can be heard

If chords roam out of a narrow stratum, their top notes may make an unwanted and uncontrolled melody

clearly, but not overwhelmingly, in support of the melody stratum above them.

Because the top note in each stratum of sound is the most penetrating in its stratum, *the stratums must be kept separate and distinct from each other.* That is the only way to keep the members of the skeleton separate and easily identified. If the chord stratum, for example, is not sharply and rigidly contained —if the chords are allowed to jump about in a loosely defined layer of sound— their top notes would penetrate as an unwanted and uncontrolled melody, very likely distracting the mind's ear from the true melody in the stratum above.

For instance, imagine your right hand playing some melody or other for a couple of bars which require two chord changes — from C to G and back to C. If you let those chords jump about in a broad stratum like this example . . . well, as you can hear if you try it, the top notes of the chords themselves make their own competitive melody.

Not that there's anything wrong with the melody they make: *Here Comes The Bride.* It's just that it sounds a little foolish to be playing that melody in the chord stratum while the true melody stratum above is playing *Love For Sale* or *Home On The Range.*

That isn't making music. That's music making itself. And it comes across as a very careless and incompetent arrangement.

UNLIKE THE ORCHESTRA OR BAND which has a drum or bass or tuba to play down there in the bass stratum, the piano must make do with a note of the chord to produce the clockwork *oom* beat in that low stratum. What the orchestra or band does with a combination of *ooms* and *pahs*— rhythmic beats and chords— the piano must accomplish with a combination of *bass notes & chords* for its low and middle stratums.

So, in laying out the normal skeleton of a waltz on the piano, your right hand plays the melody line with one finger in the top stratum —while your left hand accompanies it in two stratums beneath by playing *bass-note-&-chord-&-chord.*

In laying out the normal skeleton of a fox trot on the keyboard, your left hand works those two lower stratums beneath the melody —the low bass stratum and the strictly contained, middle, chord stratum— to produce a combination of *bass note-&-chord, bass note-&-chord.*

And in so doing, you have divided the keyboard into three separate and distinct layers of sound and laid out the three members of the skeleton which underlies and organizes almost all of our music.

It may sound a bit old fashioned, this outright, unadorned bass-&-chord piano playing. But it is absolutely honest and straightforward, and has a gilt-edged history behind it. You don't have to know how to read much music —in fact, nothing in the bass clef— to see clearly that Chopin and Schubert are asking for high priced performers to play a basic skeleton in these samples:

SO, IN A NUTSHELL: The basic skeleton arrangement expresses the melody, rhythm and harmony without embellishment or disguise. It is only one way to make music at the piano, and isn't used much today. But it is the basic way. All other arrangements begin with it. So you have to get it into your repertoire.

The basic, normal skeleton arrangement is made by playing in three separate and distinct layers of sound —stratums— on the keyboard. To wit:

One finger of your right hand plays the single-note melody of number —the melody line set out for the vocalist in sheet music. (Disregard the treble clef and bass clef for piano use. You don't need them to make music.)

Your left hand, playing in the two lower stratums, produces the other two members of the skeleton —the rhythm and the harmony. Your left hand does so by hitting a steady combination of bass note-&-chord. The bass note is a note of the chord, and is played in the lowest or bass stratum on the keyboard. The chord itself is played in a narrow middle stratum above the bass and below the

The basic skeleton arrangement is used by all sorts of people.

47

melody stratums. How many bass notes-&-chords your left hand plays in a bar depends on whether the number is in 3/4 (or waltz) time, or in 4/4 time. But in either case, the chords are kept in a narrow stratum so as to keep their top notes from wandering about and creating an unwanted and uncontrolled melody.

Which chord does your left hand play? Obviously the chord called for above the single-note melody line in your sheet music: the chord named by its root note in the chord symbols.

Exactly where are the stratum for all three —single note melody, chords, bass notes? The next chapter tells you.

The basic skeleton that holds all music together

9

HERE'S EXACTLY HOW TO MAKE MUSIC with the basic skeleton arrangement, and precisely where to express the three members of the skeleton on the keyboard:

1. Your right hand plays a one-finger, single-note melody. (That single-note melody is the vocalist's line, the top line on your sheet music.) But you play that single-note melody *an octave higher than it is printed or written.*

2. Your left hand plays basic three-note chords in a very narrow stratum in the middle of the keyboard. Your left thumb, which plays the top notes of those chords, *never goes lower than middle C or higher than the E just above it.*

3. Your left hand also works the bass stratum. Take the root note of the chord and play it as an octave —*the lowest possible octave on the keyboard.* (The chord you use is named above the vocalist's line. It is named by its root. So that is plainly the note to use for the bass note. But you play it as an octave.)

The reasons for that arrangement of the basic skeleton on the keyboard are easy to see.

1. *Your right hand plays the melody an octave higher than written.* First, because it floats the melody in a high but comfortable stratum safely and clearly above the chord stratum. And second, because it uses more of the piano and thus, orchestrally, makes more music.

2. *The chords are kept in a very narrow stratum.* Their top notes (your thumb) never go lower than middle C nor higher than the E just above it. That puts the chord stratum at the very bottom of the staff, well below the melody stratum. Moreover, it keeps your thumb from playing an unwanted and uncon-

The chord stratum: top notes of chords (played by your thumb) stay between middle C and E just above it.

trolled melody in the chord stratum.

To keep your thumb within that narrow stratum means, obviously, that *you cannot play every chord in its root position.* Some chords will have to be played with their root note on top or in the middle so as to stay within the chord stratum.

For instance, the G chord can certainly be played in root position as its top note, D, clearly lies between the C and E of the chord stratum. Similarly, the F chord (with its top note of C) can be played in root position. But that is not true of the B♭ chord. Played in root position, its top note is F —too high for the stratum. So you have to play the B♭ chord one position lower, with the top note dropped to the bottom.

There are other chords in the same boat, having to be played in other positions so as to stay within the chord stratum. But that is not so complicated an order. For one thing, *only seven of the chords* cannot be played in root position as the formula pulls them together. They are: A#/B♭ B C C#/D♭ D D#/E♭ and E chords. And for another thing, the position of chords played in stratum becomes an automatic reflex to your hand as you make music at the piano. That cannot be avoided. It comes naturally.

3: *Alternating with the chord, to create the beat, is a bass note played by your left hand.* That bass note is the root note of the chord. It is played double —as an octave —in the lowest possible place on the keyboard. Try it on your piano. Try the lowest possible E♭ note simultaneously with the next E♭ above it.

There are three good reasons for playing the bass note that way. First, the lowest note of the two is more a *noise* than a musical pitch, so it gives you a *feeling of the beat* the way a drum does in an orchestra. Second, the upper note of the two is more of a musical pitch than a noise —more clearly the tone of the root note— so it is heard as part of the chord as well as part of the clockwork beat. And third, having to reach for that lowest possible octave not only uses more of the piano orchestrally, but it also gives your hand an education in distance on the keyboard. That's very necessary when it comes to playing by ear, too.

SO, THAT'S HOW TO MAKE MUSIC with the basic skeleton —using those three elementary orchestral stratums to express the three members of the skeleton. And for that very reason, you don't have to read any more than the vocalist's single-note melody line and the chord symbols above it. The plain fact is, the two lines written for the piano on most sheet music *make less music* than the basic skeleton.

That is because the basic skeleton would *look* too forbidding to play if it were printed on sheet music, and would discourage the people who know only how to read music but not how to make it.

Chord Chord
Bass
The basic skeleton setting
for a melody in 3/4 time.

Chord   Chord
Bass   Bass
The basic skeleton setting
for a melody in 4/4 time.

Take a look for yourself. You don't have to know how to read the bass clef or the chords in the treble clef in order to see what kind of music is called for in the two lower piano parts. You can see that the right hand plays in one stratum and the left in the stratum immediately below it. You can see how few full chords are called for, and how little work each hand does.

THIS CAN'T BE LOVE

The original arrangement— left hand plays single notes and octaves in mid-keyboard.

Now that kind of music *looks* very easy to play. Childishly simple, in fact. And it sounds just that way, too. But it is not easier to make than a skeleton arrangement, and it is a whole lot more expensive. With this kind of music —two stratums close together in the middle of the keyboard, and mostly single notes played — it is a great waste of money to invest in a full-size piano when you are going to ignore the piano's orchestral ability. You could do just as well, and save lots of money, with a piano of only three octaves.

Settings written for the piano often make less music than you can make with your basic skeleton arrangement.

For most people, however, the skeleton printed on the page would be too overwhelming in appearance —what with the melody printed an octave higher than usual, the bass notes as octaves in the the lowest possible register, and (help!) all those chords in stratum. Take a look:

THIS CAN'T BE LOVE

SO, IN A NUTSHELL, the basic skeleton means:

Right hand playing single note melody one octave higher than printed or written; and left hand playing a combination of bass note-&-chord.

The chord is played in stratum (your left thumb, the top note, going no lower than middle C and no higher than the E above it). Consequently, some chords cannot be played in root position. And as for the bass note, it is the root note of the chord. You play it as an octave, the lowest octave possible on the keyboard.

In numbers where there are four beats to the measure, your left hand plays a steady clockwork of *bass-&-chord,bass-&-chord* per measure (fox trots, blues, sambas, Charlestons, etc.). In numbers requiring three beats to the measure, your left hand plays a waltz-time oom-pah-pah —a steady clockwork of *bass-&-chord-chord* per measure.

Inasmuch as you are now beginning to make music and not just to play it, you need only the single-note vocalist's melody line and the chord symbols above it.

You're the arranger now. So, you need only the vocalist's line and the chord symbols above it to make music at the piano.

Try it on your own piano

10

THE PURPOSE OF THIS CHAPTER is to give you a couple of melody samples to play in basic skeleton arrangement. As you will see, these bars are taken from old standards (or semi-classics, depending on whether you are over 35 years of age or under).

There are two reasons for using these samples. First, you know the melody line, so your ear will be able to tell your hands at once when they have made a mistake in either the melody stratum or the chord stratum. And second, there are generally no more than two chord changes per measure. In fact, most of the time there is one chord in a bar. And that is a great saving of energy and nerves when you are learning to put the basic skeleton together. It is engrossing enough to coordinate both hands at the outset, and to keep your left hand working in steady cadence. But to have the added distraction of having to find a new bass note and a new chord each time your hand comes down on the keys —that is too much. And that is just what you have to do with each chord change in basic skeleton arranging *because the clockwork combination of the beat goes on despite any change in chords.*

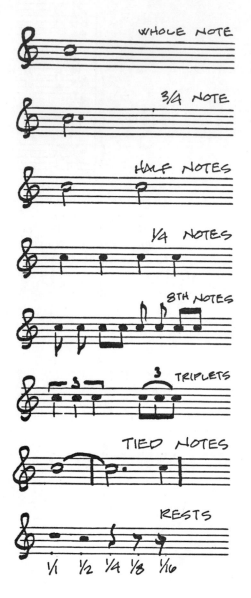

WHOLE NOTE

3/4 NOTE

HALF NOTES

1/4 NOTES

8TH NOTES

3 TRIPLETS

TIED NOTES

RESTS

1/1 1/2 1/4 1/8 1/16

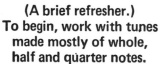

(A brief refresher.)
To begin, work with tunes
made mostly of whole,
half and quarter notes.

In other words, regardless of how many different chords are called for in a bar, the overriding principle of the basic skeleton remains the steady bass note-&-chord rhythm. And that principle calls for a bit of fancy left hand work when there are four chord changes in a bar.

Obviously the basic skeleton can be used on thousands of other numbers than those sampled in this chapter. So if you want to work with melodies of your own choosing, make sure they meet two requirements: mostly one chord change per bar, and simple melodies — few eighth notes, few tied notes, few triplets. Or, put the other way, the melody should be made mostly of whole notes, half notes and quarter notes. A very partial list of numbers in that category:

By Jerome Kern: *Look For the Silver Lining; Why Do I Love You; The Way You Look Tonight; All The Things You Are; The Last Time I Saw Paris; Smoke Gets In Your Eyes.*

By George Gershwin: *Love Walked In; Somebody Loves Me; Embraceable You; But Not For Me; Our Love Is Here To Stay.*

By Irving Berlin: *Say It With Music; Always; Easter Parade.*

By Richard Rodgers: *My Heart Stood Still; Some Enchanted Evening; O What A Beautiful Morning; Small Hotel; Where Or When.*

By Sigmund Romberg: *Will You Remember; Deep In My Heart; One Alone; Lover Come Back To Me; One Kiss; When You Grow Too Old To Dream.*

By Vincent Youmans: *I Want To Be Happy; Sometimes I'm Happy.*

By Victor Young: *Love Letters; Golden Earrings; Stella By Starlight; My Foolish Heart.*

THE BASIC SKELETON IS THE FIRST STOP on the way to complete music making. But it is only a stop. Your goal *isn't* perfection and speed. What you want is rather a good working knowledge of the keyboard and its stratums, and an ability to express bass note-&-chord combinations. This basic skeleton experience should give you some facility in finding notes and combinations on the keyboard and —just as important —an unwavering feel for the beat. The awful truth is that people will put up with a mistake in the melody quite readily (and, in fact, if you make the same mistake twice they will applaud your creativity). *But they will not stand for a pause in the tempo or an uneven, uncertain beat.* So:

1. Play slowly enough to produce a smooth bass-&-chord rhythm. It doesn't matter how slowly as long as the beat is steady.

2. Play these left hand combinations several times without the right hand melody before you put both hands to work together.

3. Use any crutch, any device that will help you to get your left hand to play a steady clockwork beat.

For instance, jot down all the chords required by the number you're working with. Then write out the component notes of each chord in their stratum position, and indicate to yourself which is the root note (to be used as the bass note).

4. In getting a steady beat —and a feeling for it— it is a help to count the beat out loud.

In a waltz (three beats per measure) you naturally count "ONE Two Three" in each measure. And in 4/4 time, you count "ONE Two THREE Four" for each bar. That steady counting goes on throughout the entire number without pausing for the lines which separate one bar from the next. Further, that counting is done very loudly to make sure that your left hand knows who is boss. That way you will *play as you count*. The counting is the feeling for the beat, and by and by it becomes part of your nature.

5. If you work with melodies other than those in this chapter, don't pay any attention to the small numbers attached to some chord symbols, such as Gm6 or A7.

You are playing *basic* skeleton, so you use only the basic three-note chord and its three-note alterations: minor, diminished and augmented. So, for A7 you play the basic A chord; for Gm6 you play the basic G minor chord.

Those small added numbers indicate a fourth note added to the basic chord. That is the way most chords are played nowadays (and will be explained repeatedly in the next section on filling out the skeleton). That is another reason for not becoming perfect in playing the basic skeleton but rather aiming to master the fundamentals.

6. No matter what the melody does, no matter which of its notes are sharped or flatted, the chords always conform to the formula.

The C chord is always the C chord, even if the melody is written in six flats. An E♭ chord is always that, even if the melody note at the time is a C or a D♭ or something else.

7. Be warned: smooth coordination of both hands and a steady beat with the left may not come in a day or two. But it doesn't take a half-year to achieve, either.

What is required is simply making music at the piano for about fifteen minutes a day. Be further warned: the keyboard at the outset may appear to be a sea of shiny, undifferentiated ivory. But that only means your mind is starting to reorganize the matter—transforming it from a piano into *your* piano. This sorting out, this falling into place, does not happen a little bit at a time. It comes in leaps. One week it is spaghetti and, suddenly, one day it is . . . well, ravioli. Between the two will be a plateau of no seeming progress. Don't worry. Stick with it.

And with that word of encouragement, here are a couple of melody lines to try with basic skeleton —all festooned and filigreed with reminders and explanations.

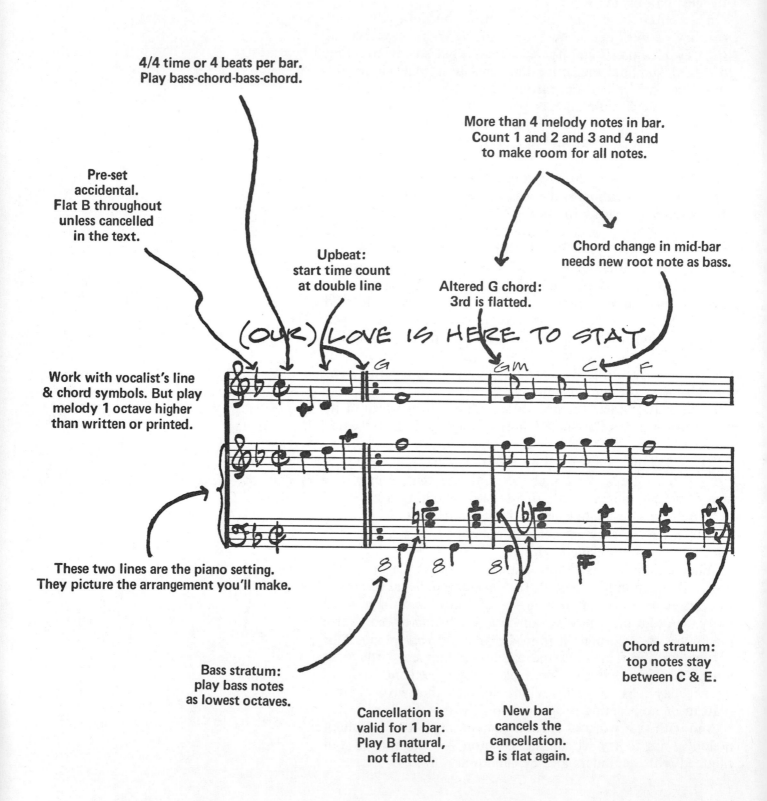

4/4 time or 4 beats per bar.
Play bass-chord-bass-chord.

More than 4 melody notes in bar.
Count 1 and 2 and 3 and 4 and
to make room for all notes.

Pre-set
accidental.
Flat B throughout
unless cancelled
in the text.

Chord change in mid-bar
needs new root note as bass.

Upbeat:
start time count
at double line

Altered G chord:
3rd is flatted.

(OUR) LOVE IS HERE TO STAY

Work with vocalist's line
& chord symbols. But play
melody 1 octave higher
than written or printed.

These two lines are the piano setting.
They picture the arrangement you'll make.

Chord stratum:
top notes stay
between C & E.

Bass stratum:
play bass notes
as lowest octaves.

Cancellation is
valid for 1 bar.
Play B natural,
not flatted.

New bar
cancels the
cancellation.
B is flat again.

LOVE'S OLD SWEET SONG

Tunes to try on a
basic skeleton
setting.
Just remember:
your aim
is smoothness,
not speed.

ADESTE FIDELES

How to play the piano despite years of lessons

THE MYTH: There are a lot of rules and regulations in music.

THE FACT: There is only one rule in music, namely *if it sounds good it is good*.

Part four

Up from the basics and fundamentals with three ways to fill out the skeleton. First: how to make and use four-note chords— the *7th* chord, the *6th* chord and the *Major 7th* chord. Next: how to fill out the skeleton with *alternating bass notes*. Last: how to put *block notes* beneath the melody.

Four-note chords— the 7th

11

SO MUCH FOR THE BASIC CHORDS, the basic skeleton, the basic bass. It's all right to visit the basics. Very educational and all. But you really wouldn't want to live there.

Basic music—like basic food, basic shelter and basic clothing— is a drab and boring existence. Only people with no choice in the matter put up with it. The rest of us put up draperies, hemlines and strawberry jam, which are hardly what you would call the fundamentals of living. That is to say, basically people are not very basic by nature, but are forever experimenting and adding onto the basics.

Clearly that is what people have done with the basic three-note chords in this part of the planet. And as a result, most of us organize the oncoming single tones of a melody with *a four-note chord* —the basic three notes with one note added to them.

Exactly when that happened is impossible to say. But you can see how it came about . . . .

Say you're a composer living in a time long ago, and you're bored to the teeth with the basic chord which lets you make only those three notes comfortable in the melody and forces you to keep the remaining nine possible notes on the move because they are non-chordals. One day, you can stand it no longer. The idea comes to you —or, rather, to your mind's ear— to let the melody you are creating linger on the B♭ even though the harmony beneath it is a basic three-note C chord. In other words, you have asked your listeners to put up with a clash of a sustained non-chordal in a chordal setting.

What happens? Why, your audience throws tomatoes at you, and quite likely at your colleagues who hear in your experiment something new, interesting, exciting —and try it in their compositions.

But year after year, concert after concert, the barrage of tomatoes slackens and finally stops altogether. It has become accepted by the audience to hear that B♭ as a comfortable tone with a basic C chord. There is no more said about it —except by a few composers who are becoming tired of that hackneyed sound of the settled B♭ tone with the settled three notes of the basic C chord. And with that, you can see that the B♭ has been *incorporated into the chord* and is an integral part of it.

That doesn't mean it is the basic chord with a note tacked onto it. Not at all. It is a completely comfortable organization. It can never again be taken apart and returned to being a basic chord of three comfortable tones and an unresolved, unsettled non-chordal note. No matter how long it has taken for that to happen, there is no going back. Or, to put it another way, *we hear what we are used to hearing*. What sounds good changes.

The 7th is really the flatted 7th, and you can always find it 2 intervals below the root.

But it changes only when its time has come. Take this business of the Bb added to the basic three. By rights and reason, it shouldn't have been that way at all. And it doesn't take a mathematical genius to predict how it should have been. After all, the basic chord is a series of the odd-numbered notes of the basic seven-tone scale — the 1-3-5. So, if a note were to be added, obviously it would be number 7. And in the basic seven-tone scale beginning on C, the seventh is obviously B, not Bb. But it didn't happen that way. The note added to make the four-note chord was *the flatted 7th — the note two intervals (not one) below the root note.* Try it on your own piano. Take a basic three-note chord and add to it the note two intervals below the root, the flatted 7th. And there you have the common, comfortable, indispensable four-note *7th chord.*

With the same recipe, naturally, you can add a note to any altered chord and make it a 7th, too. By adding this note two intervals below the root you can turn the minor, diminished and augmented chords into the min7, dim7 and aug7. And with the basic7 chord, that makes *four* 7th chords very possible (although the dim7 is seldom used today).

Exactly where you add that flatted seventh note to the basic chord and its alterations depends on the chord stratum. The top note of the chord, whether it is a three-note or a four-note chord, cannot go below middle C or past the E just above it. So the placement of the added 7th note depends on where there is room for it *within the chord stratum.* If it won't fit at the top, then you have to put it in the middle or at the bottom.

For instance, the basic F chord can be played in root position, and even the addition of the 7th —the note two intervals below the F— at the top of the structure still stays within the chord stratum. But that will not work with the Ab chord or its alterations. As a three-note chord, Ab can be played in root position and stay within the chord stratum. But adding the 7th —the Gb— at the top takes the chord out of of stratum. So the 7th has to be added at the bottom. That is also true of the G chord for example. But it does not work with the C chord. In this instance, the added 7th —the Bb— has to be inserted above the bottom note.

Try some 7th chords on your piano —particularly the basic

Two ways of counting into the next octave. But if a 9th chord is called for, play a 7th. Chances are the 9th is the melody note.

3	10	E
2	9	D
1	8	C
7	7	B
6	6	A
5	5	G
4	4	F
3	3	E
2	2	D
1	1	C

The 7th can be added to the basic chord and to the altered chords. But the Aug7 isn't used much and the dim7 almost never.

chords with the 7th added, and the minor chords with the 7th added. They're the ones to know as soon as possible. (The diminished 7ths and the augmented 7ths can wait for a long time.) But for heaven's sake, don't practice making 7th chords. They are only abstractions. They don't become real until they are used in making music. And the order of their notes will become automatic soon enough when you call on them again and again.

As for the way to finger them, that will become automatic, too. Your left hand will find its own comfortable arrangement. But it's easiest if your outer fingers —pinky and thumb— fall on the outer notes of the chord.

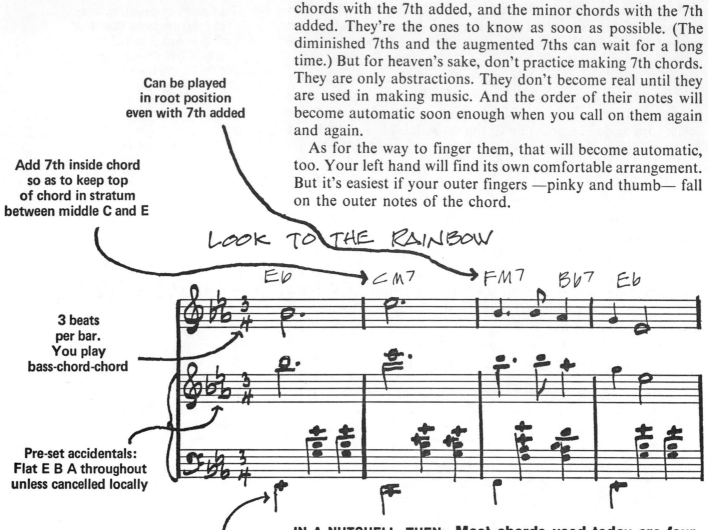

Can be played in root position even with 7th added

Add 7th inside chord so as to keep top of chord in stratum between middle C and E

LOOK TO THE RAINBOW

Eb   CM7   FM7   Bb7   Eb

3 beats per bar. You play bass-chord-chord

Pre-set accidentals: Flat E B A throughout unless cancelled locally

Remember to play basses as lowest possible octaves

IN A NUTSHELL, THEN: Most chords used today are four-note chords. The one in longest use is the 7th (sometimes called the dominant 7th). It is made by adding to the basic chord or to its alterations *the note which lies two intervals below the root on the keyboard*. It makes the 7th, the minor 7th, the diminished 7th and the augmented 7th.

Pay particular attention to mastering the 7th and the minor 7th. (The augmented 7th is occasionally used; the diminished 7th almost never. So, when you see a *dim7* called for in sheet music, please disregard it.)

The four-note chords can be played in four positions. But with skeleton arranging, the chord must be played in stratum position. That determines where you add or insert the 7th among the notes of the chord.

In the event a chord higher than a 7th is called for —a 9th, say— play it as a 7th and you'll probably be making the correct sound. The 9th is exactly where you think it is: just above the 8th. And the 8th is another way of naming

60

the root or 1st note of the basic scale once you pass the 7th as you go up the keyboard.

If the chord called for is C9, the chances are that the melody note at the moment is D. And as you can see, a C7 chord in the chord stratum with a D added in the melody stratum makes for an *over-all sound* of a C9 chord. And with that you have made a *five-note chord* — but it is divided between your two hands. That is, the chordal notes are spread out over two stratums.

You can do that with any chord —a three-note or a four-note chord —for a startling sound. But not yet. We're still fleshing out the skeleton. And properly so.

Four-note chords— the 6th

AND THE SAME IS TRUE of the 6th note of the basic scale, the note lying *two intervals above the 5th.* What had once been a restless tone longing to come home has become a comfortable chordal note which *is* at home, is a bona fide member of the chord.

Like the flatted 7th tone, the 6th has very gradually come to be heard as part of a four-note chord rather than as a note not-of-the-chord. In fact, there are evidences that it was becoming comfortable as far back as Bach's time. But it remained for the jazz bands of this century to make it a legitimate chordal note by giving it a name: *the 6th chord.*

Whose band did it first and on which number is impossible to find out. But you can see how it happened.

Let's say you're a band leader with four saxophones playing in the chord stratum. That would give each sax its own note to play in an accepted four-note chord such as the 7th. But what do you do when the chord changes from G7, say, to C —a three-note chord? Either you tell one sax to be quiet or else to double-up and play softly the same note another sax is playing. But either way the effect is unhappy: four saxophones now, then three playing, then back to the four voices as the chords change from four-note to three-note and back to four-note chords again. It comes out like music played on a very windy day with intermittent gusts carrying pieces out of earshot throughout the number.

Under the circumstances, you would look around for a fourth note to be added to the basic chord so that the sound from the chord stratum did not drift from four voices to three voices and back to four again. And the added note to the basic

12

The 6th note is found 2 intervals above the 5th.

The 6th can be added to the basic and altered chords. But you can forget the Aug6.

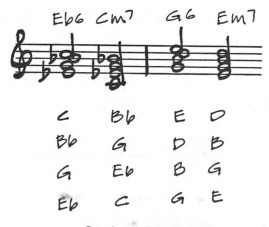

One basic 6th chord is another minor 7th chord. The identity is bestowed by the root notes in the bass.

chord was the 6th. So, when the chords changed from G7 to C, for instance, four saxophones moved from a G7 chord to a C6.

The use of that four-note setting as a named chord is still relatively new —relative to the history of music. So you'll still see plenty of sheet music in piano benches which doesn't mention the 6th chord at all. If it says anything about the matter, it may call for "C ADD 6" or perhaps "C ADD A." But there is just as good a chance that sheet music will simply call for C and leave it to you to play it as a C6.

As you would expect, the 6th note can be added to any basic chord or to any altered chord. And, of course, the resulting 6th, minor 6th, diminished 6th or augmented 6th can be played in four positions. However, in skeleton arranging the chord is played in stratum position only, which limits and determines where you add the 6th among the chord tones. Furthermore, only the *basic 6th, the minor 6th,* and the *diminished 6th* are widely used, so pay attention to them. In fact, pay particular attention to them as they will save you untold time and energy in making music as both the basic 6th chord and diminished 6th are magical labor saving devices.

You don't have to be a magician to make the magic work. Look at it this way. There are only twelve notes to work with in making all possible chords. So there is a limit to how many different four-note combinations you can make. It doesn't take too many 6th and 7th chords before you run out of new possibilities and begin to give *two names to the same combination of four notes.*

Try it on your piano. Take a basic C chord in stratum position and add the 6th —the note two intervals above the 5th —to make a C6 chord. Then take an A minor chord in stratum and add the 7th (the note two intervals below the root) to make it an Am7 chord. They ought to sound exactly the same; if they don't you've made a mistake.

What that proves is, *one 6th chord is exactly the same as another minor 7th chord.* What makes the difference to the listening ear is the bass note —the root note played as a low octave. A bass note of C makes the combination sound like a C chord whereas a bass note of A makes the very same group of notes in the chord stratum sound like an A minor chord.

Under the circumstances, then, the labor-saving device works this way. Unless the sheet music specifies otherwise—

Play every minor chord as a minor 7th chord.

And play every basic chord as a basic 6th chord.

Naturally, that rule doesn't apply when the chord symbol on the sheet music specifies an Am6, for example, or a C7. But there are usually more than enough un-numbered basic chords in most music to make this labor-saving device very worthwhile for piano players.

THE ADDED 6TH NOTE BRINGS a great saving of time, energy and thought to another chord, namely the diminished. By playing every diminished chord as a dim6 (no matter what the sheet music says) you are making a magical, four-way reversible chord. It is four chords in one. Every note in it can be the root.

In other words, a Cdim6 chord can also be an E♭dim6, an F# (or G♭)dim6, and an Adim6. It depends only on which bass note, which root note, you play with it.

And as that chord takes care of four diminished chords out of a possible twelve, it requires only *two more* of these reversible combinations to learn in order to have mastered all of the diminished chords.

How the dim6 chord comes to work in this lovely way is easy to see. As you recall, the diminished chord is an alteration of the basic chord, made by lowering the 3rd and 5th notes of the basic chord one interval each. So the added 6th is no longer two intervals above the 5th (as it is in the basic scale). The added 6th is now *three* intervals above the 5th, making four notes evenly separated from each other. That is a very gratifying condition. No matter which note in a dim6 chord you take for the root, the chord always contains the same four notes.

Try it on your own piano with the Fdim6 chord. But you have to try it in skeleton arrangement —in a combination of bass note-&-chord —in order to hear how the change of root note magically changes the sound of the chord even though the notes in the chord don't change.

If you want to take advantage of the great bargain offered by this chord, remember:

Play every diminished chord as a dim6 —even if the sheet music calls for an un-numbered dim or a dim7.

That way you need only three dim6 chords in your repertoire of chords to cover all of the possibilities.

(Usually when sheet music calls for dim7 chord, it really means *dim6*. That is a remnant from the days before the 6th chord was a named chord. What arrangers were specifying was a dim7 chord *with the 7th flatted*. Well, if you play a 7th chord and then play it with that 7th note flatted, you have turned it into a 6th chord. Try it on your own piano and see . . . and see how a dim7 can mean dim6 if part of the instructions are taken for granted.)

THE AUGMENTED CHORD —the basic three-note chord with its 5th sharped —is also a great labor-saving device *just as is*. It doesn't need an added fourth note in order to be a reversible sound. Its three-note formula puts even spacing between all the notes. Four intervals beyond the sharped 5th is the root again. So, you can make any note of the three the root without having to change any note in the chord.

The reversible dim6 chord.
The same 4 notes make 4
different dim6 chords.
Which one you mean
depends on the root bass.

The reversible Augmented.
The same 3 notes make
3 different Aug chords. But
only if it's a 3-note chord.

Try it on your piano. Take a basic C+ and try the other two notes in the combination —E and A♭— as roots. The E+ and A♭+ chords are the same as the C+ chord. The difference among them is the bass note, the root note, you hit in the bass stratum.

Under the circumstances, there is no sense in upsetting this bargain by making the augmented chord a four-note Aug6 or Aug7. Left as a three-note chord, it gives you three different chords for the price of one. That means you need only *four* different augmented chords in order to have made all of the possible twelve.

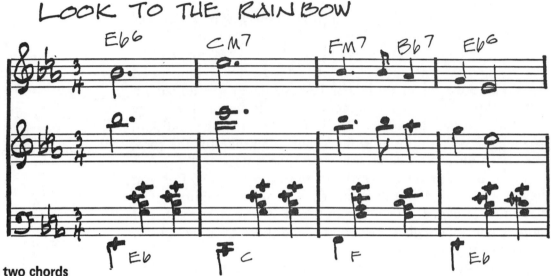

LOOK TO THE RAINBOW

The first two chords called for are identical. The difference between them is in the root notes you hit in the bass.

SO, IN A NUTSHELL: The 6th tone is located two intervals above the 5th of the basic scale (and chord). It has been a settled, comfortable tone for two centuries at least. But it has been a named "6th chord" for only a generation or two.

The 6th can be added onto the basic three-note chord and its alterations to make them four-note chords. But only the basic 6th chord, the minor 6th chord, and the diminished 6th chord are widely used — and very effectively. After all, there are only twelve notes to combine into chords. So this 6th chord will be that minor 7th chord. This diminished 6th chord will be simultaneously three other 6th chords. What distinguishes and identifies a chord from its exact look-alikes is the bass note, the root note, you use in association with it. You can use these duplications of chords to save time and energy in making music —as long as you say clearly which chord you mean by striking the proper root note in the bass.

I. *Play all un-numbered basic chords as 6th chords.* If an F is called for, play an F6. But if F7 is called for, play F7.

2. *Play all un-numbered minor chords as minor 7th*

chords. **If Am is called for, play Am7. But if Am6 is called for, play Am6.**

3. *Play all diminished chords as diminished 6th chords.* Even if they're printed as dim7, the arranger probably meant the reversible dim6.

4. *Play all un-numbered augmented chords as is.* The three-note augmented chord is the reversible one. The four note variety won't work that way.

Now, the world won't come to an end if you ignore these suggestions. But if you use them, you'll make much more music a whole lot faster. In any case, try some of four-note 6th and 7th chords in real-life music. If you use sheet music of your own choice, go through it and mark the chords as you'll be playing them —and, if you need to, write in the notes of chords you have to work out.

Four-note chords— the Major 7th

THERE IS ONE LAST FOUR-NOTE CHORD. Or, rather there is one latest addition to the basic three-note chord. Without any doubt, the human ear in this part of the planet is still developing, still turning unresolved, non-chordal tones into comfortable notes-of-the-chord.

This latest four-note chord is the Major 7th.

The Major 7th note is located one interval below the root. And it is plainly named in the chord symbols on sheet music. But being a newer chord than the 6th, it is almost never called for in the original editions of the old standard numbers.

Try a Maj7 on your piano. Try a basic C chord in root position and add this fourth note to it. Clearly, the Maj7 note is the B, being one interval below the root note C. In stratum position, of course, the C Maj7 chord, like the C7 and the C6, can be played with the the G on the bottom and the added fourth note just above it.

As usual with added fourth notes, this one can be added to the altered chords as well —but it's not. Not yet. However, there are doubtless composers here and there who are bored with the min7, the dim6 and the old three-note Aug. Doubtless they are working with *the Maj7 min, the Maj7 dim and the Maj7 Aug.* Should the day come when those chords are called for on sheet music, you will know how to make them. (Simply by adding the Maj 7th note to the altered three-note chords.)

As of this writing, and for some time to come, the only Maj7 to work with is the basic chord with this fourth note incorporated into it.

Major 7th note
is 1 interval
below the root.

Now, this is not to say that the Maj7 is completely acceptable —completely comfortable —as are the 6th and 7th chords. Until the early 1950s, this note one interval below the root was heard hereabouts by many of us as an uneasy, unresolved sound. A generation is really not very long when it comes to taking new sound combinations for granted.* So, don't be surprised if you begin by hearing the Maj7 chord as an uneasy marriage of the basic three-note chord to the alien Maj7 tone.

Now, why did it take so long for this *logical* sequence of tones —this 1,3,5 and 7 of the basic scale— to become chordal? The answer is to be found in old-fashioned music teaching, namely: "We're not here to discuss that. Just play the chords and don't waste time with questions."

The 4-note chords. Try them on your piano. Remember to play melody an octave higher than written, and basses as lowest possible octaves.

TRY TO REMEMBER

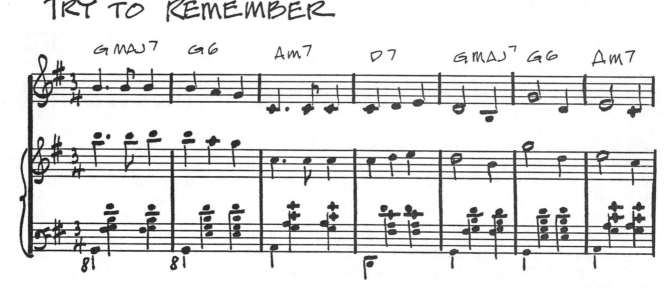

Use a Maj7 chord wherever you would use a basic or 6th chord. As of now, the altered Maj7 chords aren't widely used.

IN OTHER WORDS, IN A NUTSHELL: The major 7th tone lies one interval below the root. It is added to the basic three-note chord to make the Maj7 four-note chord. As of now, there are very few altered Maj7 chords called for. In skeleton arranging, the Maj7 is played in stratum.

As for where to use the Maj7 chord —well, as of now it is only *the basic chord* with the added fourth note, and not the minor, diminished or augmented. So you can try it wherever an un-numbered basic chord is called for. That is, you can try a Maj7 chord wherever you try a basic 6 chord.

---

*The same curious notion of "modern" obtains in painting. In a conversation overheard in a Boston museum, an earnest man asked the guide: "When did contemporary art begin?" And she replied without a moment's hesitation, "In 1913."

Alternating the bass notes

THE FOUR-NOTE CHORD IS A big step up from the basics, and makes for a much more interesting sound in the chord stratum. Unfortunately, there isn't the same possibility down in the bass stratum. About the best you can do to fill out the skeleton down there is to hit *alternate bass notes*.

The plain fact is that the bass-note-&-chord combination of the basic skeleton gets to be a big bore after a while. (That is true of basic skeletons of any sort, and explains why people who speak in basic words only are dull and tedious. It also explains why people, even in the hottest weather, never take off their skin and sit around in their bones.) But you can get a little variety by using two different bass notes in combination with the chord —when possible.

Which two different bass notes? Well, one of them —the first bass note you hit —has to be *the root note of the chord*. That gives the chord its identity and tells your listener whether you mean an Eb6 in the chord stratum or a Cmin7, for example. So, your only real choice is the second or alternate bass note you hit. And that's not a big choice, either, because the best-sounding alternate bass note is *the 5th of the chord*. (As you would expect, that 5th, that alternate bass, is played as the lowest possible octave, which is often lower than the root bass octave.)

ALTERNATING BASS NOTES ARE POSSIBLE only in one situation, to wit: when there is room for two bass notes *under the same chord*.

Obviously, that leaves out a bar of 4/4 music where the chord changes in the middle. You change bass notes in that measure to be sure —but you move from root note to new root note as the chord changes in the next stratum. (Remember, a new chord is a new chord, even if it is built on the same root note as the previous chord.)

Similarly, you can't use alternate bass notes in a bar of 3/4 tempo, either, because there is only one bass note used (in combination with two chords). Only if the same chord continues over two bars can you begin the second bar with an alternate bass, namely the 5th note of the chord played as a low octave.

WHERE YOU GET SOME CHOICE of alternate basses in 4/4 time is in two bars with the same chord used for both. In that case, you have to hit four bass notes for the same chord. And while the first has to be the root, and the next ought to be the 5th of the chord, there is no prescription for the remaining two bass notes. Or, rather, almost none. What will sound best, you will

The first bass note is the root, giving the chord its identity. If there's no chord change, your next bass note can be the 5th. As lowest octave, naturally.

SKATER'S WALTZ

In 3/4 time there's room
for only 1 bass per bar.
If chord holds beyond,
you can alternate basses.

Chopin: Single bass notes
close to the chord stratum
in the interests of speed.

Schubert: no alternating
bass notes in the interests
of an obstinate sound there.

discover, is *another note of the chord* used as a bass note. The 3rd note of the chord, say. Or maybe the root again. Or the 5th. And then perhaps the root for the last attack.

Obviously you need three bars of 3/4 time with the same chord used for all three to give you a chance to choose an alternate bass note. Inasmuch as you have three bass notes to hit, and inasmuch as the first has to be the root and the next ought to be the 5th —that leaves you one remaining attack to choose the 3rd of the chord (or the 5th or the root again).

Naturally, when you use the 5th or the 3rd as alternate bass notes, you use them *as they appear in the chord.* If the 5th is sharped in the chord —in an augmented chord— you use the sharped 5th as your alternate bass note. If the 3rd is flatted because the chord is a minor, then the flatted 3rd is your bass.

THAT IS NOT TO SAY that you have to alternate bass notes —any more than you have to play bass notes as the lowest possible octave. Music is not a machine running by means of inviolable mechanisms. Not at all. Music is an organization of possibilities. And the more possibilities you know, understand and can see in the music around you, the more music you can make.

The Minute Waltz, for example, begins with a basic skeleton arrangement of bass-&-chords in stratum. But as you can see, Chopin used single bass notes rather than octaves. And moreover, he put those bass notes very close to the chord stratum rather than way down in the lowest possible register on the keyboard. (It's amazing how much you can read in music even though you don't know the names of the notes.)

Chopin's reason for those single bass notes close to the chord stratum is obvious: speed. The waltz was written to be played *molto vivace* —"as fast as possible" (which is why the audience re-named it "The Minute Waltz"). And you lose speed when you have to reach way down the keyboard. You lose speed, too, when you have to hit octave basses.

Most of the popular numbers and semi-classical pieces, however, are slow enough to allow for a treatment which uses the full range of the keyboard rather than only the middle third of the possibilities. But now and then you find a number which has to be played in shorthand, such as *Nola* or *California Here I Come.* Like the Chopin waltz, they don't leave time for a long reach to the bass stratum or for basses played as octaves or for more than a single-note melody.

As for alternating basses, that is not an imperative, either. Look, at a sample of Schubert's *Moments Musicaux.* His bass notes, as you can see without knowing what they are, do not alternate but continue obstinately on the same tone for a meaningful part of the composition. Obviously he had his reasons for doing that. Which means that being obstinate is a possibility in organizing tones and making music.

Suffice it to say that there are very few hard and fast laws when it comes to making music. You can bend almost any principle —as long as you have a good reason for doing so. And the best reason of all is that the result sounds good.

IN A NUTSHELL: Alternating the bass note is a step up from the basics in the bass stratum. It helps to cover up the raw-boned skeleton combination of bass note-&-chord.

Bass notes are notes of the chord. The indispensible bass note is the root note of the chord because it gives the chord which follows its identity. If there is room for an alternate bass note, the best bet is the 5th of the chord —*the 5th as it appears in the chord*. If there is room to alternate the bass still another time, you can return to the root or use *the 3rd* as it appears in the chord. Whatever the bass or alternate bass in skeleton arranging, it is played as the lowest possible octave.

Any change of chord demands a return to the root note for the first bass note, even if the new chord has the same root has the previous chord —such as a change from E♭6 to E♭m7. When, as sometimes happens, there are more than two changes of chord in a measure, it may be most reasonable to dispense with bass note-&-chord combinations entirely. The best sound may be the chords only (in stratum of course) without any basses, alternate or otherwise. You can begin the bass-&-chord combinations again when the chords don't change so often. Or else you can dispense with all the chords and play only one with bass note and alternating bass note —as you can see in the opening measure of the sample below.

Try it on your own piano. Bass notes and alternates are named. Play them as lowest possible octaves.

Block notes
for the melody

15

AND, FINALLY, UP FROM THE BASICS in the right hand. Or, to put it more clearly, now we flesh out the skeleton in the melody stratum by filling in the block of space between the melody note and the four-note chords in their stratum.

That block of empty space is usually quite large, what with the melody notes played an octave higher than printed, and the chords anchored below in a narrow stratum around middle C. Consequently, what fills in that block of space are *a couple of duplicate notes of the chord*. Regardless of what the melody note is, your right hand blocks in the empty space with *a couple of the same notes which your left hand is playing* in the chord stratum.

Now, that is certainly child-like. So, if you were to take a bar or two and look straight up from the bass stratum to the top of the melody stratum, you would have to be a little embarrassed at what a lot of grown up, accomplished and sophisticated piano players are really doing with this full orchestral arrangement. Viz:

1. The bass note (an octave) is a duplicated note of the chord.

2. The chord in stratum is, of course, the four notes of the chord.

3. Two notes of the melody stratum are duplicates of two in the chord stratum.

4. And at the very top of the whole setting of doubled, duplicated and re-duplicated notes of the chord sits the single melody note —which may, or may not, be a note of the chord.

All of that proves three things. First, that the top note of the top stratum of sound is the most penetrating and can be heard clearly regardless of the activity below. Second, it proves that the chord is quite obviously a setting on which oncoming melody notes are heard as comfortable notes-of-the-chord or uneasy notes-not-of-the-chord. A melody note which is different from any of those stated and re-stated in the stratums below it can be heard plainly as being different, being *unsettled*. And finally, it all proves that you don't have to be a genius to understand the basics of music-making in this part of the planet —or to make music yourself on your own piano.

EXACTLY WHICH TWO NOTES of the chord you elect to echo in the block below the melody depends on how intelligently lazy you are. After all, many different chords share common notes with each other. E♭6 and Cm7 and F7 and A♭6 and Adim6, for example, share the C and E♭ notes. So you can use them for

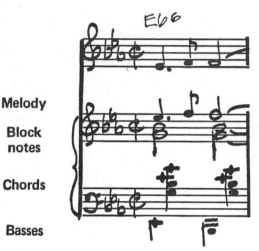

HAUNTED HEART

E♭6

Melody

Block notes

Chords

Basses

E♭6   Cm7   F7   A♭m

E♭	E♭	E♭	E♭
C	C	C	C
B♭	B♭	A	A
G	G	F	F♯

Many chords share common notes. So, one pair can serve in several blocks.

block notes below the melody whenever any one of those five chords is called for (provided you can reach them while you play the melody note).

That is not fakery in any way. That is simply making basic music —fulfilling the requirements of the skeleton which holds almost all of our music together.

Try a few examples of this basic lazy intelligence on the following fragments. Use your right hand only: pinky or ring finger on the melody note; and thumb and index finger (or thumb and middle finger) for two block notes below the melody. The chord symbol above the melody line tells you which four notes you can choose from for your two block notes.

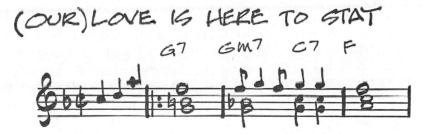

Too much blocking can choke the melody stratum. Blocks may sound better on numbered beats only.

It will become apparent to you as you begin to try a full right hand that too much blocked melody —too many chordals hung from the melody note —is an overbearing sound. And, moreover, a fast or intricate melody of eighth notes and sixteenth notes becomes very cumbersome to play if you block each melody note. So, a good principle to keep in mind is: *block only melody notes which fall on numbered beats.* And, in fact, if the melody is very fast or intricate (*Nola, Stumbling,* etc.) you will probably make better sounding music by not blocking at all but rather by playing a one-finger melody.

SOMETIMES THE MELODY NOTE is too low in its stratum to leave room for a two-note block beneath it —or even for one block note. Well, if there's no room for a full block or even a half, then there's no room. That's not a principle in music-making; that's plain horse sense.

The principle is: *the two notes of the block are merely an extension of the chord,* filling the space between the melody note and the chord stratum. This duplication is expendable. But the full four-note chord in its stratum is not. So if it comes to a choice between playing a block or a half-block vs. playing a full chord-in-stratum, forget the block and play the chord.

THERE'S JUST ONE MORE THING to be said about being intelligently lazy about the block notes. And like the other advice, this one will become increasingly obvious as you play blocked melodies. And that is: use the same pair of block notes as long as you can under a climbing melody line or a descending melody line.

If the melody climbs, begin with a narrow block — with your fingers close together— and let your melody finger do all the walking while your block fingers continue to hit the same two chordals. It's not only easier than changing block notes constantly, but it also sounds better to keep the melody notes on the same setting for as long as possible.

Likewise, if the melody comes downward under one chord, then start with a wide block —with a good distance between the melody note and the two block notes. Again, let your melody finger do the walking while your block fingers hit the same two chordals as long as possible so that you finish with a narrow block.

Obviously one lazy block may not serve for every melody note in a sequence. There is a limit to how far you can extend your fingers for a wide block. There is a limit to how narrow you can make a block when the melody continues to descend. So, sometimes you have to change the block —you have to take two different chordal notes from the same chord —to play comfortably.

Be lazy. Use one block as long as possible and let your melody finger do the walking to or from the block.

Naturally, if the melody note drops too low to leave room for a two-note block beneath it, then use a one-note block—if there's room for one. There's simply no point in crowding in a block note if it gets in the way of the laziness principle. Moreover, if a block note is too close to the melody note, you will make a muddy sound of both. So, be sure to leave at least three intervals between the melody note and the first block note below it.

AS FOR THE NUTSHELL: Your right hand fills in the skeleton by blocking the melody —putting in a couple of duplicate

notes of the chord below the melody note and above the chord stratum. if the melody note is too low to leave room for two block notes, or for one, then use one block note, or none. (There should be at least three intervals between the melody note and the first block note.)

The blocked melody is not a chord (because the melody note may be a non-chordal). Rather the block is an extension of the chord. Consequently block notes are expendable —for reasons of crowding or because they impede a fast or intricate melody. In any number, however, block only on the numbered beats.

Be lazy about block notes. Use the same two block notes for as many chords as they will serve comfortably. Keep the same two as long as possible while the melody moves up or down. Change block notes only for comfort or because a change of chord requires that one or both notes be different.

The melody note remains at the top of the block where it is most penetrating. Looked at that way, the block is a fourth —but moveable— stratum of sound at work.

With vocalist's line, you can make a full skeleton arrangement of blocked melody, 4-note chords and alternating basses.

ON TOP OF OLD SMOKEY

How to play the piano despite years of lessons

THE MYTH: There is real music . . . and then there is popular music.

THE FACT: There is music. And when it comes to making your own music, you can learn a lot of tricks-of-the-trade from the great composers.

Part five

How to camouflage the skeleton —another step up from the basics. Six ways to vary the 3/4 time *oom*-pah-pah combination. Six variations of the 4/4 bass-&-chord attacks, including ragtime as a way to disguise the skeleton. Moving the stratums around as a further camouflage device. And how to arrange a number.

Variations of 3/4 bass-&-chord

16

IT IS NOW ABOUT A CENTURY since the waltz came into full flower. Just let an orchestra play that old, familiar *oom*-pah-pah, *oom*-pah-pah in two lower stratums, and your mind is immediately transported back to the middle of the Nineteenth Century and into the parasol days of Johann Strauss.

What was it actually like to be back in that heyday of Strauss with his Royal State Orchestra playing his latest waltz? Well, it must have finally become quite a bore. There is, after all, a limit to how much unvarying bass-&-chord-chord you can put up with year after year. Most especially if you are expressing it at the piano.

That may explain what happened to Johannes Brahms, who was making waltzes at the piano while Strauss was working with a full orchestra. As a result, in only one collection of sixteen waltzes, Brahms came up with a dozen ways to vary and thus camouflage the *oom*-pah-pah of the skeleton. A few of those ways are set out below —not to be practiced and memorized but rather as pictures, as windows on a vast world of ways to vary and thus camouflage the bass-&-chord combinations of the skeleton when you make music.

Once you are aware that variation is possible, you will begin to hear new possibilities everywhere— in classical compositions by master pianists of the past; in popular arrangements; in your own mind as you experiment at the keyboard. Which variations you use will depend on one thing. And that is whether it sounds good to you.

FOR MOST OF US, THE SKELETON arrangement no longer sounds as good as it did in the Late Parasol and Early Speakeasy era. Today, this combination of the two low stratums is usually used for purposes of nostalgia— to evoke reminiscences of days which few people remember. Nevertheless, it is still *the standard clockwork,* the fundamental way for dividing the silence in an *even pattern.* It is the original *tick*-tock-tick for keeping 3/4 time, and it continues to beat beneath any camouflage variation. So the first principle in camouflaging the bass-&-chord

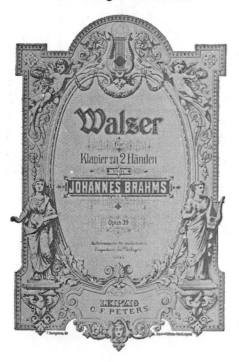

The good old Strauss waltz oom-pah-pah, and how Brahms got tired of it.

76

combination of the skeleton is, *provide the unexpected.* And just about any departure from this *oom*-pah-pah will do it —at least for a while.

That brings up the second principle of camouflage, namely: the variation, whatever it is, has to *provide an even pattern.* If you have jumbled one variation after another with no thought to order or arrangement, then it is not camouflage at all. It is inept, silly sounding music.

THE FIRST VARIATION changes the picture very little. The silence is divided into three equal ticks of the clock with the attacks coming along on the numbered beats— just as in the skeleton arrangement. What is unexpected, however, is the combination of bass-&-chord and thus the combination of emphasis. What is the standard *oom*-pah-pah of the skeleton has become the surprising *oom*-pah-*oom* (because we are so used to hearing the bass note as the first, and therefore main, beat).

You will find this variation in that Brahms' waltz collection, numbers 1 and 6. Also in di Capua's *Maria Mari;* and in Chopin's *Grande Valse Brillante* (Opus 18) and his *Mazurka* (Opus 7, No. 1.)

THE SECOND VARIATION again divides the silence into three equal parts. And again the attacks on the silence come along on the numbered beats. So, the basic skeleton is clearly at work. But once more the expected bass-&-chord combination —the expected, standard pattern of emphasis —is changed. The *oom*-pah-pah of the skeleton is camouflaged with this chord-bass-chord beat of pah-*oom*-pah.

This variation can be heard in many places, among them in three places mentioned above: in Brahms' waltzes No. 1 and No. 6; and in Chopin's *Mazurka.*

Now, each of those variations can stand alone as a camouflage technique. Or each can be combined with the skeleton itself to produce an unexpected and therefore interesting beat. Take a look at a bar of skeleton followed by a bar of the first variation followed by a bar of skeleton, and so on. What Chopin can do, you can apply.

No. 1:
Bass-chord-bass
(oom-pah-oom)

No. 2:
Chord-bass-chord
(pah-oom-pah)

TRUE LOVE

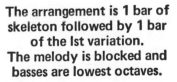

The arrangement is 1 bar of skeleton followed by 1 bar of the 1st variation. The melody is blocked and basses are lowest octaves.

What you must do, however, is to keep the combination —whatever it is— going long enough to make for an *even* pattern. A couple of bars of this variation and a couple of that camouflage technique are guaranteed to sound awful.

On the other hand, very simple variations such as those two just mentioned can be as unexpected and as surprising as anything the master Brahms himself can devise. By using a bar of the first variation (bass-chord-bass) in tandem with a bar of the second variation (chord-bass-chord), you begin a bass-&-chord pattern of: bass-chord-bass-chord . . . And that, as your ear will tell you very quickly, is the *emphasis pattern of a 4/4 time fox trot* —even though your ear is hearing the usual three beats per measure of 3/4 waltz time. Oh absolutely, it is unexpected, surprising, very exciting and consequently a wonderful camouflage of the skeleton beat. Try it on your own piano.

The 1st and 2nd variations for 4 bars. It's still a waltz. But the combination produces a 4/4 skeleton's bass-chord-bass-chord.

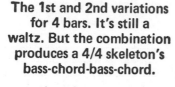

Now that the window is fully open on the world of possibilities for varying the bass-&-chord combination of the skeleton, a few further examples will suffice.

IN THE THIRD VARIATION, it is not the pattern of emphasis which is camouflaged but rather the number of attacks on the silence which are changed —reduced from three to two. There is a one beat delay between the *tick* and the tock, so to speak. But it is an exact delay, precisely as long as the missing beat, and it calls upon the listening ear to supply that beat. It makes the listener create the camouflage. You can see and hear this variation throughout Brahms' waltz No. 8 in that book.

**No. 3:
Bass-rest-chord
(oooom-pah)**

IN VARIATION NUMBER FOUR, the silence is divided somewhat differently. Here, the third beat —the last *pah*— is missing. The beat comes off like *oom*-pahhhhhhh. Only the one chord per bar is struck. And while it is held for two beats, it calls upon the listener to supply the second attack in the chord stratum. You will find this variation used throughout Brahms' waltz No. 9; as a patterned alternative woven in and out of Scharwenka's *Polish Dance;* and in Chopin's *Minute Waltz.*

**No. 4:
Bass-chord-hold
(oom-pahhhh)**

THIS FIFTH VARIATION increases the number of attacks, and so divides the silence into smaller pieces of beats and after-beats. To make this variation work, you have to divide each bar into six parts —by counting ONE-and-two-and-three-and— and playing the bass note and first chord on the first beat and its after-beat (ONE-and). That busy camouflage, of course, works to the best advantage under a slow-moving melody of mostly whole notes and half notes. Brahms uses this one throughout waltz No. 2. Chopin uses it widely in his *Mazurka* (Opus 30, No. 3).

No. 5:
B-ch-chord-chord
('m-p-pah-pah)

IN THE SIXTH VARIATION, the same principle of camouflage applies. The expected three attacks per bar are increased to four —with two of them only a half-beat in duration. It works out as *oom-pa-pa-pah*. Like the fifth variation just before (which comes out as m-pa-pah-pah, so to speak) this one ought to be saved for slower melodies —or slower parts of melodies.

Look for it in Brahms' waltz No. 11 and Chopin's *Mazurka* (Opus 50, No. 3). In fact, look for it in old ballroom arrangements of waltzes where it was used in tandem with the skeleton —usually as a vamp to establish the 3/4 beat for the dancers before the melody started. The combination is certainly worth having in your repertoire in case you ever get lost in an old ballroom.

No. 6:
Bass-ch-ch-chord
(oom-p-p-pah)

"Vamp till ready."
A bar of basic skeleton
alternating with
a bar of variation No. 6.

Now, none of this is to suggest that the surface of variation technique has even been scratched. Why, even the bolero beat —one of the most important camouflages of all —hasn't been mentioned. And it won't be mentioned until Part Eight, along with other special cases. Actually, there is only one purpose in this chapter.

AND IT IS, *IN A NUTSHELL*: The first way to cover up and conceal the underlying skeleton is by varying the expected clockwork combination of 3/4 time bass-&-chord-chord. (That skeleton beat is so ingrained in us that you can play a one-finger rendition of a waltz melody and the mind's ear will fill in the missing clockwork —the *oom-pah-pah* of the two lower stratums.) So, any alteration of that pattern, any variation from the expected order of attacks or the ex-

pected number of them per bar, will surprise and distract and thus conceal.

Like good camouflage of any sort, variation of the bass-&-chord combination must make an even pattern. There is often good sense in combining the standard, expected skeleton with an unexpected variation. But a combination of more than two variations at a time, even if one is the skeleton, will make for a jumble. But whatever the variation you use, you should have a reason for it within the context of the number —such as a busy variation under a slow passage in the melody.

Now that you're aware of variations, don't expect to hear music the way you used to. Your ear is changing, and there's no turning back to just plain ignorant listening.

Variations of 4/4 bass-&-chord (including ragtime)

17

NATURALLY, THE SAME PRINCIPLE of camouflage for the skeleton continues into 4/4 time. The whole idea is to vary the attacks —the number of attacks per bar and/or their order of appearance — so that the expected pattern is not expressed.

There are, of course, four beats to a measure in skeleton arranging of 4/4 time. That is one beat more than a bar of waltz time . So there is 25 per cent more room for variation in this timing. Consequently, the few possibilities laid out here don't come close to indicating the full range of what you can do. What follows, like what was said in the past chaper, is merely an invitation to start breaking the rules of the skeleton's bass-&-chord combinations. Anything goes —just as long as the variation continues an even pattern so that it will *work against the expected skeleton arrangement* which tick-tocks steadily in most everybody's mind. For that reason, a bar of a variation in tandem with a bar of skeleton itself is also camouflage because it presents the expected and the unexpected hand-in-hand.

The basic skeleton pattern of attacks — bass-chord-bass-chord.

THIS FIRST VARIATION leaves the expected number of attacks per bar intact, and on the numbered beats. But the skeleton's order is reversed. You play chord-&-bass, chord-&-bass, and thus *the expected accents are reversed.* The mind's ear, used to counting ONE-two-THREE-four, is presented with what sounds like one-

TWO-three-FOUR. That is because the bass notes, those usual accent beats, arrive on what seems to be the wrong numbers. You can hear this variation in obvious use in Grieg's *March of the Dwarfs;* and in Tschaikowsky's *November Troika.*

IN THIS SECOND VARIATION, the attacks again come on the numbered beats. And again the bass &-chord order is changed from the expected, thus changing the pattern of emphasis. The count per measure, at least to the unwary listeners, seems to be ONE-two-three-FOUR —which is not at all what they are used to hearing.

You can find this variation woven in and out of the first part of Beethoven's *Turkish March,* where it alternates frequently with the skeleton arrangement of bass-&-chord. You can also find this variation in the introduction to *The Procession of the Sardar* by Ippolitov-Ivanov (in his *Caucasian Sketches).*

THE THIRD VARIATION alters the number of attacks. There are none for the third and fourth beats of the skeleton. Instead, one chord is held for the expected beat and on through the remaining two beats. That forces the listener to supply silently the missing bass note and the missing chord —against the background of one sustained chord.

Among the many places you can hear this variation is in Chopin's *Butterfly Etude* (Opus 10, No. 5). (Another place you can hear it is on your own keyboard.)

THIS FOURTH VARIATION alters both the number of attacks and the type. In a sense, you can read it as bass-chord-pause-bass. And looked at that way, it is the foundation for both the tango and the bolero beat variations because it calls for *an interior number of a measure to be left without an attack.*

So give this variation some attention because it is excellent and easy preparation for more complicated-sounding camouflage techniques. They will be treated in Part Eight, where bass-&-chord camouflage is continued. In the meantime, to hear this fourth variation at work, listen to the opening few bars of Tschaikowky's *Chanson Triste.*

ANOTHER VARIATION POSSIBILITY ought to be mentioned because it gets away from the skeleton in yet another way. Namely by breaking the rule of chords in stratum. As you can see, it is a combination of one bass note followed by three chords (a variation of the skeleton itself).

Only the first chord fulfills the expectation by remaining in chord stratum. The next chord moves up one notch —the bottom note moves to the top of the structure for the third attack; ad so on with successive attacks in the measure.

1. chord-bass-chord-bass.

2. bass-chord-chord-bass.

3. bass-chord (and hold it).

4. bass-chord (hold) -bass.

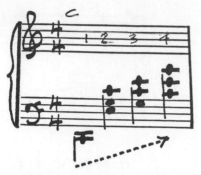

5. bass-chord-chord-chord
(climbing above stratum).

This variation, of course, can only be used in support of a *climbing melody* because you need room in the melody stratum for your climbing chords. Just remember to play the first chord attack in stratum. (Don't play chords below stratum because they will sound muddy.)

You can hear this camouflage technique used throughout Chopin's *Nocturne* (Opus 9, No. 2); and throughout Dvorak's opening section of his *Humoresque*.

PROPERLY SPEAKING, RAGTIME is not a variation of skeleton. But it is a proper camouflage. As you can see from this excerpt of *Eleanora —A Ragtime Two-Step* by Lawrence Kluger, the left hand plays an undisguised skeleton bass-&-chord combination.

The camouflage in ragtime is carried by the right hand which plays rapid attacks of syncopated eighth notes. Often, the melody is so busy that the left hand's octave basses are omitted in the interests of speed. So, really, the tick-tock of the skeleton is pretty well covered up, as these opening bars of Scott Joplin's *The Entertainer* show.

THE ENTERTAINER

Ragtime: a fast bass-&-chord
skeleton. The camouflage is
in the rapid, syncopated melody.

ELEANORA

Some other examples of ragtime: *Kitten On the Keys, Muskrat Ramble, Maple Leaf Rag.* You can also hear ragtime used in Debussy's *Golliwogg's Cake Walk* (from his *Children's Corner Suite).*

THIS WHOLE CHAPTER HAS BEEN A NUTSHELL: But it's worth saying again that there are hundreds of ways to camouflage the skeleton's bass-&-chord combination by varying the number of attacks per bar and the order of bass notes and chords. But a little bit of variation goes a long way. So keep it to a minimum and keep to an even pattern. It's the only way to avoid confusing the listening ear.

An understanding of the skeleton arrangement coupled with an understanding of the way variations differ from the skeleton is a valuable tool —not only in making your own music but also in understanding a composer's architecture. Once you see how a composer varies his arrangement from the skeleton, you can begin to commit his work to memory (if that is your aim) by remembering his blueprint of camouflage.

Moving the stratums around

18

VARYING THE BASS-&-CHORD COMBINATIONS is only one way to conceal what is really holding the music together. Any rearrangement of the expected order of things in the skeleton tends to be a camouflage. And that includes rearranging the expected *stratums of sound*. There are two effective ways to create this sleight-of-ear.

MELODY IN HARMONY

Here is the most surprising of them. The recipe is simply this— take the melody out of the top stratum and *play it one octave lower than written*. In that way the melody notes are sandwiched between the bass notes and chords.

Your right hand plays a single-note, one-finger melody down there in that low register. And your left hand *crosses back and forth over your right hand* —playing the bass notes (as octaves of course) below the melody, and then jumping over your right hand to play the chords just above the melody.

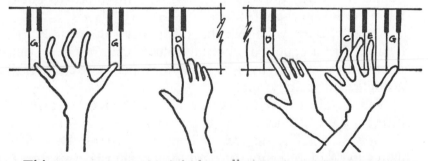

RIGHT HAND: single-note melody an octave lower than written. LEFT HAND plays octave basses below right, then jumps over it to play 3-note chords.

This rearrangement might be called Early Eddie Duchin. But it is more widely known as the "crossed-hands" style.

About the chords: there's no point in trying to keep them confined in their usual narrow stratum. The melody may climb up into that stratum and force you to move the chords up a bit. Moreover, there's no point in complicating the gymnastics further by playing four-note chords. The three-note kind will do just as well —and on occasion you can get away with a two-note chord. But whatever size chord sounds good to you, keep it as close to the melody notes as you can — certainly no farther

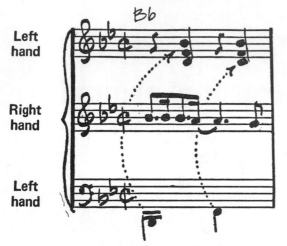

NEVERTHELESS

Left hand

Right hand

Left hand

Another view of the crossed-hands technique or melody inside harmony.

Play the melody as an octave where written and sandwich a pair of chord notes inside it. Basses are lowest octaves.

away than three or four intervals above the melody.

A couple of additional things to know about this crossed-hands camouflage. First, *put some weight on the melody notes* as you play them. After all, they are now in a lower stratum than the chords, so you need some added power to have the melody penetrate. And second, *don't give too much weight to the chords.* If you lean on them, their top notes —being at the top of the highest stratum now —will be heard as an uncontrolled and meaningless melody line.

This is really a very elementary kind of playing. But it has a very startling effect. So don't waste this camouflage by using it too often, or for too long in the course of one number. Four bars is often quite enough, particularly if it is the second time the theme is being stated. More on that —ways and means of using variations —will be spelled out in the next chapter.

If you want to listen to this melody-in-harmony variation, you can hear it in the opening twenty bars of Liszt's *Nocturne No. 3* (but with broken chords above the melody); and in the very same style in the opening eight bars of Robert Schumann's *Romance* (Opus 28). It also appears throughout the first part of Anton Rubinstein's *Melodie in F* (Opus 3, No. 1), but not written for crossed-hands playing.

HARMONY IN MELODY

The other effective way to rearrange the stratums of the skeleton is to sandwich the harmony inside the melody. That sandwich is almost made for you in a melody with its two chordal notes in the block just below. It requires only another, duplicate melody note at the bottom of the block to put the harmony inside the melody.

Actually, then, your right hand is playing the melody as an octave, with a couple of chordal notes within it. Or, to put it another way, your right hand is playing a two-note chord inside a duplicated melody note.

Well, if your right hand is playing the chord, that leaves very little for your left hand to do except to play the bass notes —as the lowest possible octave, of course— just as the skeleton demands. And as there is no need for any chords in stratum (or any chords at all, for that matter, from your left hand) *you move the melody down and play it where written,* with the rest of the sandwich hung below it.

Consequently, you are playing in only two stratums: the bass stratum, and the duplicated melody stratum which carries the harmony inside of it. All in all, it is an arrangement which looks very easy to play.

And it is very easy to play. So easy, in fact, that it is often called for in fast skeleton numbers such as *Stars and Stripes Forever, Lady of Spain,* etc. And what makes it doubly easy is that a lot of the time your right hand is playing only the duplicated melody without any chord notes inside. The chords have to be expressed only on the numbered beats — just as in the skeleton arrangement. Similarly, you strike bass notes only on the beats which require them in the skeleton arrangement.

Try it on your own piano.

Naturally, that is not a picture of a law. It is a plan for a camouflage of the skeleton by rearranging the expected stratums. So play what sounds good. The chord-in-between doesn't have to be a two-note sound; sometimes it can be one note; sometimes three.

Certainly the bass-&-chord pattern can vary from the skeleton's, too. Sometimes your right hand plays a chord while your left plays a bass on the same beat. Sometimes the octave melody can be used alone when a chord would be expected at the same time. The important thing is to preserve a *feel for the beat* beneath the camouflage.

If you want to hear a couple of examples of this harmony-in-melody device, listen to Grieg's *To Spring, Tempo I,* from bar 65 to the end; and to Schumann's *The Merry Peasant* (Opus 68, No. 10). In that one, however, the melody note in the right hand is duplicated by a note in the left, with the chords played between the two by the right hand.

THERE IS ONE FURTHER WAY to reorganize the stratums of the skeleton. But as it is very florid and gymnastic, there is no need to dwell on it. Suffice it to say, this camouflage device puts the *harmony above the melody.*

This treatment is usually reserved for original classical compositions, or for piano translations of orchestral music, or for very fancy renditions of popular numbers. In essence it is the melody played by your left hand —usually as a single-note

It's really the skeleton, but played in 2 stratums. Top layer holds both melody (as empty octaves) and interior chordals played as chord attacks.

melody— with your right hand doing all sorts of fancy filigrees and fandangoes about it.

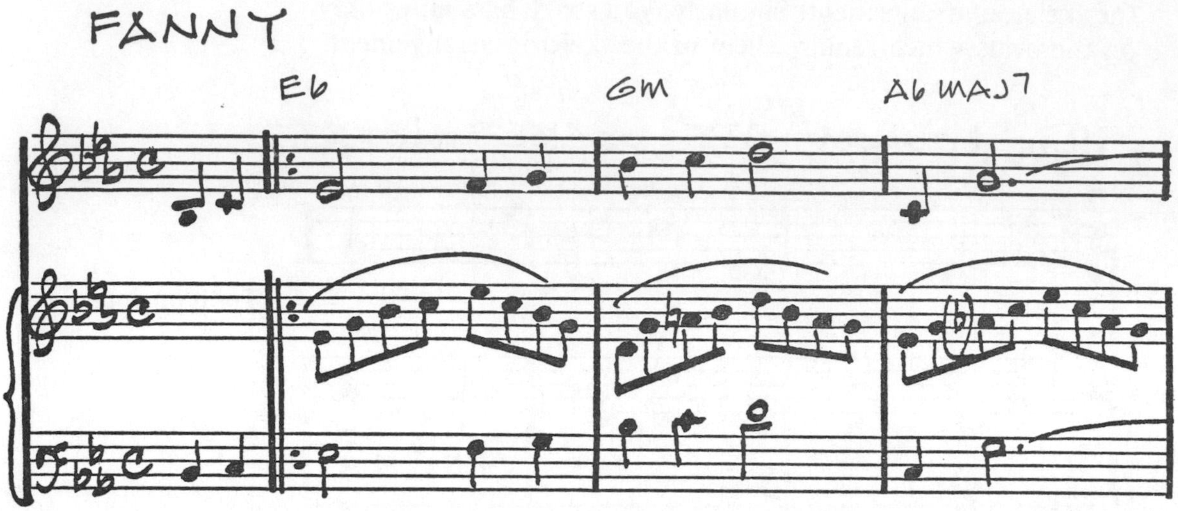

FANNY

Chord stratum

Melody stratum

Melody under harmony is another 2-stratum setting. Your right hand does most of the fancy work with either full chords or an arpeggio treatment.

The melody seems to trot along under a heavy downpour of chords, or else the wind sweeps through and breaks the chords up into a harp-like run. All in all, it's like a day late in March. Consequently, you can find this technique in Grieg's *To Spring* (first 42 bars); Sinding's *Rustles of Spring* (first 30 bars); and Schumann's *The Merry Peasant* (first 8 bars).

WELL THEN, IN A NUTSHELL: The first effective way to rearrange the skeleton's stratums is the crossed-hands technique of putting the melody in the harmony —putting the notes of the melody in the stratum between bass notes and chords.

So, play the melody notes with your right hand one octave lower than written. Your left hand hits the bass note octave and then jumps over your right to hit the chord. Don't worry about keeping the chord in rigid stratum. Don't worry about hitting four-note chords. Just keep the chords close to the melody.

A second effective way to camouflage the skeleton by moving stratums around is to put the harmony inside an octave melody. Your right hand plays the melody where written and duplicates the melody note an octave below, dropping two (or one or three) chord notes in between. Your left hand plays only bass notes, as lowest octaves. Together, your hands preserve a feel for the beat — a bass-&-chord combination more or less like the skeleton's.

There is a third way to reorganize the stratums. And that way is to put the harmony —chords and/or broken chords— above the melody.

How to arrange a number

SOME ENCHANTED EVENING

WHEN IT COMES TO PATTERNS of oncoming single notes, that is one of the best-known in American popular music —the opening four bars of Richard Rodgers' *Some Enchanted Evening*.

19

What makes it a pattern is the repetition. The first two bars are echoed in the second pair of bars. From pair to pair you will see congruent patterns of high and low notes, exact duplications of wide and narrow durations in time, and similar sequences of chordal and non-chordal notes.

And in addition to all of that, there is also a *sparse-and-busy* pattern repeated in each of the pairs.

The tune makes attacks on the silence, a pattern of sparse-&-busy measures

And with that sparse-and-busy pattern, you have a form in which to lay out your arrangement —your patterned use of the skeleton and its variation.

In other words, the arrangement ought to be busy where the melody is sparse, and sparse where the melody is busy. If arranging a number can be reduced to a principle, it is this: In making music, you should have *something* going on all the time. And that is quite different from having *everything* going on all the time.

To be specific, you might want to have each pair of bars in this pattern combine two variations of skeleton arrangement. The first bar of each pair, being rather busy in the melody, it could do nicely with a three-attack bass-&-chord combination; and the second bar of each pair, being less busy in melody, it could take a four-attack combination of bass-&-chord.

SOME ENCHANTED EVENING

An arrangement made of variations No. 4 and No.2. The setting is sparse where the melody is busy, and busy where the melody is sparse.

That's hardly the only way to arrange these opening bars. But whatever variation of skeleton or camouflage device you elect to use (and that includes the use of the skeleton arrangement itself), keep two things in mind. First, remember that any new combinations of bass-&-chord must make a pattern —must be repeated in an understandable way. And second, keep the texture of the new arrangement out of conflict with the texture of the melody, just as you did in the opening bars.

So, don't use more than a couple of different devices in arranging a part or a half part of a number. Too many devices will prevent your repeating them —making a pattern of them— within a part or half part. In the same way, too much going on in both melody and arrangement will make for gibberish instead of pattern.

THAT BRINGS UP THE MATTER of parts and half parts of numbers.

Most popular music and show tunes are written in two parts —an A part and a B part. Each is eight bars long, usually. And each part is repeated once, twice or three times —in any event, enough times to make the number thirty two bars long.

In many instances, the thirty two bars come along this way. The melody runs through Part A twice for openers (that's sixteen bars). Then the melody takes one lap through the release or Part B (bringing the total to twenty four bars now). And to finish, there is a repeat of Part A again, to make the final total thirty two bars.

That is an A-A-B-A form. And you can hear it this very moment if you will invite the neighbors in to help you sing *September Song*.

In many other numbers, the thirty two bars come along in an A-B-A-B form —with both parts repeated twice. (There's no release in this form.) And while it isn't quite so common as the other, there's enough of it in use so that you and your neighbors can swing right into *I Could Write A Book* and *Getting To Know You.*

There are other variations, to be sure. There is A-B-A-C, for instance, in which Part C is a variation of Part B. And there are expanded forms which follow the usual A and B layout of parts but make one or the other sixteen bars long so that the final number is much longer than thirty two bars. *(Some Enchanted Evening* is an A-A-B-A form basically. But Part A is sixteen bars long, Part B is eight, and following the final Part A, there is a six-bar *coda* or tail which brings the number to a finish.)

In any event, with an A-A-B-A number such as *Some Enchanted Evening,* you have three occasions to play that Part A —three occasions to arrange and rearrange it. How you do so depends, naturally, on what sounds good to you *at the time.* The next time you play it, an entirely new arrangement may be much more to your liking— particularly as you are now alert to all sorts of camouflage techniques. (And still others will be set out for your inspection as this book moves along.)

But just for example, you could play all of Part A the first time through with two variations of bass-&-chord combinations illustrated at the opening of this chapter. For the next time through Part A, you could change the arrangement to crossed-hand style —dropping the melody an octave below where it is written and putting it between the bass notes and the chords. And for the final Part A of the number which finishes most A-A-B-A tunes, you could . . . well, whatever sounds good is good —as long as it makes an understandable pattern.

On the other hand, there's no reason why you can't break the parts in half —if the melody makes half part patterns— and give one treatment to the first half-part and another patterned treatment to other half-part. (In *Some Enchanted Evening* a half of Part A is eight bars long. In traditional, thirty-two bar numbers, a half-part is four bars long. But the principle works either way.) Whether you repeat these half-part arrangements when Part A comes around again is up to you and your ear.

But there's a word of caution about arranging in half-parts: *Don't change the melody stratum in mid-part.* Don't pull the tune from the high stratum of the skeleton down to the low stratum of the crossed-hands technique. It is as though you were dividing a sentence (which is what a half-part usually is) between a soprano and a basso—

SOPRANO: Where seldom is heard

BASSO: A discouraging word.

SOPRANO: So what

BASSO: Can an antelope say?

As for Part B or the release (or bridge), that eight-bar pattern could be set apart by playing it as a one-finger melody where

Part B, alias the bridge or release.

A few of the millions of numbers written in the A-A-B-A form.

Blue Moon
The Man I Love
Bewitched
Body And Soul
Harbor Lights
Heart And Soul
If I Had You

TOMORROW IS ANOTHER DAY...

written with a chord at the beginning and middle of each bar. Or you could . . .

But even with extended patterns of sixteen-bar parts and other combinations of parts (A-A-B-B as in *My Heart Belongs To Daddy* by Cole Porter), the fact remains that just about all of the material you will be working with has only *two* developed themes or patterns. And moreover, no matter how many single notes are in each full part, the part is almost always only eight bars long —and the final tally, the complete number, is usually thirty two bars long.

All in all, it is a very handy form for organizing oncoming notes —a very easy form for your ear to identify, to follow and to remember. It's a form that makes for lots of repetition of each pattern, so you don't have to pay very close attention to get the picture. If you miss something the first time, you can be certain that the pattern will be on re-run in a moment or two. Under those circumstances, it's only reasonable to call this form "popular music."

SO, IN A NUTSHELL: As you would expect, there are no neat rules to lay down for proper arranging. There are, as usual, only a few principles —all of them tested by time, and all available to be altered or even disregarded. Some of those principles are:

I. Don't attempt to treat a melody with any sort of arrangement until you understand its form and know how its patterns are delivered. You have to know whether each part can be subdivided into half parts. You have to know whether the parts are delivered as A-A-B-A or in some other form. You have to know what the sparse-and-busy texture of the melody is. The lyrics will help you recognize that texture.

2. Don't begin to play an arrangement until you have made a plan on paper. Keep a pencil at the keyboard and make notes to yourself on the sheet music, telling yourself which device to try here or there. Don't use a pen and ink because, as that immortal eraser, Ludwig van Beethoven, once said, "Morgen ist ein anderer Tag."

3. But even though tomorrow is another day, don't pattern a treatment simply for the sake of pattern. The object of arranging with variations and camouflage techniques is to make the music interesting, not merely intricate. There is no profit to the ear if it has to referee a competition between the melody and the setting. Being interesting at the keyboard means keeping *something* going on all the time. It doesn't mean keeping *everything* going on all the time. The personality of the melody will decide the simplicity or complexity of the arrangement.

True, you have quite a few interesting camouflage devices available —basic skeleton; full skeleton; all sorts of bass-&-chord combinations; reorganized stratums; and no device other than a solitary one finger melody. And you will have quite a few more techniques available to you before this book ends. But that doesn't mean you have to use them all In each setting. In fact, the fewer you use —as long as you have a reason for using them— the easier it is to make an interesting pattern and texture for your arrangement.

4. You can arrange in full parts (full eight-bar parts) or in half parts in most slower numbers. But you generally can't work in hunks smaller than four bars because your arrangement has to be repeated so as to form a pattern.

If you elect to work in half parts, make sure that the melody divides that way —into four-bar, easily identified patterns. (*September Song* does not break readily at the four-bar mark, for instance.) Furthermore, don't move the melody from one stratum to another in mid-part for most numbers. (An exception to that rule is *Little Sir Echo*. In that one, you can —and should— move the melody from one stratum to another when the echo answers for the vory reason that another county is being heard from.) For the vast majority of numbers, however, you should keep the melody in one stratum throughout a whole part. If you want to change stratums, do so when you play the full part again.

One last item about arranging with combinations of variation techniques and camouflage devices. And that is, you haven't seen anything yet. The next chapter opens a great cupboard full of new possibilities. With those and what you now know, you could become the most popular kid on the block.

Try some arranging on your own piano. The suggested variations are numbered according to the way they appear in this chapter.

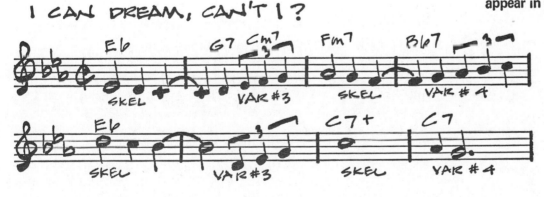

How to play the piano despite years of lessons

THE MYTH: Music is another language.

THE FACT: Music is the same simple language spoken over and over again, this way and that.

Part six

Camouflaging the skeleton (cont'd): The arpeggio — or how to amaze your friends and relatives. The arpeggio looks and sounds a whole lot harder to play than it really is. How to turn the arpeggio into a counter-melody. And, to put it to still further use, how to employ the bottom of the arpeggio as the 10th chord or open position chord.

The arpeggio
and how to make it

20

THERE ARE A COUPLE OF VERY GOOD reasons why the skeleton arrangement —and even some of its variations— can sound so old fashioned, tacky and boring. For one, everything is pretty much where you expect it to be. The four-note chords are in stratum. The melody is blocked. The clock ticks along audibly at four attacks per measure or three. The chordal notes stand like a vertical scaffold beneath the oncoming melody tones. And all in all, the whole affair could be like a dull conversationalist, saying the obvious over and over again about where each melody note belongs in time and space.

The other reason why the skeleton might sound so boring and abrupt can be traced to the nature of the piano itself.

Unlike the strings, woodwinds and brasses, the piano cannot sustain its sound. A violinist, for example, can make a steady tone last for the full length of his bow and arm. A clarinetist and trombonist can sustain a steady tone for as long as they have air in their lungs. But a pianist, no matter how deeply he inhales nor how hard he presses the key and pedal, cannot keep the piano tone from dying away. On each attack —on bass or on chord —the sound is stated sharply. But immediately thereafter it begins to fade until the next attack produces the next sharply stated sound. At best, the overall effect is like the waves of the ocean —alternating crests and troughs on a choppy day.

That is the case with all percussion instruments: they are all abrupt and choppy because *they cannot sustain a tone*. The closest they can come to it is a rapid number of attacks —a drum roll, say, or the familiar arpeggio sound of the harp —which are pulled together by the mind's ear into what sounds like one continuous, sustained sound.

Like its colleagues in the percussion division, the piano can do the same —can increase the number of attacks, thus putting the crests of sharply stated sound closer together. That is the making of an *arpeggio* of tones, a roll of attacks which the mind's ear will pull together into what sounds like a continuous and sustained sound. And that is a different kettle of drums from the choppy attack of bass-&-chord combinations.

THE WORD ARPEGGIO COMES FROM the same origin as the word *harp*. In plain Italian, arpeggio means notes played in a harp-like manner. And in plain English, that means separating the chord into its individual notes and playing each one after the

Percussion instruments can't sustain a tone. They tend to be abrupt and choppy.

other across more than one octave.*

To be specific about the arpeggio, take a basic C chord in root position. That chord can be dismantled quite easily and separated into its individual notes C E G. And then, if you play those three notes one after the other over and over, across more than an octave range —from one C to the next and beyond it— why, you have produced an arpeggio arrangement of the C chord.

Now, that seems simple enough. But when that plain fact is laid out on the staff, it can drive terror to many hearts. Even when it is put into the treble clef for easy reading, that very same C chord arpeggio takes on the look of an impossibility —an acrobatic feat which requires superhuman skill to play. (To start that arpeggio in a lower stratum so that it would be written to begin in the bass clef and roll up into the treble, that picture would be too cruel and heartless, even though it is very easy to understand and to play, once you know the root note of the chord— the starting note of the arpeggio.)

When it comes to the arpeggio, it appears that a thousand words of explanation are better, or at least more reassuring, than one pictue. And anyway, that picture is a little misleading. For all its simplicity, it is twice as difficult to play as the arpeggio you will be using in making music. But if you can understand how that difficult one works, you can make the simple one much more readily.

An arpeggio.
But if this picture
makes you nervous,
don't look at it.
Read the text instead.
It's very reassuring.

AS A REPLACEMENT FOR YOUR left hand's bass-&-chord combination in skeleton arranging (and those camouflage devices which use bass-&-chord combinations), the arpeggio arrangement provides two obvious benefits.

First, it gets rid of the choppy sound of attack-pause-attack of bass-&-chord combinations. In their place you have what sounds like a sustained, continuous harmony running up through the stratums to the bottom of the melody block. Consequently, you get *a much fuller sound out of the piano.*

The second benefit of the arpeggio arrangement in place of bass-&-chord combinations is *camouflage* of a vast magnitude.

The skeleton's chords stand *vertically* under the blocked melody and tick-tock *horizontally* across time. But the arpeggio, as you can see if you can bear to look at the illustration again, rolls along a *diagonal* path from bottom left toward top right, or from top left toward bottom right (or both, as in the picture).

That diagonal arrangement camouflages the four-square

---

*Breaking up the chord into individual notes and playing them one after another within an octave range is not properly an arpeggio. Rather, it's a broken chord.

C E G   C E G C G E C

scaffolding of the skeleton very nicely without leaving the music unsupported by its framework. Each individual attack in the arpeggio is still the tick-&-tock of the clockwork which measures each oncoming melody note's duration in time. And what appears to be a sustained tone created by the arpeggio is still the chordal sound, the setting which identifies each oncoming melody tone as comfortable or restless.

Clearly, this camouflage device was not invented for the occasion of this book. It has a long and very legitimate history. So, if you want to hear it at work in piano literature, tune in to Grieg's *To Spring* from bar No. 65 to the end; to Rubinstein's Kamennoi-Ostrow (Opus 10, No. 6) throughout most of the piece from bar No. 42 to the end. The shorter version of this device which is played within one octave —the broken chord— also abounds in classical music. It is heard throughout the first movement of Beethoven's *Moonlight Sonata,* (Opus 27, No. 2); and in the opening twenty two bars of Liszt's *Liebestraum.*

Beside what it offers in continuous sound and camouflage, the arpeggio has one more advantage, namely it is *interesting* to listen to. And for that reason, it can be played in its simplest form without losing anything in the arrangement. That means you can play an arpeggio of eighth notes only. And furthermore you can dispense with the added fourth notes of chords and make your arpeggio of the basic three-note chords.

In other words, you need only eight attacks per bar in 4/4 time; and only six per bar in 3/4 time. And those eight or six attacks do not have to include any 7th notes, 6th notes or Major 7ths. Instead, you use only the three notes of the basic chord or of its three-note altered forms. So, that lush, full sound of the arpeggio —which *looks* so impossible to make on the keyboard —is nothing more than the root and 3rd and 5th notes of the required chord played over and over.

IT IS NOT NECESSARY TO BEGIN the arpeggio in the lowest possible place on the piano. In fact, it's not advisable to do so because the tones down there are more like growls and you can lose the effect of the arpeggio in blurred and muddy overtones. It is much better to start the roll in the next higher stratum.

There is still the problem of overtones there, as you can hear if you try three attacks —root, 3rd and 5th— to begin an arpeggio. But that problem can be solved very neatly by separating those bottom notes, opening them up, ventilating that bottom to let the growling overtones escape. That way, the individual three attacks of the beginning of the arpeggio can be heard as tones rather than as noise.

How to open up those notes? Simply by playing them out of normal order so that you leave a gap between each attack. That is done by playing the first three notes of the arpeggio in this

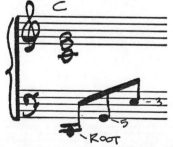

order —*root note,* followed by *5th note,* followed by *3rd note.* (Thereafter the arpeggio continues in normal order, by the numbers. It picks up with the 5th note as reason indicates, and moves on to the root, to the 3rd, to the 5th and so on.)

Try that open position of the first three notes of the arpeggio on your own piano. Try it with an arpeggio built on the basic F chord. Instead of playing the normal order of notes (F A C), play it as root- 5th-3rd —F C A. Naturally, it is played with your left hand in the next-to-lowest starting place on the keyboard.

Not only will you hear that ventilated sound of the open position. But in addition you will hear another logic at work, to wit: the first two attacks —root and then 5th— mark the *outer shape* of the chord. The next attack, the 3rd, gives the chord *its own personality* as basic, minor, etc. And once that news is announced to the listening world, the arpeggio can continue in the expected, normal, closed position order of notes.

THERE ARE A FEW ITEMS to keep in mind about using an arpeggio in place of the skeleton's bass-&-chord setting.

Item. The separate attacks of the arpeggio can be described as the ticking of the clock, measuring the exact duration of each oncoming melody note. In 4/4 time there are eight ticks of the clock; in 3/4 time there are six. How you count those ticks is up to you. But whatever method you use, keep it *steady and accurate.* A missing attack or an extra attack will make uneven clockwork and consequently oncoming notes of the wrong width in time. (It will also make bars of uneven length.) You might be trying to play *Red River Valley,* but by wrong timing you could miss the mark and instead be playing Beethoven's *Sonata No. 2 in A* (Opus 12, No. 2). So count out loud. And, of course, play what you count; never count what you play.

Item. The fingering you use to play an arpeggio depends solely on what is comfortable for you. But experience teaches a couple of things. For one, hit the first note of the arpeggio —the root note of the chord —with your pinky. After all, the arpeggio demands that you come up the keyboard with your left hand, and moreover that you open the run with three wide-

Eight attacks in a bar of 4/4 arpeggio. Six in a bar of 3/4. So, you have to count with "ands" to make room.

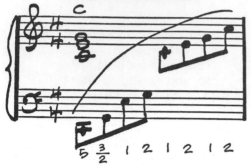

ly spaced attacks. Your index finger or middle finger will be best for the second attack. And that leaves your thumb in position to make the leap to the third attack.

In fact, it's not a bad idea to count the beats of the bottom, open part of the arpeggio by combining the names of the notes with the stretch you have to make in order to hit them. Instead of counting, "One, five, three, five" and so on, you might try the count of "One five, *stretch,* five . . . ." Or, if you need more room for additional melody notes in a bar: "One and five and *stretch* and five and . . . ."

As for the fingering required to play the upper, closed remainder of the arpeggio, you can probably do the job most easily with your thumb and index finger alternating with each other.

Item. The blocked melody, of course, is played one octave higher than printed. But that is no guarantee you can finish a bar of arpeggio without colliding with the bottom of the block. If the melody (and block) are low, and a collision with the arpeggio is unavoidable, you can avoid it by turning back —reversing the arpeggio, retracing your steps, and playing the last note or two going down the keyboard the way you just came up. But having to retrace your steps that way is necessary only occasionally. And almost always it is only a note or two which have to be played on the return route. But regardless, it is still the same arpeggio of three notes stated over and over whether it rolls upward, or retraces its path downward.

Item. In addition to being a steady clock for measuring the duration of oncoming notes, the arpeggio is also a sustained and continuous setting —a chord— which bestows on the

HOW HIGH THE MOON

single melody notes comfortableness or restlessness. Consequently, the arpeggio has to tell the mind's ear how to separate the oncoming melody tones into chordals and non-chordals. To accomplish that job, the arpeggio *must begin anew at the beginning of each bar* —unless two successive bars call for the same chord. In that case, you can keep the arpeggio going without starting anew at the beginning of the second bar. And, naturally, if the chord changes in the middle of a bar, why, you have to start a new arpeggio right there. From the root, of course.

In other words, you play two half-arpeggios for a bar where the chord changes mid-way through. But just where you place the bottom of each half-arpeggio is up to you. Obviously a half-arpeggio in 4/4 time is only four notes long. So you can either begin each considerably closer to the middle of the keyboard without worry about a collision with the block beneath the melody, or you can combine the two half-arpeggios into one run made of two chords.

Now and then in a number, a chord change may come on the last beat only. In that event, a new arpeggio has to begin at the bottom for the new chord, even if the chord lasts for only one beat (two arpeggio attacks). The two attacks you play for that brief chord are just what you would expect — the root and 5th notes, the outer shape of the chord —just what you would play to begin any arpeggio with the open position of chord notes.

Item. You can achieve the full sound of the arpeggio with the help of the right pedal —the sustaining pedal. But don't overdo it because holding down that sustaining pedal too long will pile tone on tone until the full sound you want becomes a muddy glop.

A good way to use that pedal is by the numbers —the numbered beats. In a bar of 4/4 time, hold it down on No. 1, release it on No. 2, hold it down again on No. 3 and release it for No. 4. So, in an arpeggio of eight attacks, it's two down, two off, two down, two off. That kind of pedal work not only makes for a good, clear sustained tone; it also helps you with your counting out the time.

Item. This elementary arpeggio of the basic three notes makes for a camouflage device which sounds like the most accomplished kind of music-making on the block, if not in the whole neighborhood. But because the arpeggio is so lush and full and busy, its texture can work against busy melodies or busy parts thereof. For instance: Gershwin's *Someone To Watch Over Me* or Fats Waller's *Honeysuckle Rose* do not sit happily on an arpeggio —not even during rests and sparse bars.

On the other hand, some numbers were born to be treated with an arpeggio, at least in parts and pieces of bars. Look at what you can do with a combination of chord-&-arpeggio as a setting for *Some Enchanted Evening*.

If the arpeggio could collide with the melody block, retrace your steps for the last note or two.

A chord may last 1 beat, getting 2 attacks only.

SOME ENCHANTED EVENING

**How to amaze your friends.
The arpeggio combined
with skeleton or one
of its variations.
Remember to block melody.**

And what that further proves is this. When your right hand (with the melody and block) isn't doing much, your left hand is busy with the arpeggio. Conversely, when the melody becomes busy and your right hand is working, your left hand isn't. But with a skillful combination of arpeggio and even skeleton, you can sound as though you had somehow devised a way to play four-hand arrangements all by yourself. However, the lily can be painted (or gilded, if you're that sort). And so, the next chapter will provide you with palette and brush. But first—

THE NUTSHELL: The arpeggio is played by the left hand as a replacement for the bass-&-chord combinations of skeleton and its varieties. The purpose of the arpeggio is to produce a full, sustained, continuous sound and thus eliminate the choppiness of bass-&-chord combinations. The arpeggio can be used very effectively to give movement —a sense of something happening— to a slow number or a sparse passage or bar in the melody.

The elementary arpeggio is made by a succession of rapid attacks —the notes of the basic three-note chord played as individual eighth notes one after the other. In a bar of 4/4 music, there are eight notes in the arpeggio; in a bar of 3/4 music, there are six attacks.

The arpeggio starts an octave or so higher than the lowest possible root note, and crosses stratums up the keyboard to the bottom of the block. If a collision with the block looms, avoid it by retracing the steps of the arpeggio and playing the last note or two going back down the keyboard. *All eight or six attacks must be stated in each bar.*

The arpeggio begins with the open position of the chord

notes —root followed by 5th followed by 3rd. Thereafter the arpeggio continues in closed position, picking up with the 5th and thence to the root, etc.

Begin a new arpeggio at the beginning of each bar. Begin a new arpeggio whenever there is a chord change, no matter on which beat it comes, and even if there is room for two attacks only (if so, the root and the 5th). Half-arpeggios and smaller can be started closer to the middle of the keyboard because they have fewer attacks and run less risk of colliding with the bottom of the block.

Steady accurate counting out loud is a must in order to develop a smooth, even arpeggio. Which fingers you use, however, depends on which is most comfortable. But it's advisable to start with your pinky on the root.

The diminished and augmented chords are a little more difficult to play as arpeggios and may require a bit of practice. But don't bother to practice them until you encounter them.

A fluent arpeggio of the basic three chordal notes will. . . .well, all right, it will amaze your friends when you sit down to play. They'll never miss the 7ths, 6ths and Major 7th notes. They'll never realize that your right hand is idle or under-employed by the melody while your left is so very accomplished —and vice versa. All in all, an arpeggio is a very handy device. No piano should be without one.

A few numbers to try with
an arpeggio setting
either throughout
or for a part.

The Way You Look Tonight
Where Or When
If I Loved You
The Song Is You
All The Things You Are
Embraceable You
Love Walked In
Over The Rainbow
I See Your Face Before Me
April Showers
Deep Purple
Good Night Sweetheart
Yesterdays

Turning an arpeggio into a counter-melody

21

IN ONE WAY, THE ARPEGGIO is merely the notes of the chord played as a succession of attacks up the keyboard and heard as a continuous, sustained sound. But looked at another way—

You could say that the arpeggio is an assortment of on-coming, single tones. And that begins to sound like the definition of a melody. Further, you could say these oncoming tones make an altitude pattern (low to high), a duration pattern (they're all eighth notes), and a chordal-non-chordal pattern (they're all completely comfortable). So, really, you could say that the arpeggio is a melody.

True, it is a very simple, unsophisticated melody of the sort found in children's songs and folk tunes. But that does not alter the case. We've got a melody here. And consequently, you could say that a melody with an arpeggio setting is actually an arrangement of *two tones at work simultaneously,* one opposite the other. On the one hand (your right hand) is the melody organized by the composer and distributed by the publisher— a melody blocked with a couple of notes of the chord. And on the other hand (your left) is a *counter-melody* of single notes only which you are composing. All by yourself. Alone. With no help.

All of that could have been spelled out in one short paragraph. But it has gone on at length because there is a great public mystery about this business of counter-melody. In fact, the topic is so dark and forbidding that it is usually referred to as "counter-point" —and then only in a very quiet, tentative voice with the hands touching at the finger tips. Generally, statements on this matter begin, "We here at the Institute have been working with counter-point and find that..."

The arpeggio's basic duty
is its chordal sound.
(The first 3 notes and last.)
That leaves place enough
for substitute notes to
make it a counter-melody.

BY PLAYING ONE MELODY AND *making a counter-melody below it* at the same time, you are producing fuller and more interesting music than you can with the obvious and repetitive family of skeleton arrangements —with the chords kept in their narrow stratum in order to avoid making an unwanted and uncontrolled counter-melody.

How interesting you make the arpeggio—how sophisticated you make that single-note counter-melody in your left hand —depends on the kinds of notes you insert amidst the three basic chordal notes which make the fundamental arpeggio sound. One or two other notes inserted as substitutes for one or two of those basic chordals can turn the arpeggio into a much more fascinating and adult counter-melody beneath tunes which everybody knows by heart.

Actually, there's not a whole lot of room for substitution. The arpeggio has its first duty to the chord setting for the oncoming notes of the melody. So, the first three attacks have to be the three basic or altered chord tones (played in open position, of course). In addition, the final note of the arpeggio must be one of those three basic chordals for the same reason: the setting for the melody above. So that uses up four notes of the arpeggio —four of the six in a bar of 3/4 time, four of the eight in a bar of 4/4 time.

But that leaves plenty of room for the one or two substitute notes needed to pull the arpeggio out of the strict, legal definition of a melody and into the sophisticated actuality of being a real counter-melody. Naturally, any note you use to substitute and insert must take its place in the upper, closed part of the arpeggio. As for which notes to use, you have quite a few choices:

1. Prescriptions in the printed chord symbols are a possibility, but a tame one.

If the chord called for specifies the added fourth note —6th, 7th, Major 7th —you can use that note in place of a chordal (or even two) in the arpeggio.

Even if the chord doesn't call for a 9th, you can often use that note as a substitute. (The 9th is also the 2nd —the note named two intervals above the root.) But listen to what you play. If the 9th doesn't sound good in the arpeggio under the particular melody bar you're arranging, don't use it.

2. If the chord is un-numbered —*a plain C, say, or a Cm* —**try substituting the numbers you would use if you were playing four-note chords in stratum.**

As you recall (as you had better recall), one minor 7th is another basic 6 chord. So, for un-numbered basic chords, try a 6th —or even a pair of them— in the arpeggio. Or try a Major 7th, or a pair of them, if there's room. The only requirement is that you end the arpeggio on one of the three basic chord notes and not on any other kind —not even if a chord number is specified in the chord symbol.

For an un-numbered minor chord, of course, your first choice of a substitute in the arpeggio is the 7th (or a pair of them).

3. If playing the prescribed or implied numbers in the arpeggio gets to sound a bit tame, try using more than one substitute in making your counter-melody.

No law says you must incorporate the numbers prescribed in the chord symbols, or even those implied when the chord has no number with it. Try using non-chordals and let your ear be the judge of the counter-melody.

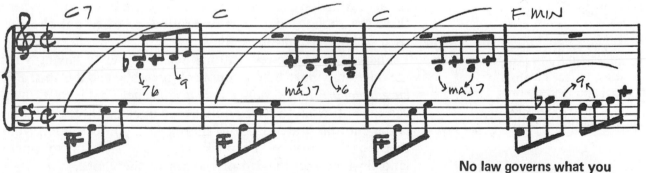

When it comes to arpeggios made of diminished chords, your first choice can be the added 6th note which makes the *dim6*—that four-way labor-saving device. For an arpeggio made of an augmented chord, your first choice might be the added 7th note. And then again, it might not. It depends on how it sounds to you. But you may find that the bare bones of the three-note diminished and augmented chords are interesting enough when played as arpeggios. After all, the arpeggio is a very lush, rich sound even when purely chordal.

No law governs what you can toss into an arpeggio between its first 3 notes and the last. The only test for the result: How does it sound to you?

BECAUSE THE BOTTOM, OPEN PART of the arpeggio has to be three pure, undiluted, basic chordal notes, any substitute note must be played in the upper, *closed run* of the arpeggio. That means substitutes are always sandwiched between chordal notes. No matter which non-chordal note you add and insert in the closed run, it is always just a step or so away from one of the essential three — root, 3rd, or 5th. So, when the bar is finished and it is time to play the final, chordal note of the arpeggio, you will find it no more than an interval or two away.

Melodies can leap over many intervals, usually taking off from a chordal and landing on one.

Obviously, melodies do not always move as a stepwise string of oncoming tones, each sitting no more than two intervals away from the next. A lot of the time melody notes jump across many intervals, even in simple, unsophisticated children's songs. Moreover, melodies seldom move only up or only down. Most often there is considerable backing and forthing along the path.

You can ask your arpeggio counter-melody to do those things, too. But, of course, on a rather limited basis. After all, you have to start a new arpeggio at the beginning of the next bar —with the obligatory three basic chordal notes to begin it. So, leaping about and reversing direction and generally behaving like a melody is really only for 4/4 time measures where there are enough notes to mess around, or when one chord is used for more than one bar.

There is only one restriction when it comes to having your melody jump more than a couple of intervals, and it is this: *You have to depart from a chordal and land on one.* That is to say, you can take off from the third note of the opening three because it is the chordal, the 3rd of the chord. And you can jump from there to the bottom of the block —but only if you make sure to land on the root, the 3rd or the 5th of the chord.

Once you have landed, your melody can do anything you like (as long as it sounds good to you).

You can move to a non-chordal — as long as you get there without crossing more than two intervals. And from that non-chordal you can move to another chordal (as long as it is within two intervals). And from that chordal, you can leap back to the chordal you departed from in the first place . . . But too many chordals may sound timid and uninteresting.

Well, it is absurd to waste time pointing out what you can do about making your counter-melody move. You can do

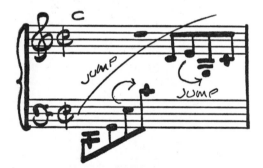

If you want your counter-melody to leap, it's best to leave from a chordal and land on one. From there, you can move to a non-chordal.

anything you like if it sounds good. The only thing you cannot do is to leap over three intervals or more *from a chordal note to a non-chordal note —or, naturally, from a non-chordal note to another or to a chordal note.* The only allowed leaps are from one of the chordal three to another. All other motion has to be stepwise, by one or two intervals, forward or backward.

The final note of the measure has to be one of the three chordals, naturally. But how you get there is limited by the note you played just before it. If that next-to-last note is a non-chordal, then you have to move stepwise to a final note one or two intervals away. Otherwise, you can leap tall buildings to finish the bar.

More amazement
for your friends.
A skeleton variation
combined with
a counter-melody.

IN A NUTSHELL, THEN: The elementary arpeggio can be considered a melody —a counter-melody to the tune you are playing in your right hand. But it is a very simple melody. However, it can be made much more sophisticated and interesting by doing a bit of fooling around with the upper, closed part of the run. (The bottom must be left intact: three chordals played in open position to establish the setting for the oncoming single notes of the composer's melody. And the final note of the run must be another one of the three chordals —root, 3rd or 5th for the same reason.)

But within those confines, there are still two very important and creative changes you can make:

1. You can vary the content of the closed, upper part of the run by inserting substitute notes. Your first choice may be any numbered notes prescribed by the chord symbols. You can use substitutes over again, or use several different substitutes within a bar, just as long as it sounds good to you. But whatever you insert must be connected stepwise (no more than two intervals away) to chordals or to other substitute notes. It must also sound good to you.

2. You can vary the movement and direction of the arpeggio counter-melody. You can jump across three or

more intervals. You can reverse direction, and reverse it again. But you can only jump those distances from one of the three chordals to another of the three. To move to or from a non-chordal note, you can only go stepwise —no more than two intervals— to the next note you play.

A little bit of this variation within the elementary arpeggio goes a long, long way. Just keep the beat even.

The 10th chord or open position

22

OF ALL THE SIMPLE-MINDED THINGS in this whole book, the message in this chapter really takes the cake. It is this—

If you play the three bottom notes of the arpeggio all together and at the same time, you will be playing a basic chord (or basic altered chord). That is because you took that chord apart to play the notes separately for the bottom of the arpeggio.

The chord you will play by striking those bottom three notes all together and simultaneously is a chord in its *open position*. That is because you made the bottom of the arpeggio by playing the three basic chordal notes as root, 5th and then 3rd —out of order and thus in ventilated or *open* sequence.

This ventilated, out-of-usual-order, open position chord is also known as *the 10th chord*.

That is because the open position puts the 3rd on top of the chord rather than in the middle (where it usually lives in the closed position). To put the 3rd on top requires that you take it from the next octave up on the keyboard. And up there, that note is Number 10 of the basic scale (just as the 2nd note up there becomes the 9th, and the root becomes the 8th).

The 10th chord sounds its best in a low register on the keyboard, and is usually played there. But just how low on the keyboard you can play it depends on your piano. The bigger and finer the instrument —the longer the strings and better the sounding board —the lower you can produce a clear, mellow, unmuddied 10th chord. So its location on the keyboard depends, as usual, on what sounds good to your ear.

As for the use of this ventilated and consequently cool sounding chord, it is obviously one more device for camouflaging the skeleton and varying the kind of music you can make.

1. You can use the 10th chord in place of the first bass note of the skeleton —a substitute for the root note used as a low octave.

In that event, you hold the open position chord for one beat

Bottom 3 notes
of the arpeggio
played together:
The l0th chord
or chord in
open position.

—and follow it with a closed position chord in stratum, and thereafter onward with the regular, beloved, boring skeleton.

2. You can use the 10th chord in place of the opening, bottom three attacks of the arpeggio.

And from there you can proceed with the standard, closed position, upper part of the arpeggio —with or without substitute notes incorporated. Or you can state the 10th chord and then jump a distance to a chordal and continue the arpeggio there.

There is a great economy and bonus in this variation of the arpeggio.

In the standard arpeggio bottom, you begin with *three attacks* —three eighth-notes-in-succession, to state the complete chordal sound. But when you use the 10th chord for the bottom, you have only to state it for one beat — *for only two attacks' worth of time.* In that way, you free an eighth note for use in the upper part of your arpeggio or counter-melody. Just remember to count your opening 10th chord as one beat ("One-and") in order to save that third attack for later in the bar.

3. You can use the 10th chord for a prolonged bottom of your arpeggio.

You can play the 10th chord as one attack lasting half-a-bar, and then play a half-arpeggio for the remainder of the bar. In that sense, the chord is not really part of the arpeggio but rather a device all of its own. And the half-arpeggio is on its own as well.

4. You can use the 10th chord as the only device, the only setting, your left hand plays— one 10th chord after another in that open position stratum you have marked off on your piano.

That is a particularly effective technique during a measure or two where the oncoming melody is made of whole notes or bar-long rests. Then, a progression of these cool chords can be very effective. If, however, only one chord is called for where the melody is sparse, you can sound like a terrible bore if you strike *the very same chord sound* over and over.

In that instance, you have several options open (if you want to use chords only with no bass notes or arpeggio). You can get the feeling of motion by changing the placement of the notes within the 10th chord —moving the root to the top for one attack, moving the fifth to the top for the next, and so on —but keeping the whole in its open position. Or, you can move from a statement of the 10th chord to the same chord but in closed position and in stratum —and from there to another chord exactly like it but one notch higher on the keyboard . . .

It's the same chord over and over, whether in open position or closed position. But by re-ordering the notes within the chord on each attack, you have it move notch by notch up or down the keyboard.

Some uses of the l0th chord. In place of the first bass in the skeleton, and the first half of the arpeggio. Or as 1 attack to begin it.

Four l0th chords in a row.

The 3-note basic chord is a circular relationship. Turn it clockwise, the chord climbs in closed position. Counter-clockwise, it is the l0th chord which climbs.

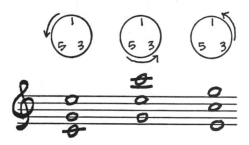

The l0th chord as the first bass attack alternates with a low bass octave, adding another possibility. Remember: block the melody.

THAT'S NOT THE SAME THING as getting the harmony to move. But it's an artful dodge that has the appearance of movement. It's sort of the same effect you get by sitting in a stationary train and watching a train move by on the next track. It looks for all the world as though you're in motion. It even feels like it. But when all is said and done, you're still standing at the depot in Paterson, New Jersey.

There's nothing wrong with that trick of the ear — as long as it sounds good. But there are a couple of things to keep in mind if you're going to have one chord give the impression of movement when it is really only shifting from foot to foot while time and the melody pass by on the adjoining track.

For one thing, there is no law which requires an attack on every beat in the measure. Two chords only per bar of 4/4 time —especially if they are airy and resonant 10th chords— can provide plenty of what seems to be motion. But you must count evenly and accurately so that each attack arrives on exact time.

And for another thing, you cannot play the succession of chords on the exact same spot. Something has to move. That is the whole idea. So, in moving the chords up or down the keyboard, make sure they follow each other very closely. To move the chords from root position up to (or down to) the next root position leaves a vast gap of sound between each attack. That's not the sound of *going somewhere*. That's the sound of having gone.

How to get a chord to follow itself very closely?

Very simply. The basic chord is really a circular relationship of its three notes. No matter how you spin the dial, regardless of which note comes out at noon, or at 4 o'clock or at 8, the three always make the same chord. So, to move a chord up the keyboard notch by notch *in the closed position,* turn the dial *clockwise* notch by notch and play what you read at each stop.

If you're working with the 10th chord —*the open position* of the chord —you have to read the dial *counter-clockwise.* That is the relationship of the basic chord notes (or altered basic chord notes) in the open, ventilated condition. In actual operation, it works out like this:

TRY TO REMEMBER

One further item remains to be mentioned in this matter of the 10th chord, namely the fingers to use for playing it.

Well, why not use the same fingers you use for playing the bottom three notes of the arpeggio? After all, the chord is exactly the same as those three notes, except that they are struck all the same time —or pretty close to it.

The difficulty may be that your hand is too small to reach all three notes at the very same moment. And so, then you will have to roll them. That is, you will have to rock your hand from pinky toward thumb —either hitting the three in as close succession as possible, or else striking the bottom and middle notes simultaneously and rolling quickly to hit the top note of the chord a twinkling later. But whichever way you may have to roll the chord, the last note you hit must be *on the beat* and not after it.

If you can reach all three notes simultaneously, it may take some stretching to do it. So don't expect to be able to do it at the first try. You can also look forward to the feeling that comes with stretching unused muscles. But sooner or later (mostly sooner) your hand will learn to make that stretch easily. And if you can't make the reach but must roll the 10th chord, by and by it will become as easy as pie. In fact, you will soon think of it as a pie rather than as a roll.*

THE NUTSHELL OF IT IS: The bottom, open part of the arpeggio can be played all together as a chord. It is called the 10th chord or chord in open position. And it can be played considerably lower than the skeleton's chord stratum.

The 10th chord has all sorts of uses as another camouflage device —from replacing bass notes to being the only setting under a melody. But regardless of how you use it in an arrangement, make sure the arrangement makes a pattern.

---

*You may find the second combination of the open position — the one with the 5th on the bottom — a lot easier to play or roll. But if so, don't tell anybody you read that here. This inversion puts the root at the top and thus makes for an un-rooted, free-floating sound. But, on the other hand, if it sounds good...

How to play the piano despite years of lessons

THE MYTH: Playing by ear is inferior to playing what is written.

THE FACT: Even the great composers played by ear. That's how they wrote what is written. You have to play by ear—you have to listen to what you play— to know if it sounds good.

Part seven

Open voicing. The over-all sound, and some ways to alter it. How to produce a cool, ventilated, sophisticated arrangement. How to add tension and —just as important— how to reduce it. Where creativity and personal style begin to take over at the keyboard.

The open voicing arrangement

23

THIS ENTIRE PART SEVEN is very short for two reasons.

The first is that the camouflage device of open voicing is very short. Only four or five notes high, including the melody. No bass notes (unless *you* feel the need for an occasional bass.) No chords in stratum. No blocks beneath the melody. The whole business is made only of the single melody notes supported by the 10th chord (and a couple of little variations of it). And all of it played right in the middle of the keyboard.

The second reason that open voicing is so briefly considered here is that there is no way to say, "Just keep in mind that . . ." and "Remember to do the following if you want this device to sound its best . . ." The awful truth of the open voicing camouflage is this: what sounds good is good. And that is up to your ear.

So, just keep in mind that you have no alternating bass notes, no variations of attack, no lush and full arpeggios and counter-melodies to keep your arrangement going. You have only four or five notes, all played together in the middle of the keyboard, with which to be interesting. What this camouflage loses in orchestral, many-stratum arrangements it has to make up with *tension.* As you will see in a moment.

Melody

Basic chord in open position

Only 4 notes in all. So, each is 25% of the over-all sound. One changed or added note makes a big difference.

THE OPEN VOICING ARRANGEMENT is probably the easiest of all to play (next to a one-finger, single-note rendition). It is simply the melody note played *where printed,* with the 10th chord or open position chord beneath it. And to make the production even easier, you *divide the work of the open chord between both hands.* No stretch, no rock, no roll to reach the three open notes. Basically, your left hand plays the root and 5th notes; your right hand adds the 3rd of the chord and plays the melody on top.

Essentially, then, your left hand is playing two notes: pinky on root note and thumb on 5th — the outer shape of the chord. And your right hand is playing two notes in the next octave above: thumb on 3rd note to complete the chord, and pinky on melody note above that. So, both hands are working together to produce the *complete over-all sound in two adjoining stratums.* (Of course, you can play the full 10th chord with your left hand if you can reach it.)

It is that *over-all sound* which produces exactly the effect the name "open voicing" implies: airy, cool, clean, controlled, spare and tense —in short, a sound that is still known after a generation of widespread use as "modern."*

Now, this term "over-all sound" is not a matter to take lightly with a nod and a simple, "Yes, yes —the three chord notes and the melody note spread across two stratums." The over-all sound includes considerably more than what you hear stated outright.

For one thing, this cool arrangement is careful to stay within its two stratums in the middle of the keyboard because originally it was not a solo piano arrangement. It was kidnaped from its place in small combos —trios and quartets— where it had to take care not to tread on the stratums of the bass, clarinet and/or saxophone. So, open voicing having been taken out of a larger context, it is a sort of *abstract art.* And it therefore asks the listening ear to supply the missing over-all sound.

In addition to asking listeners to remember what used to be played, open voicing also asks the ear to remember *what is usually played* in piano arrangements — namely a setting which repeats and re-repeats all the chord notes again and again, from bass notes up through chords in stratum and on up through their extension in the block beneath the melody. Open voicing, however, says its piece only once (and sometimes not even that). As a result, part of the over-all sound within this spare, bare arrangement is *what isn't there but should be.* That is, open voicing asks the listening ear to keep in mind sounds that may have been said briefly and in passing, or maybe weren't even said at all but only hinted at.

There is one more item to be included in the over-all sound. And that is the melody note. Unlike most all piano arrangements where the melody note sits *up on top* of the entire setting, the open voicing arrangement pulls the melody note *into* the over all sound. With so very few chord notes beneath it —and those few notes so spread out —the melody note becomes a much greater percentage of the over-all sound. And that can make for a very interesting sound, particularly if the melody note is an uneasy non-chordal or if the chord spread out below is made to sound tense (which is readily done by changing one note or adding one note in the structure). All in all, the over-all sound can change with one note more or less or different and distorted in the arrangement.

Such effects are easily achieved with open voicing. But they require a particular kind of material to work with, namely a slow-moving, sophisticated melody with plenty of sparse bars

---

*The word "modern" continues perplexing. Bach most certainly used the Maj7 chord (without naming it). On the other hand, one magazine editor says that she hates modern music. She likes semi-classics. Her favorite: <u>Blue Moon</u>.

SEPTEMBER SONG

2 attacks per bar in 4/4 time states the beat for your listeners.

throughout. A fast or busy number is too breathless for this arrangement and will inhale all the air from the ventilating system. A melody of child-like, mostly chordal notes will sound foolish if you try to create tension with it. And if there are no stagnant or sparse places in the number, there is no room to let the effect of open voicing sink in.

And with that advice, it is now time to try a few bars of the arrangement to hear the over-all sound and see what it does —and does not— accomplish. The sample is the opening of *Try To Remember*, a number in 3/4 time. You need play only *one attack per bar* with your left hand —on the first beat of each bar, naturally —and ask your listeners to supply the remaining two beats of the over-all sound.

1 attack per 3/4 bar is enough.

TRY TO REMEMBER

One further item regarding that over-all sound. That feeling of tension and, more important, the feeling of change from *tension to release* and from *rest to tension* is much more apparent in the over-all sound of open voicing than in the over-all sounds of skeleton or arpeggio settings. In those, the melody note is one of nine, ten or eleven in the arrangement, and consequently it doesn't have nearly so great an effect on the whole sound. If you try these few bars with a full orchestral treatment —using bass stratum, chord stratum and blocks beneath the melody note— you will hear the difference. Oh, for heaven's sake, go on and try it.

Now, on to the next sample. This one is the opening of

Spellbound, the theme from the famous Hitchcock film with Gregory Peck and Ingrid Bergman, together again for the first time, skiing their way into your heart.

As you can see, it is in 4/4 time. And while you could state one beat only per bar and ask your listeners to supply the remaining three, that is a bit too demanding for all thirty two bars of the number. It sounds better to the over-all sound if you hit two chords per bar —on the first and third beats, naturally. And if you want to vary that sound, you can do so quite easily by replacing the second chord of the bar with a bass octave. (See the second and third bars of the illustration.)

There are other ways to vary the sound of those two chords per measure. For instance, on the first attack, you could play the basic, open, root-&-5th. At the mid-point of the bar —on the third numbered beat —your left hand can change the configuration and play the root-&-7th. As for the note you dropped, the 5th note? Why, you stated it once at the opening of the measure, *and now it has taken its place in memory* —which is a decided part of the over-all sound.

And now one last example of what you can do with open voicing. This one is *There's A Small Hotel.* And it raises the question, what do you do with a sequence of bars where no chord change is called for? After all, the very same root-&-5th played twice per measure bar after bar can be a worse bore than too much tension.

What do you do? The same thing you would do if you were playing chords in stratum. You'd start trying the possibilities of a fourth note to hear what sounds good. You'd try a 6th, a Major 7th, a 9th. But in this instance your left hand would try them as *the outer configuration of the chord.* That is, your left hand would try root-&-6th, root-&-Maj7, etc.

And in that regard, there's something else you would do in a larger setting to vary the repetitious sounds— *you'd alternate your bass notes,* moving from the root to the 5th and back again. So, you can try its parallel in this instance, too. Your

1 or 2 attacks per bar, add or change notes to raise tension. But use the basic chord, too, to resolve the tension.

first attack being root-&-5th. Your second could easily be 5th-&-root.

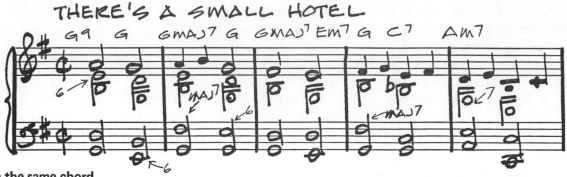

When the same chord lasts for several bars, change the over-all sound on each attack.

When one melody note lasts for a bar or more, your left hand can change the outer shape of the chord on each attack

There's something else you can do, too —and not only in this kind of number but also in any open voicing arrangement. And that is, you can throw an additional, higher tension into your right hand configuration. That will give your right hand *three notes* to play —a big addition which changes the over-all sound by 20 per cent. (You cannot add notes to the bottom of the chord because they would close the ventilation of the open voicing sound.)

Which note do you add to your right hand? That depends on what sounds good to you. It could be almost anything, and not only a 6th, Major 7th or 9th. Or it could be nothing added at all. It's sort of like trying everything including the kitchen sink just to hear what it sounds like. But despite the allure of added higher tension, don't work this side of the street all the time. If you add tension at every moment, your playing will surely become expected and, finally, boring. Too many sinks spoil the kitchen.

Besides, no law says that you have to change the outer shape in your left hand. Root-&-5th may be perfectly acceptable for several bars in a row. Nor do you have to add a third note to your right hand and try to increase the tension, even for a half-measure. Nor, in fact, do you have to strike more than one attack per bar with your left hand, even in 4/4 time.

Those matters have been mentioned here only as a kind of first aid supply kit —a What To Do In-the-event-of. As it turns out, the odds are that you will come back to this chapter again and again and ask it what to do in the event of boredom and the need for change. That is the curious thing about people who *make* music. No matter how rudimentary, primitive and halting the music they make, their mind's ear changes, develops, grows. And by and by what used to sound insupportably glorious (and an amazing feat of two-hand coordination) starts to sound very old hat.

That is the real hazard of playing by ear —of *making* music and *listening* to what you play. Sooner or later you start to yearn for a more interesting sound, and you begin to work at ways to produce it. On the other hand, if you're very careful not to listen to what you play, you will probably never have this ailment.

OKAY, THEN, IN A NUTSHELL: Basically, open voicing is the 10th chord spread out between both hands. Your left plays root-&-5th with pinky and thumb. Your right plays 3rd and melody note (with thumb and pinky if you can reach those notes; otherwise your left hand plays the full 10th chord). In any case, you play the melody note where printed, and move the open position three-note chord up the keyboard to support the melody note.

Essentially, open voicing is an arrangement of four notes (sometimes five if you try an extra note in your right hand). That is the best arrangement for fooling around with at the keyboard because each note in it makes so great a difference in the over-all sound. Further, it is a very relaxed, cool style of playing. Your left hand has to produce only one attack per bar in 3/4 time and no more than two per bar in 4/4 time.

If there is no chord change and you want to vary the sound of the bottom of the chord, you can follow the root-&-5th with the 5th-&-3rd, or root-&-6th, root-&-9th, etc. It all depends on which chord is called for and how it sounds to you.

Similarly, you can raise the tension of a trite sound by adding a third note to those in your right hand —preferably a non-chordal. (Now and then you can add two notes there to increase the tension still more. But that can get to sound very crowded and destroy the open-voiced effect.)

Which notes you add depends again on what sounds good to you. But don't try to distort every sound. Tension is comparative. The plain, primary, resolved chordal sound is necessary, too, because distortion can become trite.

Use the open voicing arrangement on numbers where the over-all sound has a chance to sink in —slower melodies, those with long, sparse bars, those whose melodies do not climb and fall all over the staff but move within a narrow up-and-down pattern. The melody should be sophisticated, too, with a good amount of non-chordals in its personality. *Home On The Range* is slow enough and sparse enough. But it isn't sophisticated enough for this cool, high tension arrangement.

How to play the piano despite years of lessons

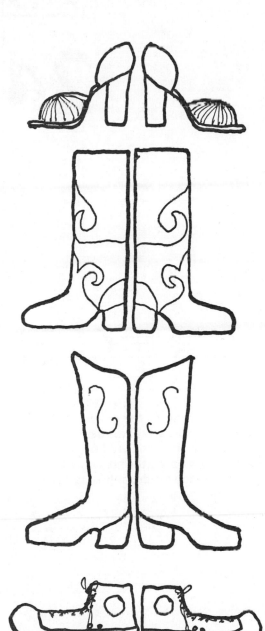

THE MYTH: What with all those stems, dots, flags and notes, music is a very hard language to read.

THE FACT: Yes, if you want to touch-type it perfectly. But if you only want to know what it's saying —why, it's telling you how and when to break up the silence.

Part eight

Camouflaging the skeleton (concluded): Special arrangements and settings. The bolero, including the rhumba and the beguine. Calypso and how to spot it. The tango, with some mysteries of 2/4 time explained. And two kinds of cocktail piano —full-block style and locked-hands (or Early Shearing). Also shuffle rhythm for cowpoke and slowpoke numbers.

Special cases—bolero (including rhumba)

24

DINNER, THE SIGN SAID. *And Dancing.* Remember those days? The dinner was always the same —flaming breast of sword and baked Alaska. But the dance music . . . .

There was a twelve-piece band for the fox trots and waltzes —three instruments in the rhythm section (bass, drums, piano), and the remaining nine (usually brasses and woodwinds) working the harmony and melody stratums. And when the set finished, they were replaced by the Latin band for the rhumbas and such.

Actually, "replaced" is a little too strong a word. Transformed is more like it. What really happened was that three instruments disappeared —a trumpet, a trombone and a saxophone. And as if by magic, those three instrumentalists became members of the rhythm section. One with a pair of maracas. Another banging a tambourine. The third with claves and jawbone . . . . In any event, the upshot of it was that the rhythm section had suddenly *doubled in size.* What had been only one-third of the orchestra a moment ago was now a *half.*

Well, you can see where that puts the emphasis in Latin arrangements: on the beat, on the steady clockwork, on the time-keeping member of the underlying skeleton. And that, for the piano, means another member of the skeleton has to yield some of its equality. So, the chords in their stratum are dismissed from the arrangement, and the harmony is turned over to the blocks beneath the melody notes.

In essence, then, the bolero arrangement (also very suitable for beguines and rhumbas) camouflages the skeleton by emphasizing one member and minimizing another. It is really a three-stratum device —the single-note melody; the uninterrupted, unwavering and immediately recognizable beat of the bass notes; and the two or three block notes below the melody which take over the job of the chords completely, not only producing the harmony but also working in combination with the bass notes to produce the distinctive bolero beat.

Now, to take a closer look at these three stratums at work so that you can add the bolero arrangement to your repertoire.

1.

The melody is played where written, rather than an octave above as the skeleton arrangement requires. After all, there are no chords-in-stratum —in fact, no full chords at all— in this bolero device. So, the melody can be moved down to use that

**The heart of the bolero beat:
Bass-rest-bass-bass
on the numbered beats.
As usual, the bass notes
are lowest possible octaves.**

area of sound. (The block notes are played just below the melody notes, naturally.)

2.

The bass notes are the crucial attacks in this arrangement. They make the bolero what it is. And what is it? Why, it is simply an arrangement in 4/4 time in which the bass notes, played as octaves of course, are heard on the numbered beats of *One, Three and Four,* but not on *Two.* That is, you count as you always do for 4/4 time. On the main, numbered beats you count: One, Two, Three Four. But the attacks you play on those numbers are *bass, rest, bass, bass.*

The notes you hit on those bass attacks are, as usual, the root of the chord called for. But as there are only three stratums at work, your basses don't have to be played in the lowest register on the keyboard. You can move them up so that they are in closer support of the block notes.

As usual, too, you can vary the basses by playing the 5th in place of the root —if there is room to do so before the chord changes. But that variation is nowhere near as important as *keeping that steady bass, rest, bass, bass* beat going throughout the number. (This beat, like all Latin rhythms, is so strong that you cannot arrange only a few bars with it, or even a part. Once you start it, you cannot stop it until the number is finished.)

Try a couple of bars on your piano —just the single melody notes with your right hand (where printed) and the bass note octaves somewhere beneath.

Essence of the bolero: melody played where written without blocks, and steady bass-rest-bass-bass below it. Try it on your own piano.

FANNY

You will probably have to count good and loud until you get a feel for the bolero beat. But that shouldn't take you too long because this rhythm is just about as standard in our music as waltz time. In fact, numbers which once were crooned sweet and low —*Blue Moon,* for instance— are very likely to show up nowadays in a bolero setting. Try it in your own mind and hear how it sounds.

Block notes serve as chords, attacking on after-beats (the "ands" after numbered beats).

3.

The two or three block notes beneath the melody are a sort of replacement for the skeleton's full chords in the chord stratum. The block notes play the harmony, true. But much more important in an arrangement where the rhythm is half of the enterprise, the blocks work in combination with the bass notes to reinforce the bolero beat.

That is accomplished simply by playing the blocks in between the bass notes — or, rather, between the numbered beats. Or, to make the matter relentlessly clear, in bolero rhythm, you play the blocks *on the un-numbered, unaccented, after-beats.* And it is this business of putting an unmistakable attack on the unexpected, unaccented after-beat which gives the bolero beat most of its protective camouflage coloration.

In the skeleton, as survivors will recall, the bass-&-chord combinations attack only on the numbered, accented beats of the measure. But in the bolero rhythm, the bass notes alone strike on the expected, numbered beats. (But only on three of them so as to surprise the listening ear with silence where there should be an attack. So, the bass notes attack this way: "One, Rest, Three, Four.")

The block notes attack on the commas between—on the unexpected, unaccented after-beats. That stress on the unaccented after-beat goes by the name of *syncopation,* and it is one of most widely used camouflage devices in the whole bag.

All right, then, you can see how the arithmetic works. Your left hand playing bass notes has to attack (or rest) on the four numbered beats. Meanwhile, your right hand playing blocks has to attack on the four after-beats. All of that adds up to eight places necessary per bar. And to make those places available, you have to count, "One AND Two AND Three AND Four AND." Otherwise you won't have the even, steady beat necessary to play *Left Right Rest Right Left Right Left Right.* Take a look at it, and try it out. Slowly to begin with.

The full 4/4 bolero with main beat basses-&-rest and after-beat blocks.

Now, it is a mistake to think that this typically Latin beat was devised in some candle-lit taco stand on a slow Tuesday night by a poor but dishonest bandido (played by Leo Carrilo) and then appropriated for Tin Pan Alley by Cole Porter (played by Cary Grant) during a summer vacation from Yale (played by Harvard and beaten soundly). Quite the contrary. The bolero rhythm with its unmistakable accented after-beats has credentials of the most legitimate sort, having been given to the world in holy matrimony by real classical composers.

You can hear such accented after-beats —and you should listen to it to make your playing of it much, much easier —in Tchaikowsky's *None But The Lonely Heart;* in Schumann's *Warum;* in bars 29 through 40 of Beethoven's *Piano Sonata* (Opus 101); and in the familiar opening theme of Schubert's Symphony No. 8, *The Unfinished Symphony.*

With all that business of beats and after-beats accounting for half of the arrangement, the remaining half had better be a rather simple melody —a fairly slow-moving line of whole notes and half notes and not too many quarter-notes, and most certainly no triplets or other kinds of syncopation. If there are too many attacks by the melody notes, they will make for chaos when added to the busy rhythm.

Besides, if there are too many melody notes to play, your right hand will become angry with you. But with slow-moving melodies, your right pinky can sustain those long notes while a couple of other fingers hit the block notes on after-beats.

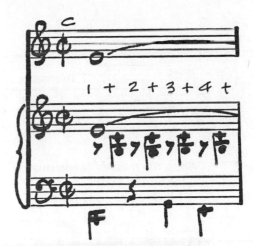

Pinky strikes melody note and holds it while 2 other fingers play the block on the after-beat.

If there are too many melody notes to play comfortably with blocks, don't play blocks. But the bass beats must continue always.

But even slow-moving melodies speed up from place to place, using quarter notes and even eighth notes. In that event, there are several things you can do to make life easier for your right hand and its after-beat work.

1. Forget about the after-beats entirely and play the melody as

When the melody is too busy
for blocks on after-beats,
block all melody notes.

plain octave-duplicated notes only.

But keep the bass beat going. That's what makes it a bolero, and it can't stop or you'll lose the arrangement. Once the melody slows down again, you can put your right hand back to work with its after-beat attacks.

2. When the melody becomes a succession of eighth notes, block the second of each two notes or block them all.

The second of each pair is the after-beat —the beat which gets the right-hand block attack in bolero arranging. The first of each pair of eighth notes is the main beat, as you recall. You can play each first eighth note as a single note without a block because your left hand is at work on those beats.

3. When the melody becomes a succession of quarter notes, each will probably fall on a numbered beat.

In that case, your right hand has two jobs to do for each quarter note. First, your right pinky strikes the melody note as a single note —and holds it while a couple of other fingers play the block on the after-beat.

4. When the composer's melody becomes too complicated for bolero —measures filled with dotted quarter notes followed by eighth notes, or triplets, and so on— you have a couple of options.

One: you can turn the page and look for another number to play in a bolero setting. Or, two: you can help the composer by re-timing his melody notes so that they will fit the bolero. Your goal is to make those melody notes fall on the main beats and after-beats —and not on after-after-beats. To do that, you may be making some of his notes longer and some shorter in duration. But nobody will notice what you've done for a measure or two out of thirty two measures. It is the bolero rhythm which rivets the attention, not the melody movement.

If that seems to be too complicated to do, then go back to the first advisory. Play the melody in single note octaves without blocks at all through such difficult bars of melody. Let your left hand bass beats carry the bolero by itself until the melody comes to its senses and you can start playing after-beat blocks again.

5. The skeleton calls for the melody to be played at the top of the structure and the block notes just below.

But sometimes the melody falls too low for comfortable sounding block attacks below. Moreover, you may want to further camouflage the skeleton's expected sound. If so, you can reorganize your right hand's work, and perhaps make the work somewhat easier to do.

You can play the blocks above the melody. In that event, your right thumb plays the melody notes (one octave below printing) and three fingers play the block attacks above your thumb. Or you can put the harmony inside the melody. You can play the melody as an octave, with your right pinky playing the notes where printed and your thumb duplicating those notes an octave below. And in between pinky and thumb, you play a few chordal notes for the block attacks.

But no matter where you play the blocks —below, above or within the melody— they are still the after-beat attacks. And so you play them only on the *ands* after the numbered beats.

6. As reported, the bolero arrangement will serve nicely for numbers marked "Beguine" and "Rhumba." But very strictly speaking, the bolero and the rhumba divide the attacks differently in both right and left hands.

This is not to suggest that one is easier or more preferable than the other. It is only to say that there are a number of variations of this kind of syncopation around, and if you find yourself playing a somewhat different arrangement of main beats and after-beats, it may be because you *feel the Latin tempo* somewhat differently. If so, it will be a lot easier to play your way. Just keep your syncopated arrangement even and steady throughout the number.

To look at one variation, just for reassurance—

Where the bolero breaks the four numbered beats into four pairs of beats and after-beats, the rhumba (or, rather, one kind of rhumba) gets the same total of eight attacks in a different combination: a set of threes, followed by another set of threes, followed by a pair. (Strictly speaking, this is not a bolero variation. The bolero had it origins in Europe; the rhumbas came from Africa. But human hearts —the basis of rhythmic beat— beat the same way everywhere.)

Composer's melody

Your version

A bar of melody too complex for bolero treatment. Re-time notes to fall on main beats and after-beats.

Bolero beat vs. rhumba. The bolero breaks up the 8 beats into 4 pairs. The rhumba breaks them into two sets of 3 and a pair.

Well, with that kind of subdivision of the main, accented, numbered beats, this one variety of rhumba further camouflages the skeleton with syncopation. The principle of it is simply this: Play the bass note on the first of each group *whether or not it is a numbered, accented beat*. And with that pattern, you can see how the expected attacks are varied. The bass, traditionally used only on numbered beats, is silent on

The calypso beat is spread
across 2 measures:
a bar of plain skeleton
yoked with a rhumba bar of
beats and after-beats.

A few numbers to try
with a bolero setting.

Amor
Perfidia
Green Eyes
Misirlou
Amapola
Autumn Leaves
Orchids In The Moonlight
Strangers In The Night
The Shadow Of Your Smile
I Could Have Danced All Night
If Ever I Would Leave You
What Is This Thing Called Love
Night And Day
Begin The Beguine
In The Still Of The Night
Why Was I Born?
Blue Moon
All The Things You Are
That Old Black Magic
Speak Low
Love Walked In
Yesterdays

two of them and moreover is heard on one unaccented after-beat. And the block notes, usually used only for after-beats, are heard on two numbered, main beats. That's a lot of camouflage because it's a lot of the unexpected.

If you come across a Latin type of rhythm which seems to present a mystery or a problem —calypso, say— take a look at a piece of sheet music for the answer. The attack pattern in the bottom, piano parts will often tell you how to arrange your own playing. In the case of calypso, the complete beat is spread across two bars. The first is plain, straight skeleton. The second is a straight rhumba system of beats and after-beats with right hand blocks.

It could be reversed, of course, with the rhumba bar stated first and the skeleton second. But either way, it has to continue in the starting order to keep the pattern coming along as expected in two-bar shipments.

If you want to take a look at some calypso music, see *Jamaica Farewell, Yellow Bird, Rum and Coca Cola,* and *Marianne.* It's very reassuring to do so. It lets you know that you don't have to know how to read every note in order to know what's going on.

IN A NUTSHELL, THEN: The bolero arrangement (usable for beguines and rhumbas as well) is a variation of bass-&-chord combination in 4/4 time.

There are no full chords or chord stratum used in this camouflage technique. Usually, the melody is played where printed and the blocks are played below it. And in the stratum or two below the blocked melody, the bass notes are heard (played as octaves as usual).

The bass notes attack on the numbered, accented, main beats — but only on beats No. 1, 3 and 4. (Beat No. 2 is silent. It is counted, but as a quarter rest.)

The melody blocks are used in place of chords. They play the harmony called for in the chord symbols. And they attack only on the after-beats —on all four *ands* after all the numbered beats. So, keep your blocks simple. And count good and loud: *One AND Rest AND Three AND Four AND,* until you get a feel for the beat.

If the melody is too fast or intricate for blocks to be played, leave them out until the melody slows down. Play only the melody notes (as octaves if possible) until you can play the after-beat blocks again. But under no circumstances can you neglect the three bass note attacks per bar. They keep the bolero arrangement together.

The bolero rhythm is a form of syncopation because it puts emphasis on the normally unstressed (usually silent) after-beat. Because this syncopated beat is so strong and

so large a part of the arrangement, the bolero (or rhumba, beguine or calypso) must be used throughout a number and not just for a part or combined with any other device.

Special cases—tango rhythm

IN SOME WAYS, the tango is similar to the bolero. Both are in the Spanish temper. Both are all-or-nothing arrangements and must be used throughout a number rather than as a setting for a half-part or even a whole part. Both are most effective used with slow, sparse, simple melodies. And both the tango and the bolero are devices to camouflage the skeleton in 4/4 time —both are syncopated arrangements, emphasizing the unexpected, unaccented after-beat.

But there the similarity ends, and the tango goes on with its own personality —which is quite a bit like the full skeleton, viz:

1. Your right hand plays a straight, blocked melody one octave higher than printed.

2. Your left hand is in complete charge of the tango beat, and produces it with a combination of bass-&-chord —or, to be precise, a combination of bass-&-broken chord.

Your left hand plays that combination in four attacks. First, the bass note as an octave (but not necessarily the lowest); or as a single note (in which case the lowest). Then the chord, more or less in stratum —5th note, then root-&-3rd together, and finally the 5th again. (Those three attacks of the broken chord can be made by rocking your hand from pinky to thumb-&-index finger together and back to pinky.)

Tango's 4 attacks per bar:
(1) a medium-low bass octave;
(2) the 5th note of the chord;
(3) root-&-3rd together;
(4) and the 5th note again.

The only complication (if that is the word for it) is that you play the second attack on an after-beat. And you can only locate that solitary after-beat by dividing the whole measure into main beats and after-beats. That is, you have to count out eight places per measure —even though you need only four for

The 2nd attack falls between numbered beats. So, count 8 places to provide the one necessary "and."

Similarly with 2/4 tango: the 2nd attack lies between numbered beats. But you need only 6 places to make room for that syncopated attack.

your four attacks.

Well, it cannot be helped. You need that one, lonely *and.* So you have to count *One and Two* AND *Three and Four and.* But it does the trick. Your attacks fall into place.

Oh yes, one other minor matter about that broken chord business. Inasmuch as the order of attacks is from the 5th up to the root-&-3rd (and then back to the 5th again), the chord has to have the notes in that order. But that's no problem. At least half of the chords you play in stratum now are in that line-up, with the 5th on the bottom and the root and 3rd on top.

NOW AND THEN YOU WILL COME ACROSS a tango in 2/4 time, particularly if the number was published first in Latin America or Europe. Consequently, you have to get all four attacks of the tango rhythm into this seemingly smaller measure.

But fear not: 2/4 time is a trick of the eye only. You don't have to speed up your mind's clock and your hands to squeeze the four attacks into a two-beat measure. What you do, simply, is to divide the two beats into a measure of *two main beats and two after-beats* —One and Two and. That gives the measure a total of four places —which is what you have when you count only the main beats of a 4/4 measure. In other words, a measure of 2/4 time is played at the same speed as a measure of 4/4 time.

That takes care of the whole problem except for what to do with that second attack —the one which does not fall on a main, numbered beat in 4/4 time and does not fall on *and* in 2/4 time.

Well, you do for the 2/4 measure what you did for the 4/4 measure: you create an after-beat space for that unaccented attack, that 5th note of the chord. (Actually, it is a misnomer to call it an after-beat in 2/4 time because those *ands* are the after-beats. In this instance, you would have to call the unaccented, unexpected attack an "after-after-beat.")

What you count, then, is *One and-a Two and-a.* That little "a" is the after-after-beat, and on the first one you play your syncopated attack. On the second "a," of course, you do nothing. But don't think of it as a total loss. If you master this way of counting by "one and-a two and-a," and then get yourself a plaid dinner jacket, you can become a band leader if 1928 ever returns.

In any event, it works out to be the same tango played at the same speed whether you are playing it in 4/4 time and counting *One and Two* AND *Three and Four and,* or in 2/4 time and counting *One and-a Two and-a.* The advantage of 2/4 time is that you have less to say as you count, which is a great saving of breath and thought.

If all of that is agreed to, then try a little bit of tango on the piano. As you will see, there are two samples to go at —one in 4/4 time and one in 2/4. But that is only reasonable because, as everybody knows, it takes two to tango.

O SOLE MIO (DI CAPUA)

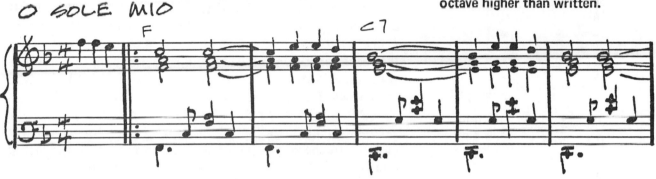

O SOLE MIO

A 4/4 and a 2/4 tango. Both run at the same speed, but the count is different. Play blocked melody an octave higher than written.

AND THAT'S IT IN A NUTSHELL: The tango, like the bolero, is a distinctive Latin rhythm and therefore is used as an unvaried setting throughout an entire number.

The tango is laid out in stratums similar to the skeleton's. Your right hand plays a blocked melody an octave above printing. Your left hand produces the tango beat with a bass-&-broken-chord in four attacks per measure. (The bass note doesn't have to be the lowest possible octave, but if you play it as a single note, it should be the lowest.) From the bass note your hand jumps to approximately chord stratum for the broken chord—

a) the 5th note of the chord, the syncopated attack
b) the root-and-3rd played together
c) the 5th again.

Those three attacks in the chord can be played without lifting your hand but only rocking it.

In 4/4 time, the syncopated attack falls on an after-beat. In 2/4, on an after-after-beat.

A few melodies to try with the tango setting:

Adios Muchachos
Blue Tango
El Choclo
La Paloma
Hernando's Hideaway
Jalousie
Kiss Of Fire
The Magic Tango
Orchids In The Moonlight
The Rain In Spain
Tango du Reve
Tango Of Roses
O Sole Mio
Softly, As In A Morning Sunrise

The best melodies for a tango setting are slow, sparse, straight forward and un-syncopated. Should the melody become fast and/or complicated, you can drop the tango arrangement for those few bars. But you have to return as soon as possible.

Special cases —shuffle rhythm

26

IF YOU DOUBLE THE ELEMENTS of the tango in each bar —if you play two sets of that bass-&-broken-chord combination —you have the attacks of shuffle rhythm. But as you can see, you have to vary the timing a bit because a bar of doubled tango isn't really the same beat as shuffle rhythm.

You can hear this arrangement in the familiar *On The Trail* portion of Ferde Grofe's *Grand Canyon Suite.* This shuffle is also beloved by arrangers for such cowpoke numbers as *Don't Fence Me In,* and such slowpoke numbers as *Lazy Bones.* And the reason is, this double tango beat per bar played in a relaxed style under a sparse, poke-along melody sounds like the shuffling clip-clop of a horse on the trail —or at least what a musician thinks a horse sounds like clip-clopping easily down a trail.

Consequently, the shuffle rhythm is not an overpowering member of the arrangement. So, you can use it for the setting of one part of a number and use another variation for another part. And being a lazy-sounding arrangement for lazy-sounding melodies, you will have no difficulty in fitting all eight attacks per bar.

Basically, it is the 4/4 skeleton at work in your left hand —*bass*-&-chord-&-*bass*-&-chord. But the chord is broken each time in the tango manner so that you rock from pinky to thumb-&-index finger and back to pinky again. And as for the bass —that is either played as an octave but not necessarily the lowest, or as a single note, in which case it is the lowest. (There isn't time in the eight attacks for lowest possible octave.) And you count it: *One and-a Two and-a Three and-a Four and-a.*

I bar of shuffle rhythm and 1 of tango

For 1 bar of shuffle rhythm, double the tango combination. But count them differently.

There are 8 attacks. But you have to make room for 12 places to provide both the after-beats and the after-after-beats.

Being a relaxed, underwhelming arrangement, it is quite content to work with a variation or two. For instance, you can lower the last attack of each broken chord, and play the 5th note an octave below the chord stratum. That seems to give the shuffle more urban melancholy and less trail dust —the kind of a setting you might want for a blues type of feeling.

It's a relaxed setting and works well with all kinds of tunes and other devices.

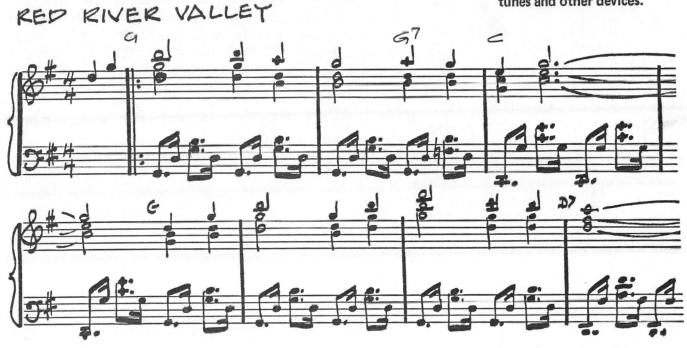

RED RIVER VALLEY

BLUEBERRY HILL

Naturally, you can suspend the shuffle rhythm attacks if and when the melody becomes too busy or complicated—as long as you have established the shuffle first so that your listeners can keep it going in their minds until you state it again.

As for the melody, it is just as you thought —played one octave above printing with block notes attached.

And that, in a nutshell, is that.

Block-style & locked-hands

27

IF THE TERM COCKTAIL PIANO means anything, then it certainly means the two arrangements set out in this chapter. Most of the time, both have the melody played where written. Both have the chords right below in support. Both do without bass note attacks. And all in all, both keep a lot going on in the middle of the keyboard where it can be plainly heard working its magic on the customers and keeping the cash register ringing up a counter-melody.

So, with everything in the middle of the keyboard and no bass notes to consider, these two camouflage devices can be used in arranging a full part (but probably not less) of a number without committing you to the whole thing, the way the bolero arrangement does. Furthermore, with these devices there is no beat expressed outright. The rhythm is implicit in the melody. So you have to keep careful count of the tempo in your mind's ear as you play. Otherwise you find yourself playing Mozart without ever knowing it.

THE FULL BLOCK TREATMENT, quite simply, puts the melody on top of a very full . . . well, block. In other words, your right pinky plays the melody. And that leaves you with nine idle fingers which you use to string out a block of nine chordal notes down the keyboard. Naturally, people with more than ten fingers can build a longer string of block notes below the melody.

With so full a block, the melody is in jeopardy of becoming swamped by the supporting chordal notes. So it's a good idea to duplicate the melody —to play the melody as an octave with your right hand and fill in that octave with three chordals. Then, your left hand can add its five-note block immediately below.

All of that may be a bit of an overstatement. For one thing, you may not be able to find three chordal notes to fill in the octave-duplicated melody sandwich in your right hand. (In that case, play only two if you can play only two, and play a non-chordal for the third.) For another thing, your left hand may have more fingers than available chordal notes. (If so, then play a non-chordal note or two. Almost any combination of tones can be put together—depending on what sounds good to you. The important thing is that *at least four fingers of your left hand must be producing tones.*)

In comparison with the ventilated, open voicing arrangement, this full block setting is stacked to the rafters with closely

The full block treatment puts the single melody notes on top of as many chordals as you can fit beneath it.

packed tones and their overtones. Consequently, the lower registers are not the best place for full block playing because the sound becomes muddy. In other words, don't use it to arrange Part A of *Where Or When*. But it will work pretty well for the release —Part B— where the melody moves up to a higher register. Similarly, the first half of *I Love Paris* is too low for full blocks. They will growl down there. But the last half of the number is in a much higher register, and there you can use this setting for an overwhelming finale.

Because full block playing is so full, ponderous and stately, it works best with slow and simple numbers. So stay away from busy, intricate and syncopated melodies. Moreover, the ponderous, sonorous, jam-packed treatment is far too overwhelming a setting for an entire number. In fact, it works best when it is used with a *contrasting* arrangement. *Part A* in full block treatment can often be followed by a part played as a single-note melody over a basic skeleton or open voicing setting.

If you want to hear full blocks in classical music, listen to Rachmaninoff's *Prelude in C♯ Minor*, parts *A 1* and *A 2.*

THE LOCKED HAND STYLE REDUCED to its essentials —and that's all it is, essentials —is simply this. The melody played as an octave. A couple of chordal notes inside the sandwich. And a little *grace note* tacked on at the very bottom —played just below and just before the melody notes.

If you count that little grace note an interval below the bottom, duplicated melody note, there are five tones in this entire arrangement. And they are spread out between both hands. To wit:

Your right hand plays the melody (where written) with a couple of block notes below it.

Your left thumb duplicates the melody at the bottom of the block. And your left index finger hits a note an interval below that duplicated melody note —and hits it an instant before the melody note is heard.

That grace note, that slurred note heard prematurely at the bottom of the arrangement discolors the lower melody note just enough to give it an interesting hue. That interesting hue, that locked hands setting, has been around since the 1930s —in supper clubs, in cocktail lounges and on records. And it still persists, doubtless on account of its combination of simplicity and color.

Oh sure, you could play most of this arrangement one-handed —with your right hand playing the melody as an octave sandwiching a pair of chordals and your left index finger hitting that grace note at the bottom a split second too soon for the melody. But that is the hard way.

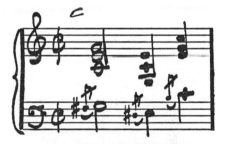

Locked hands style:
Play an octave melody with
a couple of chordals inside,
and strike a grace note
just below and just before
the bottom melody note.

Locked hands is much easier. It leaves your right hand with its traditional, skeleton work of playing a blocked melody. And it puts your left thumb and index finger to work together as the natural partners they are. That way, your left thumb can guide your right hand to the attack an instant before the grace note has sounded fully. Consequently the name: locked hands —with both hands close together along the base of the thumbs.

Now, there is no way of measuring a split second in grace note playing. There are long split seconds and short split seconds. It depends on the kind of hue you want to give to the discoloration of the melody note an interval above it. So, you'll have to try it on your piano and listen to the possible effects of longer or shorter grace notes. The only requirement is that the grace note come along *before* the melody, and that the melody arrive *on schedule*. The split second for the grace note must be stolen from the time of the melody note just before it.

Try it —first with your left hand alone, with your left thumb playing the melody (an octave lower than written) and your left index finger ruining the purity of sound with a note one interval below played a twinkling before.

The grace note is an interval below the bottom melody note. Played a split second before, it discolors the melody note.

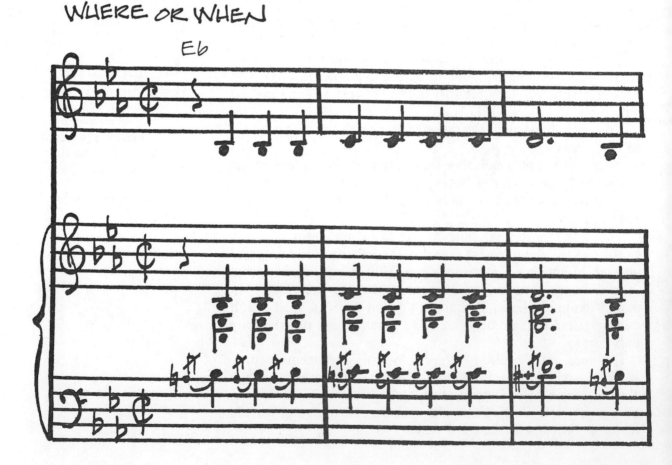

WHERE OR WHEN

Whether you choose to adorn *every* melody note in the number with a grace note, that is up to you. Here and there a part of a bar may sound better unblurred. Here and there you may want to play only an octave melody without either grace note or block notes. The fact is, if it sounds good ...

THE NUTSHELL: Full block treatment and locked hand style have all the earmarks of cocktail piano playing, whatever that means. Most of the time, both arrangements put the melody where printed. Both work best with slow, simple numbers. Neither uses bass notes nor any other rhythmic beat. Both use only blocked melodies.

1. Full block treatment is a blocked octave melody supported by another block. All ten fingers are at work —well, eight anyway. That makes for a tall tower of closely packed tones and overtones (most of them chordal, but some nonchordal if you have to use them). So reserve this treatment for melody parts in a higher register where the tones won't be muddy. Contrast makes this arrangement most effective. Follow it with a one-finger-alone treatment, say, or a cool open voice setting.

2. Locked hand style is also an octave-duplicated treatment of the melody (with a couple of chordal block notes within). But it is supported by a grace note only, an interval below the bottom melody note, and played a moment too soon. But the few notes in the over-all setting are spread out over both hands. Your right hand plays a blocked melody note at the bottom of the block, and your left index finger plays the grace note an interval below that lower melody note. (Sometimes you may have to use your thumb for the grace note and your index finger for the melody note.)

Strike the grace note to suite your ear. But the melody note must come along in its proper time. Remember: block the melody.

HAUNTED HEART

Eb

How to play the piano despite years of lessons

THE MYTH: Harmony is very mathematical and mysterious, and consequently very hard to understand.

THE FACT: Harmony is hard to understand only for those people who can't tell time from a clock.

Part nine

How harmony moves (how chords change). **The chords make the melody move. The chords move on a circle. Elementary Classical chord progressions on the circle (a little Bach, a little Schubert, most folk songs). Classical chord progressions (more Bach, some Beethoven, most popular music). Romantic progressions (a bit of Chopin, a bit of Richard Rodgers). Impressionist and Modern progressions mentioned. An alternative to the circle — chords move on a line. Chromatic and tonal progressions.**

How melody moves

28

AS FAITHFUL READERS WILL RECALL, this enterprise began twenty-some chapters ago by defining a melody as a bunch of oncoming single tones which your mind's ear sorts out and pulls together into three patterns. In other words, your mind is a musical instrument which makes melodies by organizing tones in three ways:

1. A high-and-low pattern of tones (written as notes up and down the staff, and sometimes below it and above it).

2. A wide-and-narrow pattern of those same tones, a pattern sorted out by your mind's ear according to how long or short a time each note lasts as measured by a steadily ticking clockwork.

3. And, of course, a pattern of those same high-and-low and long-and-short tones sorted out according to whether they are comfortable chordal tones or restless non-chordal tones —that is, whether they fit into the chord called for, or do not fit it.

And then, having mentioned those three patterns, this book turned around and went on chapter after chapter talking about the third pattern only —that chord setting which bestows chordal and non-chordal identity on the oncoming tones, making it possible to sort them out into a pattern of notes-of-the-chord and notes-not-of-the-chord. For twenty six chapters, in fact, this book has beleaguered and harassed that chord setting, closing it, opening it, turning it upside down, breaking it into pieces, adding to it, duplicating it, syncopating it, ventilating it —and in general behaving as though the chords made the most important pattern of all and did the most to make a melody out of the chaos of oncoming tones.

Well, if that is the message which has come through, it is a bit of an overstatement. But better that than the widespread notion that harmony is very difficult to make and even more difficult to understand —or the equally popular belief that the chords are somehow different from the *real* harmony and consequently are superfluous and unnecessary in making basic, *real* music.

Clearly, harmony is not difficult to make —as this book has gone on and on for twenty six chapters to demonstrate. Once you have the formula for the basic three-note chord, it requires very little more to alter it, to add a fourth note to it, and to force the whole enterprise into total submission.

And as for the chords being different from the harmony and somehow superfluous to real music —well, it is true that you can produce a perfect single-note melody expressing only the high-and-low and the long-and-short patterns of the oncoming tones. But that doesn't mean you are dispensing with the chord setting for those tones. Quite the contrary. The chords are there at work anyway, and so are the chord changes, whether or not

Even the simplest tunes are usually made of both notes-of-the-chord and notes-not-of-the-chord (x).

you state them out loud with your orchestra or orchestral keyboard. As it turns out, the chords and the chord changes —the harmony— will determine to a considerable extent just what the other two patterns are.

Take the long-and-short pattern of durations —the length of time each oncoming tone lasts. Obviously the longest notes, those where the melody rests and relaxes, will almost always be *chordal notes,* comfortable, resolved, settled notes-of-the-chord. Similarly, non-chordal notes will tend to be shorter in the general scheme, being uneasy, unresolved, restless tones which are *longing to come home* to a chordal note. So, whether you state the chords outright or not, they have an effect not only on the duration of oncoming tones but also on the *forward motion of the melody* as it moves toward relaxation and resolution or away from it.

The effect of the chords and chord changes on the high-and-low pattern is even more obvious, as a quick look at 400 years worth of melody development reveals.

To begin with, it is doubtful that our melodies were ever entirely chordal. Yes, such all-chordal melodies occur in bugle calls, Wagnerian leitmotifs and fanfares reserved for brass instruments. But these are not usual, although a glance at them shows an important fact about the ups and downs of chordal notes, namely that *they can jump to and from each other over any distance.*

SWORD MOTIF FROM SIEGFRIED (WAGNER)

A few kinds are made wholly of notes-of-the-chord. They reveal that melody can jump from one chordal to another over any distance.

REVEILLE

More commonly, melodies had a few non-chordal notes in the assortment as Western music began to develop about four centuries ago. But these early melodies in music as we know it today usually selected their non-chordals from the basic (diatonic) seven-tone scale. And moreover, those non-chordals were treated in the simplest way possible —*by being sandwiched one at a time between chordals* or moving in tiny one-interval or two-interval steps away from a chordal and back to it.

Restless non-chordal notes were quickly resolved into comfortable chordals. And that earliest development in the high-and-low movement of a melody made of both chordal and non-chordal tones survives today because *we have become used to hearing a melody move that way.*

We hear what we are used to hearing.

1.

Restless non-chordals were selected from the basic 7-tone scale and sandwiched between comfortable chordals. Tension was quickly resolved.

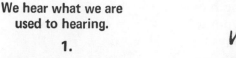

Later in the ups and downs of melody line come the use of non-chordal tones taken from anywhere in the chromatic scale —the complete set of twelve tones— rather than from only the basic seven-tone scale. Doubtless it was a shock to the ear at the time, and consequently such high tension non-chordals were quickly resolved into comfortable chordals. But over the centuries, we have got very used to hearing these *non-chordals taken from outside of the basic scale.* And so they sound completely natural— in fact, completely old hat.

We hear what we are used to hearing.

2.

Later, non-chordals were taken from outside the basic scale. As before, they were quickly resolved into comfortable chordals.

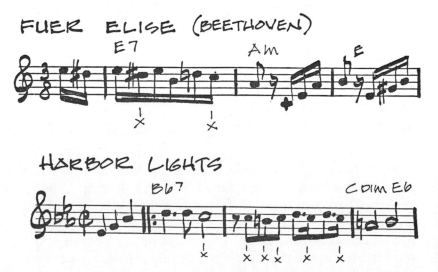

The third (and next-to-last) development saw the non-chordals take more and more time before being resolved into a chordal. Non-chordals began to jump to each other *over a resolving chordal,* and then to jump back and forth between each other for some time, before the comfortable, resolved chordal was sounded. In other words, the listening ear had become able to tolerate and to enjoy much more tension in a melody, *delaying the resolution longer and longer.*

HUMORESQUE (DVORAK)

3.

Next, tension was prolonged.
Restless non-chordals jumped
to each other over a chordal
before being resolved.

SOME ENCHANTED EVENING

The latest development is just what you would expect. *Chordals now jump to non-chordals over a long distance.* But being non-chordals in a strange place, their very next move after the jump is to resolution on the nearest comfortable chordal.

NOCTURNE No.8 (CHOPIN)

4.

Now it's common to
hear tunes jump from
chordal to non-chordal,
then quickly resolve.

I'LL FOLLOW MY SECRET HEART

SEPTEMBER SONG

Under the circumstances, it seems reasonable to expect another development in the high-and-low pattern of oncoming melody tones. And that is: a long string of *non-chordals jumping over any distance to and from each other.* That means a long delay before resolving into a comfortable chordal note of the chord being played beneath the melody. Such a long-leaping and unresolved sequence of non-chordals will create its own chord sound which will clash with the chord called for in the harmony. Will it last and become a sound we call music? Only history can decide. But try a couple of bars of it and ask yourself if it sounds good (which is the test for good music). It may be later in history than you think.

THE FUTURE (CANNEL-MARX)

IN A NUTSHELL, THEN: Even if you play a one-finger, one-stratum, single-note melody, the chords and chord changes are at work. The long-and-short pattern of duration, and the high-and-low pattern of climbing and descending melody line are also movement of chordal and non-chordal notes —notes-of-the-chord and notes-not-of-the-chord. Obviously, you can't have those unless you have a chord to begin with.

A look at history reveals how the use of non-chordals has developed. You can use that information in several ways.

First, by noticing the way non-chordals are used in a melody, you can keep the melody in mind better. Second, by applying the principles of non-chordal usage, you can make more effective counter-melodies of your arpeggio settings. And finally, by looking at a melody as a string of patterned chordal and non-chordal notes, you can see that the chords and chord changes determine to a considerable extent how the melody will move. In other words, *the melody grows out of the harmony.* In still other words, most of our composers have a sequence of chords in mind —and from that sequence their melodies are born, move, rest, leap, resolve and finish.

True, there are thousands and thousands of popular tunes, hymns, folk songs and so on. But, as you will see, there is really only one fundamental way the chords move in almost all of those tunes. And once you see how that simple motion goes —how the chords progress 99.7 per cent of the time —you are 75 per cent of the way to playing by ear.

How chords move—
progressions on the circle

29

AT THE OUTSET OF EVERY PIECE of music, between the clef sign and the time signature, is something called the *key signature*. But why it is called by that name is very hard to understand because the key fits only a box of difficulties.

To be specific, say that there are no sharps or flats up front there in the key signature. Presumably that means the music which follows is in the *key of C*. But what does *that* mean? Well, it certainly doesn't mean that the C chord is the only one called for in the number. It may be used for the first bar or two. But then the chord changes —and changes again and again before the C chord is called for once more.

Under the circumstances, it would be just as reasonable to say that the number begins in the *key of C,* and then it moves to the *key of A,* and then into the *key of D,* and into the *key of G* —and finally it moves back into the *key of C* for a while. And having said that, what have you said about keys and their uses, or about the way chords change and move?

There is another way to look at keys —a much more common way, but not much more reasonable. And that is to explain the situation by saying that the key tells you which basic seven-tone scale gives an identity to each chord called for. For example, if the key of a number is C, then a chord rooted on C is the Number I chord, a chord rooted on D is the Number II chord, an E chord is III and so on, through the basic scale beginning on C.

With that key to chord movement, you could look at a number and say that the chords go from I to VI to II to V to I again. But what exactly does that mean about the general way chords change and harmony moves?

Here's what it says. First, you have to know all of your basic seven-tone scales perfectly. Otherwise you won't know that while C is *I* in the key of C, it is also *VI* in the key of E♭, *III* in the key of A♭, etc. —and *completely non-existent* in the key of

How are the chords moving? From key of C to key of A, etc? Or, even more confusing, as a progression of the Roman numbers assigned to each root starting with C as number I?

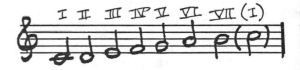

Use the key signatures as pre-set accidentals telling you the notes to sharp and flat in the melody only.

It's a whole lot easier to see the 12 possible root notes of the basic scales (and the chords) laid out on a circle according to their weight of black keys.

B. And the second thing all of that says about the way chords move is that sometimes they move from I to V to I, and sometimes from I to IV to V to I, and sometimes they move from . . .

Clearly, that is not a general principle. It is a very complicated, very mysterious business. And the nice thing is that it's not necessary to an understanding of how chords change —how harmony moves.

CHORDS, OF COURSE, ARE CALLED by their root names. To say, for example, "C chord" is to talk shorthand. It means the chord made of the root, 3rd and 5th of the basic seven-tone scale beginning on C.

Similarly, to say that the chord has changed to an *Am,* for example, and from there to a *D7* and thence to a *G dim* is the same kind of shorthand. It says that the chords called for are to be made from the basic seven-tone scale beginning on A, and then from the basic seven-tone scale beginning on D, and then from that scale beginning on G.

So, each chord in the sequence is a shorthand way of saying that one basic scale after another has been called on to supply its chords. (Obviously, it makes no difference which chord —basic, altered, added-to. The important movement is the *root note.)*

All in all, then, you could say that it is not really the chords which are changing. Rather, you could say that the list of chords called for in a piece of music *bespeaks a pattern, a layout of the basic scales.* In other words, if you want to know how chords move in almost all of our music, you have only to see how the twelve basic scales are laid out in our minds.

And that is childishly easy to see. The twelve basic scales are laid out according to how heavy they are with sharps or flats —how many black keys each scale uses. As you would expect, those scales with fewer sharps or flats are at the top and those with more are . . . well, take a look at it in real life.

The basic scale begining on C has no sharps or flats in it —no black keys. So it sits at the top of the layout of basic scales. However, the scale beginning on F has one flat in it, and the scale beginning on G has one sharp. (It isn't necessary to memorize any of this. It's only necessary to see how the layout of basic scales develops and why.)

The basic scale beginning on B♭ has two flats in it, and the basic scale beginning on D has two sharps. So they come along next, being heavier with black notes. The basic scale beginning on E♭ has three flats in it, and similarly, the basic scale beginning on A has three sharps in it. So, weight puts the E♭ and A scales next.

And so it goes for the rest of the basic scales. The basic scale beginning on A♭ has four flats in it; the scale beginning on E has four sharps. The basic scale beginning on D♭ has five flats; beginning on B, the scale has five sharps. And as for the scale with six flatted notes, that one begins on the root note of F# —or on G♭, which is the same spot on the keyboard.

And with that circle, you have a crystal clear picture of how the basic scales are laid out most of the time in the Western world. That is to say, it is along that circular path from root note to root note that our chords progress in just about every popular number, hymn, folk song and, in fact, in almost all of the music we think of as classical as well.

THERE ARE MANY ADVANTAGES in having a circular key to unlock the secret of how harmony· moves —the seemingly mysterious ways in which chords progress through a piece of music.

For one thing, there is no beginning or end to a circle. Consequently, there is always a relationship of one basic scale to the next. No matter how you turn the circle, there is no starting point or finishing place. So, you don't really need the notion of "key" for chords to move along the Roman road of I, II, III, etc. *You need only a home base* to depart from and come back to in the harmonic movement. And no matter which stop on the circle you call home, and no matter how far you go from it, there is always a crystal clear path back to your home base laid out before your very eyes.

There is another advantage to this layout: You can always remember it and recreate it for yourself. Down the right side of the circle the basic scales are set out in order of increasing number of flats. Down the left side, the scales are named according to their increasing weight of sharps. But that is almost beside the point. Once you begin to work with this circle —once you begin to see how the seemingly complicated harmonic movement of great music and trivial music follows the circle —you will find that you cannot forget how it is laid out. (That explanation begins in the next chapter, and ends very soon thereafter. Once you see how it works, there's nothing else to say.)

There is one more advantage in this layout of the root notes of basic scales rather than the use of "keys" to understand how harmony moves and chords progress. When you explain this matter by means of keys, a C chord can be I, VI, III . . . or non-existent —depending on the key in which the piece of music is written. But when you use the circular arrangement of basic scales (and, of course, of their chords), there is no such difficulty. When you see a C chord called for, you know exactly where it is: It is at the top of the circle, at 12 o'clock high. And that is also where you will find the Cm, C dim, C Aug, C Maj7, C7,

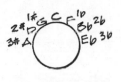

The circle at the half-way point...

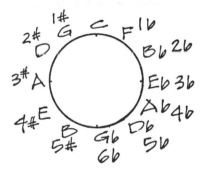

...and complete. On this path, most chord progressions move.

**Paint it, crochet it,
do it up in chocolate icing
—do anything to remember it.**

**Begin by remembering
these hours on the
harmony clock:
Noon, 3 o'clock:
6 o'clock and 9.**

C6, C9 and so on through any possible chord built on the root of C (or, rather, taken from a C scale).

IN OTHER WORDS, *with a circle of root notes,* you always know what time it is in most harmonic movements. That is because the circle of keys has all the attributes of a clock face.

It has only twelve stops, as a clock has only twelve hours. And while each stop on the circle can be called by two names —E♭ can be called D♯, for instance —that is also true of the hours on a clock: 3 o'clock in the afternoon can be called 1500 hours.

Like a clock, too, the circle of root notes can make any one of its twelve stops the appointed hour —a home base pulling time and motion toward it, the way an 8 p.m. dinner party pulls all of your effort toward it throughout the afternoon before it.

Like a clock, the circle also provides for both clockwise and counter-clockwise movement —progression away from the home base and movement back toward home base by way of the intervening stops. And like a clock, the circle is in fact a timing device. The movement of the chords from one root note to the next along the circle pulls the music forward in time. And that is why harmony —the movement from chord to chord —is frequently referred to as *a progression.*

Most of the chord progressions in this part of the planet can be traced clearly and easily on the circle. As you will see in the next couple of chapters, there is a home base on the circle (the key signature of the music), and thereafter the chords move a little way from the home base and progress back toward it in a regular fashion.

Most of the chord progressions in this part of the planet follow one of three paths on the circle —the Elementary Classical path of folk songs; the Classical path of almost all popular numbers; and the Romantic chord progression path found in a few of our standards.

There are two other routes for harmonic movement as we know it nowadays on the circle. One is the Impressionist progression of chords, the other the Modern progression. But they are used very seldom —and then only in serious music, never in popular songs of any kind. Nevertheless, both Impressionist and Modern progressions on the circle will be given a nod, a glance, and a word of explanation on the principle that a little learning is better than none at all.

All in all, then, it is a good idea to look long and hard at the circle of root notes —the circle of basic scales and their chords —because that is the route almost all of our harmonic movement takes. So, memorize the circle. Put it on your piano. Execute it in needlepoint for your piano bench. Do it up in chocolate for dessert. But get it fixed in your mind.

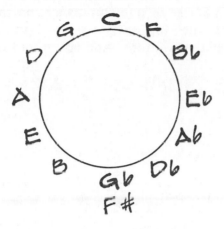

SO, IN A NUTSHELL:

Just remember that the key signatures with flats are on the right side of the circle, and the key signatures with sharps are on the left. That's very important if you want to be able to tell what time it is in the harmony.

Progressions on the circle— elementary classical harmony

30

IN THE PATTERN OF ELEMENTARY CLASSICAL harmony, the chords never move farther on the circle than *one stop away from the home base* before coming home again.

In a piece of music in the "key" of C (no flats or sharps in the key signature), the home base is at 12 o'clock. And the chords throughout the piece move no farther away than 11 o'clock and/or 1 o'clock before coming back home again. Consequently, the only chords used in the piece of music are built on C, G and/or F.

As you would expect, a chord progression which stays so very close to home is to be found in the simpler kinds of music— in most patriotic songs, folk songs, children's songs, ethnic songs, hymns and, as the term Elementary Classical implies, in many of our revered, antique classics. (In fact, that is what the word "classical" means: typical, traditional, standard, enduring.)

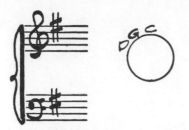

1 sharp in key signature, home base on circle is G. In Elementary Classical harmony, the chords never move farther from home than next door neighbors.

So, here it is in the opening of Bach's familiar *Minuet in G.*

The key signature has one sharp, telling you that the home base is G on the circle. And as you can see, the chords progress from that home base to one stop away and then come home before moving one stop away again— and come home immediately after that venture. And so on and on to the end.

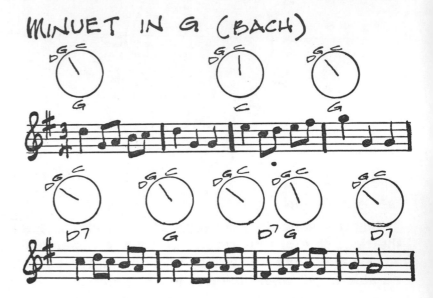

To transpose the *Minuet* into another key —to give it another home base — does not change the *pattern of chord progression.* No matter where the home base on the circle, the chords never move farther away than one stop to the left and/or one stop to the right.

No matter what the piece of music and no matter what "key" it is in, if the harmony moves in an Elementary Classical pattern, then it stays right around home —and, in fact, it touches home base before moving out again.

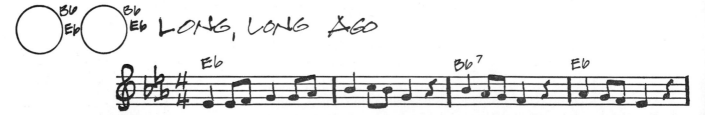

Key signature puts home base at 3 o'clock. Only 1 neighboring chord is needed throughout.

That is a great convenience in having a circular layout of root notes for chords. You can always tell what time it is in a progression. And as you can see from this most elementary of progressions, the appointed hour on the clock —the home base on the circle —has enormous magnetism. It pulls the harmonic movement toward itself. That, of course, is true of any kind of appointed hour. It organizes the hour leading up to it and often the hour after it, as anybody knows who has ever had to be sure to get home on time to go out to dinner.

As Classical harmony developed and grew out of its Elementary pattern around the home base, innovative composers learned that the appointed hour on the clock could organize many of the hours before it. The magnetism of the home base, it turned out, could pull quite a long progression of chords clockwise toward itself.

But before that discovery was made —and while Classical harmony was still in its Elementary stage —composers discovered that they did not have to touch home base after each and every venture to an adjacent chord on the circle. They discovered that it was possible to jump from one adjacent chord to the other —from one side of the home base to the other *before finally coming home.* In other words, as harmony developed, it became possible *to delay the resolution of the chord progression* for a little while.

Naturally, it doesn't matter which key you find the music in —which stop on the circle is named as the home base. When the harmony moves on a clock face, there is always an hour before the appointed hour, and an hour after it.

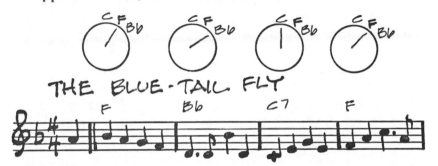

And just to clear up any doubts about progressions on the circle, the principle also applies to home bases which are *minor* (music written in a minor key).

Here, for example, is an excerpt from Schubert's familiar *Serenade.* The progression is Elementary Classical because it never goes farther away on the circle than the two neighboring stops of the home base. Further, it is an illustration of delayed resolution as you can see by the way the progression leaves the home base of 10 o'clock, jumps back and forth from 11 o'clock to 9 o'clock, and then comes home at last.

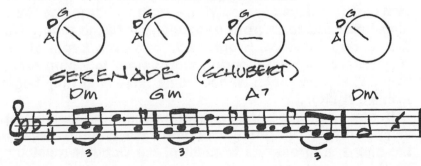

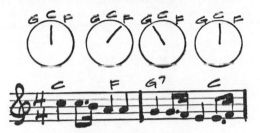

Neighboring chords can jump to each other over the home base before coming home.

This key signature can mean a home base of F or (here) D minor. The minor is to be found a quarter-circle back.

But why the home base is *D minor* when the key signature is one flat and usually means by it that the home base is F —well, that is a matter of convention, an old clause in the musical contract we have with each other hereabouts. And as of this writing, nobody has secured enough votes to rewrite that clause.

According to that clause, each key signature —each stop on the circle —can signify two possible home bases. A signature can mean what it says outright, such as that no sharps and no flats means the home base is C, or that one flat means the home base is F, or that one sharp means that the home base is G, etc. But our contract also says that *the very same key signature can also indicate a minor key* —a different home base on the circle. That minor key, that other home base, is *the sixth of the basic scale* named by the key signature. If the key signature is C, it could also mean the key is *Am*. If the key signature is F, it could mean a home base of *Dm*.

As you can see, the minor home base is a quarter-circle in back of the basic home base. On the circle, this means two possible home bases for the same key signature. And now that you know that, you can forget it. Most sheet music announces its chords in plain English letters of the alphabet.

For our purposes, the key signature is really only a signal as to which accidentals are pre-set —which notes *in the melody are to be sharped or flatted* (unless cancelled locally here or there). Consequently, the key signature affects only the melody, not the chords. They are prescribed by the chord symbols.

With the chord symbols in plain English, you can locate them on the circle and trace their movements easily, particularly now that you see how the Elementary Classical harmony moves. Whether the chords are minor or not makes no difference to the regular way they move. Whether the home base is minor or not does not affect the progression of chords on the circle.

IN A NUTSHELL: Elementary Classical chord progressions are very timid, moving from the home base (signified by the key signature) to the next neighbor to the left or right on the circle and then coming home again. Or, the progression can be delayed in resolving —coming home after jumping back and forth from one neighbor to the other. The Elementary Classical progression can even begin at the very outset on a neighboring stop before touching home base. That is, a piece whose home base is D may begin with an A chord.

In any case, this pattern never moves more than a stop away to the left or right of the home base. It is the basis for the chord progressions in most of our popular music.

WE THREE KINGS OF ORIENT ARE

Progressions on the circle —classical harmony

31

AS TIME PASSED, INNOVATIVE COMPOSERS began to see that the appointed hour on the clock could organize many of the hours *before* it —the way a noon wedding can organize the entire morning before it for those involved in the procession. As it soon became clear, the magnetism of the home base could *pull quite a long progression of chords clockwise toward itself.*

The important word in that classical principle is *clockwise*. That's what makes this most-common harmonic movement Classical.

Essentially, then, Classical harmony moves this way:

1. The progression begins, of course, on the home base.

That is the stop on the circle designated by the key signature. Take a number written in the key of C, a piece of music whose home base on the circle is C —12 o'clock high, so to speak.

2. The next move in this Classical progression of chords is a jump counter-clockwise.

That is a jump backward to an earlier hour, so to speak —a jump backward over one or more stops on the circle. As you can see here, that jump backward can be a quarter-circle. (But it could be a jump backward farther than a quarter-circle, or less than a quarter-circle.) However, at least 90 per cent of our popular music begins exactly this way— a quarter-circle jump back *over two intervening stops* on the circle.

3. Now the chords begin their march home, their Classical progression clockwise —pulled back by the irresistible magnetism of the home base.

But, as those innovative composers of long ago found, the homeward progression *must follow the circle.* The march must halt at each stop enroute home on the circle. So, having jumped backwards *over two stops* on the circle, the progression comes home by halting at each of those two stops.

In other words, after a jump backwards from 12 o'clock high to 9 o'clock on the circle, the chords set out for home base at high noon —stopping enroute at 10 o'clock and then at 11 o'clock.

4. At last the progression comes home to the home base.

And from there it can begin its Classical jump to the left again —and progress back home again, by halting at each intervening stop on the circle. Naturally, this same principle of the jump backwards and the clockwise homecoming is at work regardless of where the home base is on the circle.

How far the Classical progression jumps to the left before beginning its clockwise return home can vary widely.

It starts on
the home base,

jumps backward
over 1 or more stops

and then comes
back clockwise

touching each
stop enroute

until it is
home once again.

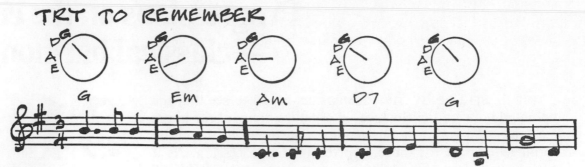

TRY TO REMEMBER

The quarter-circle jump backward is the most popular in our popular music.

Sometimes the jump is only two stops back —one stop less than a quarter-circle. Sometimes the jump backward is five stops, such as from a home base of B♭ all the way back to A, almost a half-circle. That is the case of a popular number of some years back, *Mr. Sandman*. But even with so great a leap backwards, the Classical harmony principle persists. Each intervening stop is touched enroute home, as you will see if you care to look at that song.

For the most part, however, our popular music and our classical music agree on a shorter jump backward — a quarter-circle or so. Here is testimony to that effect from J.S. Bach in the opening bars of his Prelude No. 1 from *The Well-Tempered Clavichord*. As you can see, the progression of chords is clearly Classical with its backward jumps and clockwise homecomings. The first jump is back over *two stops*, the second jump is back a *quarter-circle*. And on the way home, each intervening stop is visited.

Testimony regarding the backward jump and the clockwise, stop-by-stop homecoming from J.S. Bach.

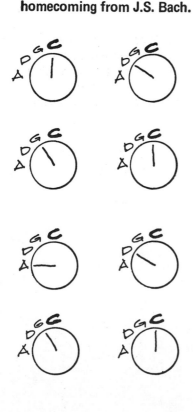

PRELUDE NO. 1 (BACH)

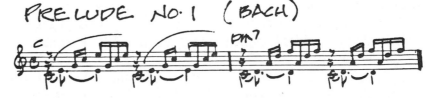

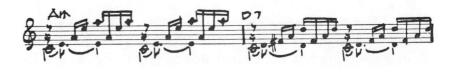

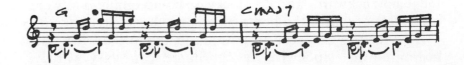

Examples of this Classical harmonic movement are everywhere, so there is no need to set out any more illustrative examples. A look in anybody's piano bench will prove the facts of the backward jump and clockwise stop-by-stop homeward journey.

As for that most popular of all backward jump and clockwise homecoming— the quarter-circle —you can hear how comfortable its progress on the circle sounds merely by playing the *root notes only* of the sequence: home base, jumped-to spot, and the stops enroute home again.

But it took a lot of musical history to get there —to get away from the Elementary Classical movement around home base and into experimentation with jumps farther away on the circle. At its time in the development of harmony, a jump backward to a chord only two stops away from the home base was a revolutionary change in sound.

Today, so standard a number as Sigmund Romberg's *One Alone* jumps from its home base backward *five stops* without provoking any emotion stronger than a reminiscence for a bygone time which was more understandable. And, of course, having made that great leap backwards, the chord progression in the number comes home as you would expect —clockwise, stop-by-stop, along the circle.*

COMING HOME STOP-BY-STOP along the circle means coming home *via chords rooted on those stops.* But exactly *which kind* of chord is called for at each root along the circle — basic, minor, diminished, 6th, etc. —that depends on the *melody notes called for at the time* and whether they make a good sound with the chord or make a clash. Take a look at how the C chord changes its personality depending on the melody notes at the time the progression jumps backward a quarter-circle.

Movement on circle is from root note to root note. But the chords themselves are altered or added-to to prevent clash with tune.

SERENADE TO CHLOË

And the same is true for all the chords built on all the root notes all along the way home. But even if there is a momentary clash here and there enroute to the home base, it doesn't alter

---

*Reversible dim6 and Aug chords can be named for each component note. Thus, from C to Cdim can also be a quarter-circle jump back— C to Adim. When harmony moves from home base to a dim6 or Aug, re-naming it usually reveals a Classical progression at work.

Enroute home, the chords
often have a 7th added.

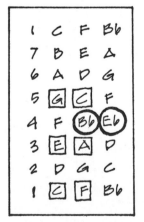

The added 7th of a chord
belongs to the basic scale
named next on the clockwise
route. The added 7th helps
pull the progression home.

the progression. In the Classical harmonic movement, all stops must be touched on the way home. A chord must be built on each root note along the way from the jumped-to spot back to home base. That is the principle of this clockwise progression: Every hour must chime enroute home. No matter what the melody does, *the circle must be closed,* even if the melody clashes with the chord for a moment.

That principle about that circle is what most of our composers have had in mind most of the time. It is what makes our patterns of oncoming single chordals and non-chordals so easy to identify and to remember. This circular layout of root notes, this progression of backward jumps from the home base and clockwise returnings is an idea we generally share about what sounds good. It is what makes popular music popular in large part.

WHETHER THE CHORDS ENROUTE HOME are basic or altered, they frequently have a 7th added to them. That is as true of what we call "classical music" as it is of popular, but it is much easier to see in the chord symbols of popular music.

Why those 7ths are added to so many of the homecoming chords is easy to explain. The added 7th —the addition of the note which lies two intervals below the root of the basic seven-tone scale (and its chord)— helps to pull the progression clockwise and thus homeward. Here's how it works:

This 7th, being two intervals below the root, it is *not a member* of the scale-and-chord whose name it uses. (In fact, this 7th is often called *the flatted 7th* to show that it does not reside in the basic seven-tone scale.) In other words, the 7th which turns a C chord into a C7 is not found in the basic scale built on C. Similarly, the 7th which makes an F7 chord is not found in the F scale; and likewise the 7th of the B♭7 chord does not live in the B♭ scale.

Where each of these 7th notes really lives is *in the next scale named clockwise* on the homecoming route of the circle. So— the 7th which makes a C7 chord is a member of the F scale.

And the added 7th which makes an F7 chord is a member of the B♭ scale —the next-named scale clockwise on the circle.

And, similarly, what turns a B♭ chord into a B♭7 is the addition of a note taken from the E♭ scale. And so on clockwise around the circle —until the story is told completely, with a G7 chord made by the addition of a note taken from the C scale.

Under the circumstances, then, the addition of this borrowed 7th makes a chord *unstable, unresolved. The addition of this 7th puts in a tone which leads the progression clockwise into the next scale —the next chord— on the homecoming route on the circle.* Consequently, jumped-to chords and those enroute home are often 7th chords because that added 7th helps to pull the progression clockwise toward home.

ALL IN ALL, THE MAGNETIC PULL of the home base is so strong that there are very few things you can do to camouflage the basic and very familiar Classical progression of chords with its circular layout, its backward jump and clockwise, stop-by-stop homecoming.

For quite a long while it was possible for composers to cover the essentials by extending the backward jump from two stops to a quarter-circle, and then to four and later to five stops. Each longer jump backward over more intervening stops was a landmark development in its day. But today, the long jump of five stops (from home base B♭ say, way back to A as in *Mr. Sandman)* sounds very pleasant and ordinary. And that is just about as far as you can jump backward on the circle —less than half-way around.

A jump half-way around begins to appear equivocal, as though it could be *either behind or ahead* of the home base. Clearly, a backward jump of more than a half-circle —from home base C to A♭, say— not only appears but also sounds like a jump *forward on the circle.* And that destroys the Classical chord progression because the clockwise pull from A♭ will take the chords to D♭ and then G♭, which is *away from the home base,* not toward it.

So there's really no room left on the circle for developing (and thus camouflaging) the backward jump. That leaves only one other component of the Classical chord movement available for camouflage, namely *the clockwise, stop-by-stop progression back home* from the jumped-to point on the circle. And that is where most of the camouflage has been developed.

Consequently, you will often come across variations of the homeward trip. But as that journey covers only a very limited path —usually a quarter-circle or a stop more— you will see very quickly through each camouflage device.

There are, after all is said and done, only three possibilities for camouflage: delayed resolution; starting out not on the home base, but enroute home; and inserting a chord-not-on-the-path for its surprise value.

1. Delayed resolution simply means that the journey back does not go directly home from stop to stop along the circle. Instead, it fools around enroute, dawdling, going back to repeat a stop, seemingly missing a stop and then coming back to pull it into the progression.

You can see this type of delayed resolution in Beethoven's *Minuet in G,* beginning with the fifth measure. It opens with the quarter-circle jump backwards from home base G. But enroute home, the progression seems to miss the first stop —A— and

Less than half-way — the apparent limit of the backward jump. Any further and it would sound like a forward jump.

goes instead to D. And now that everybody has been properly surprised (those who were surprised by that have been dead for two centuries), the progression retraces its steps to touch the by-passed A, and then goes home just as the classical pattern says it should.

MINUET IN G (BEETHOVEN)

G   G+   Em   D   A   D

Delayed resolution, a kind of camouflage. The progression seems to miss a stop (A), but goes back to include it.

This fooling around enroute home, this delayed resolution, is a very common camouflage device in both classical and popular music. Often it is laid out in a patterned way with a stop missed, a return to touch it, then another stop missed and a return to touch it . . . and so on all the way home.

But whatever stops have been missed, rest assured that they will be pulled into the progression before it is finished. Even if the home base is reached with one stop left out, the progression will go back for it —seemingly as an after-thought. And that is because Classical harmony demands that the circle be closed completely.

2. Starting out not on home base but enroute home is the second camouflage device, and means only that the home base is not mentioned at the outset. Instead, the progression begins somewhere on the way to the home base, gets home, and then begins its familiar Classical pattern of jump backwards and clockwise homecomings (delayed or not).

There really aren't many places to begin this device: a stop or two (three rarely) behind home base, and followed by a direct, clockwise, stop-by-stop march home on the circle. Typical of this camouflage of starting enroute home —presumably so that the listening ear will be mystified for a moment about what time it is on the circle —is the opening of *As Time Goes By*, written in 1931.

For a couple of other numbers whose chords begin two stops behind home base, see *Body and Soul, Honeysuckle Rose* and *I Get A Kick Out Of You*. For some numbers whose progressions begin a quarter-circle behind home base, see *Sweet Georgia Brown, Seems Like Old Times* and *There'll Be Some Changes Made*.

Now and then, Elementary Classical harmony is called on to help with the camouflage. As you recall about that early movement on the circle, the progression never goes farther away

EVERYTHING'S COMING UP ROSES

Dm7   G7+   C   Cm

Another camouflage device: The progression doesn't begin on home base but on the clockwise trip homeward.

than the stop on either side of the home base. Consequently, there is a long history in our music of hearing the chord *clockwise ahead of the home base move counter-clockwise back home to resolution.*

Now and then you will find a number which begins its opening chord progression one stop ahead of the home base, lingering there long enough to make for considerable surprise —and thus camouflage— when it moves seemingly backward to the home base. A case in point is *I'll See You In My Dreams,* written in 1924 when four bars of a chord rooted *ahead* of the home base must have been a wow, and a move *counter-clockwise* home left listeners wondering what time it was in the chord progression.

Obviously, this device of starting out on the homeward route or jumped-to spot can be combined with the camouflage of fooling around on the way home, leaving out stops and going back to pull them in. For example, this excerpt from Chopin's *Minute Waltz* (Op. 64, No. 1), transposed here to make C the home base for purposes of illustration.

...the progression may begin
with a counter-clockwise
move to home base from the
neighbor ahead

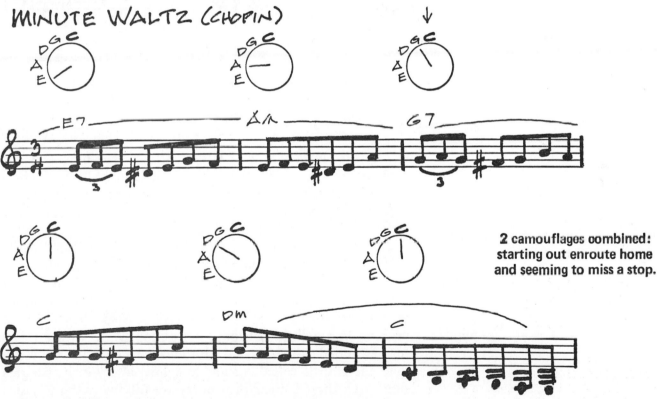

2 camouflages combined:
starting out enroute home
and seeming to miss a stop.

In most popular numbers, however, that kind of complicated camouflage is not found frequently. After all, the aim of popular music is to be popular. And you can't accomplish that by trying constantly to surprise the listening ear and making it wait too long for arrival at the home base resolution. That is why the Classical pattern of chord movement on the circle is so often used uncamouflaged in popular numbers, and any camouflage is usually easily seen through.*

3. Inserting a chord not-on-the-homeward path is the third and last general camouflage technique used to cover the usual clockwise, stop-by-stop homeward trip on circle.

Almost always when an outlandish —or out-circlish— chord is used in a progression, its only purpose is surprise. And after it has been used, the progression returns immediately to the expected pattern. For example, here is the opening progression of *September Song.* As you can see, the second chord is a jump *forward* on the circle to A♭. That is a very long jump forward, and consequently an unmistakable violation of the Classical pattern (which allows for only one stop ahead of the home base).

An outlandish chord may be used in the progression. It will come from the outland far away clockwise from home.

That second chord is there merely for its surprise, its camouflage effect. And that having been accomplished, the progression goes to its home base of C again —and then progresses through a usual, expected Classical progression.

IT IS ALSO POSSIBLE TO CAMOUFLAGE a true-blue Classical progression while still following it to the letter. Altering a chord or adding to it is a very common way to cover up the essential fact that it is exactly where it should be on the circle and in the progression.

For instance, when many successive bars of melody require only one basic chord and thus produce no real movement on the circle, you will often find the impression of movement created by the use of altered or added-to chords in the sequence. See the opening bars of *There's A Small Hotel.* There's nothing like a little tension —an added Maj7 with an even further added 9th, 11th or 13th tones —to give an impression that the chords called for are somehow alien to the progression, even though their root notes are following the Classical route perfectly.

---

*Rarely do popular numbers employ complicated camouflage. But see <u>Alabamy Bound</u>. The progression starts one stop ahead of the home base. Next it jumps backward over the home base. Then it fools around enroute home without stating the home base for thirty bars — two bars before the number comes to an end.

For this reason of creating an impression of novel chord progression, a diminished chord will be used at the jumped-to spot when a basic or 7th chord would do just as well.

NEVERTHELESS

Don't be misled by numbers or alterations. Chords move on the circle by their roots. Remember: dims and Augs can be named by each note in them. That G dim6 is also a Bb dim6.

That second chord —that B♭ *dim*— is by its formula also a D♭ *dim*, an E *dim* and a *G dim*. So, that jumped-to spot is really a quarter-circle, a very Classical jump backward from *home base* B♭ to G dim. But for a moment, the listening ear is asked to wonder about which diminished chord it is hearing.

That isn't really confusion or grand amazement. But it is enough. In popular music, a little camouflage goes a long way. The listening ear is satisfied with small tricks because they don't upset the comfortable, expected Classical apple cart.

IN A NUTSHELL, THEN: Classical harmonic movement —the way most chord progressions go in most of our popular music— calls for a jump backward from the home base over at least one intervening stop, and then a clockwise trip home touching the stop which was jumped over. Usually, the jump backward is a quarter-circle (over two intervening stops). But sometimes it is a longer jump. In any event, the Classical progression calls for each stop to be touched and a chord sounded on that root note before the progression is complete. After that, it can jump backward from the home base again — to come home clockwise, stop-by-stop, again.

The magnetism of the home base pulling the progression homeward is helped by the addition of a 7th to the chords enroute. The 7th of each chord is a note two intervals below the root —a note borrowed from the next scale named on the homeward, clockwise trip. The 7th, then, is a leading tone —leading the progression onward clockwise. But even with the added 7th helping the irresistible magnetism of the home base pull the progression clockwise home, the progression can jump backwards no more than five stops on the circle —from home base C, for instance, backward to B.

The Classical progression is the strongest pattern in our popular harmonic movement, so it cannot be too completely camouflaged or it will no longer be popular.

THERE'S A SMALL HOTEL

Almost all are G chords. But changes of tension give an impression of chord movement.

There are only three main types of camouflage used. First: delaying the resolution enroute home by seeming to miss stops and coming back to touch them as an afterthought. Second: starting the progression at the outset from a jumped-to spot (without stating the home base first) and then coming home Classically, clockwise, stop-by-stop. And third: using a chord which is not in that homeward path —an outlandish chord— for a surprise effect once in the middle of a progression.

But most progressions in most popular numbers are straight forward Classical movements on the circle. Most of the camouflage you will find is only a trick —a diminished or augmented chord called by one of its names not-on-the-homeward-route; a chord to the right of the home base (and thus a legitimate part of Elementary Classical progressions); or simply a high tension chord but rooted just where it should be on the Classical, clockwise path homeward.

Just keep your eyes on the root notes of the chords called for (sometimes you may have to re-name the diminished or augmented chord called for), and you will see that the progressions are very Classical, very expectable, very circular and clockwise.

It's a good idea to fool around with the possibilities of Classical progessions, substituting a quarter-circle jump for other, more trite progressions. But don't just try it. *Listen* to the result. And remember that the harmony is stronger than the melody, so an occasional, brief clash between harmony and melody is quite all right —even desirable. In other words, the circle must be closed (the progression completed) regardless of what the melody does.

Progressions on the circle —romantic harmony

TO RE-STATE IT VERY BRIEFLY:

Elementary Classical harmony moves only around the home base, and Classical harmony jumps backward from home base over one or more stops to come home clockwise, stop-by-stop, on the circle.

32

Romantic harmony, the next development in patterned chord movement, uses those Classical progressions around, away from and back toward home. But Romantic harmony adds the invention of using *two home bases*.

Take a real live instance of Romantic chord progressions at work. Here are the opening two bars of Chopin's *Prelude* (Op. 28, No. 20).

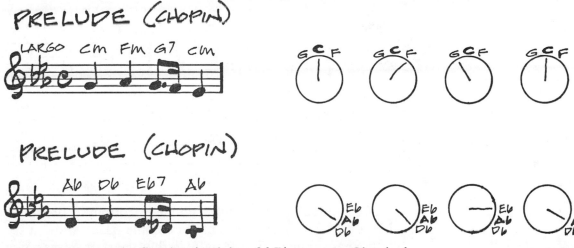

As you can see, the first bar is plain, old Elementary Classical harmony, moving from home base C to the neighbors on either side of it, and then back home to C to close the progression. In the second measure, the very same thing happens, but *the home base is Ab*.

There are three usual (and obvious) earmarks of most Romantic chord progressions:

1. The second home base is usually to the right of the first home base.

Putting the second *clockwise ahead* takes it out of Classical range where the magnetic pull of the first home base cannot pull the progression back to it.

2. The Romantic progression is usually quite obvious. There should be no mistake that a Classical progression around one home base is in operation.

To make it clear that two home bases are in use, the two

Two home bases. The 2nd home base sits clockwise ahead of the 1st on the circle.

progressions must be fairly close together —a bar or two away from each other, four at the most —so that the listening ear will be surprised at the shift from one to the other. That Chopin *Prelude* back there had the two progressions in neighboring measures. The popular number *Laura* uses one home base for four bars and a second home base for the next four bars.

3. To make the shift from the first home base to the second even more obvious, the melody in both instances is either exactly the same, or at least very, very similar.

For the same reason, the chord progression around the first home base has to be duplicated around the second home base. To wit: four bars (No. 10 through 13) of *The Swan* by Saint-Saens. Each home base is used for two bars. The melody line in the first pair and the melody line in the second pair are congruent reflections of each other. And the same is true of the chord progressions around the two home bases.

The melody patterns at each home base are exact replicas or unmistakably similar.

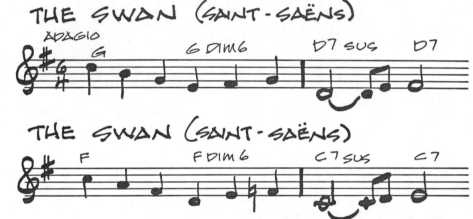

Most popular music does not use Romantic progressions. Most popular music uses only one home base. And if a second home base appears, it is usually in the B part or release of an A-A-B-A form. You can find that in *Smoke Gets In Your Eyes:* the A parts are home-based on E♭, as the key signature announces; but the release, the B part is home-based on B. In the same way, the A parts of *Once In A While* are home-based on E♭ while the release is home-based on G. But that is not a Romantic shift to a second home base because *the melody of the release is entirely different from the melody of the A parts.* Consequently, such shifts to a new home base for the release merely announce to the listening ear that a new melody is about to begin.

Occasionally you will find a number which seems to be Romantic in harmony movement with one home base for the first A part and another for the second A part. Such a number is *Tea For Two*. The first full A part is home-based on A♭, the second full A part is home-based on C. But that is *not* Romantic harmony at work. And for two good reasons. For one, the first home base is used for too long to make the shift to the second home base *surprising* —one of the ear marks of Romantic progressions. And for another reason, the second home base is a *jump backward* from the first (from Ab back to C). That is much more Classical in movement than Romantic. So, all in all, you would have to look on *Tea For Two* as an instance of transposition from one key to another and not a bona fide Romantic harmony move to a second home base.

However, there are some popular numbers which do employ the Romantic pattern on the circle, fulfilling both requirements —the second home base established *ahead* of the first, and at work within four bars of the first; and the *mirroring of both chord and melody* patterns in the first and second instances.

Take a case in point, *Show Me* where Romantic harmonic movement is clearly in use. The first home base, G, is used for eight bars, and the second home base, Bb, is used for the next eight. Not only are the melody lines mirror-like images of each other, but the chord progessions are also duplications on the circle.

As you can see, the second home base (Bb) is *clockwise ahead* of the first home base (G). So, the requirements for Romantic chord progressions have been fulfilled.

The list of popular numbers which use Romantic harmony is nowhere near as long as those which stay within the Classical pattern. But you can find plenty of numbers with progressions around two home bases, particularly now that we are a safe distance (a century and a half) from the time when Romantic progresssions were an adventurous innovation. So, see *A Man And A Woman.* See *Live For Life.* See *Moonlight in Vermont* (release). See *Laura.*

No, Romantic harmony is no novelty. On the contrary, it can be found in Beethoven's works. In fact, he employed Classical progressions at the outset of his career and then used Romantic progressions as his career developed. So, we're quite used hearing this movement around two home bases. And consequently

Some popular numbers use Romantic movement, but it's not common.

it comes as no surprise but as a pleasure to hear a good, professional pianist re-work the harmony of a popular number, taking it out of the Classical mold and playing this phrase with one home base and the next, mirror-image phrase with a second home base. Try it. You might like it.

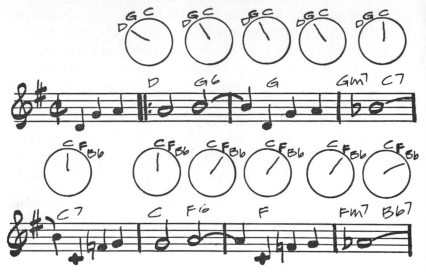

Try it on your own piano. If you like the effect of a Romantic, 2-home base progression, apply it to a number which doesn't call for it in the original.

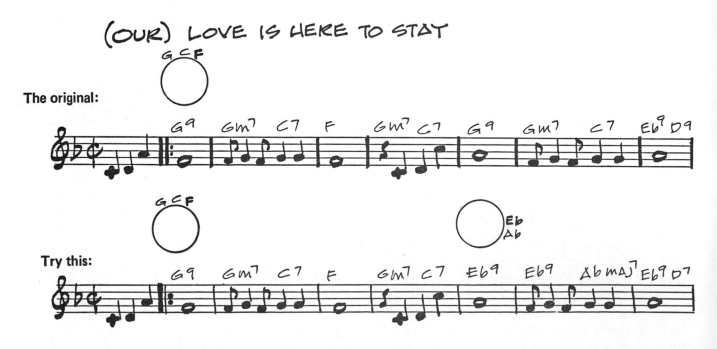

Progressions on the circle —impressionist & modern

33

YOU CAN SEE WHAT COULD HAPPEN to harmonic movement on the circle once Classical principles — traditional principles— are modified by Romantic progressions with their two home bases. The door is opened to much farther-ranging movement. It becomes easier to move anywhere on the circle away from the home base and back to it —*just so long as the movement finally reveals itself to be a pattern.*

IMPRESSIONIST HARMONY is exactly that sort of a larger pattern of chord movement on the circle which takes quite a bit of time to reveal itself as a pattern. And while Impressionist harmony does not appear in popular music —at least not yet— that is no guarantee against its ever arriving there as our music evolves.

The matter of Impressionist chord progression is mentioned here briefly for two reasons. First, it may some day be helpful to know this pattern so as to be able to make more music with popular tunes. And second, it will certainly be helpful in listening to classical compositions. (Oh yes, it is possible to find Impressionist progressions in classical music, just as it is very, very easy to find Classical chord progressions in works by Romantic composers, and so on. The history of ideas —*and music is an idea*— does not follow the same sort of calendar as the history of battles and eclipses.)

In the Impressionist chord movement, there is a home base on the circle, and there is a progression away from it and back to it. But the movement on the circle may take quite a few bars and chord changes until the pattern is revealed. In fact, the progression may take a complete trip around the circle.

You have heard Impressionist harmonic movement in the famous *Liebestraum* by Liszt. And as you will see in this version (simplified for this illustration of chord progression), it takes *twenty four 3/4 bars* of harmonic movement on the circle to reveal and complete the pattern.

Clearly, there is a home base. The key signature tells you that. And clearly there is a pattern of movement on the circle. It is *counter-clockwise* —a jump backward, *using two* stops on the circle, *skipping two* stops, using two, skipping two . . . and then repeatedly *bracketing the home base.*

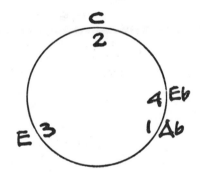

Liszt used **4 home bases** and took **24 bars** to complete the pattern.

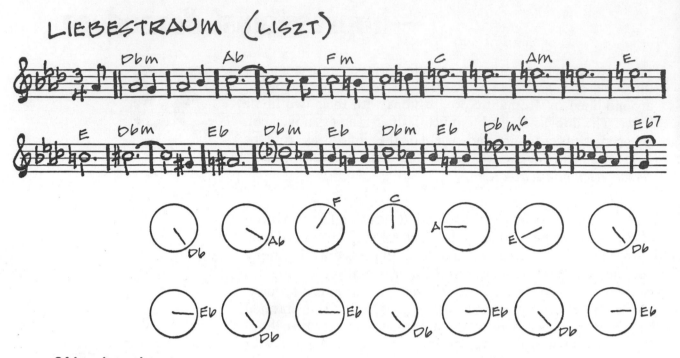

LIEBESTRAUM (LISZT)

24 bars is too long to complete a progression of chords in a popular number which is only 32 bars long.

Certainly that is a pattern of movement on the circle. But as it takes twenty four bars to complete and be revealed, it is too long for use in the popular music we know these days. After all, a popular number is usually made of eight-bar parts —and frequently a part is really a pair of four-bar phrases. And you cannot have a melody pattern which is finished before the chord pattern has been revealed. It would make for disorganization rather than organization. It would make for a lack of pattern. So, Impressionist chord progressions will probably not be used to organize popular tunes because the result could sound like gibberish.

BUT NOBODY CAN SAY FOR SURE. After all, this is an age of gibberish in almost everything else —drama, novels, poetry, painting, decoration, marriage styles and psychotherapy. And while it is true that a wide-ranging Impressionist chord pattern could be squeezed into an eight-bar part, the chords would come along so quickly that there would be no time to let each sink in —a sure way to make for chaos.

And that brings up the matter of *Modern harmony*. It can, however, be dispensed with in the same breath.

Modern harmony is a movement on the circle far too long and wide ranging to reveal a pattern to the listening ear. It could be pictured on a graph —and may sometimes be composed that way. But it has very little application in making music at home.

How chords move—
progessions on the line

WHAT WITH MUSIC BEING SO entrancing and compelling, it is quite easy to forget that what sounds good is largely made by an agreement we have with one another.

Historically, the business of dividing the octave into the twelve parts —the chromatic scale— which we use to make our music was accomplished by agreement between composers and piano tuners. And, as though to prove that it was only an agreement, some composers today are reviewing that clause by working with "treated" pianos whose octaves are divided into more than twelve tones.

Just as certainly, there is no law governing which scale is to be taken from the complete, chromatic set of twelve notes. After all, the basic seven-tone scale — the diatonic major scale— isn't the only one we use in our music. There are also the minor scale, the diminished scale, the augmented scale and the 7th scale to name a few scales whose chords you now know.

And as for the movement of chords in our usual and compelling harmonic progressions from root note to root note around the circle —well, there is no eternal, natural law which says that the circle is the only path to move chords, or that chords have to move from root note to root note.

As it turns out, we have agreed among ourselves on at least one other path for moving chords in progression.

This other path is up (or down) a *line of steps*. And this *step-by-step* order is based on the way you find the twelve tones laid out chromatically on your keyboard.

The line of notes as you find them on your keyboard (here beginning on C). The line makes a path, up or down, for chords to follow. It's called a chromatic line.

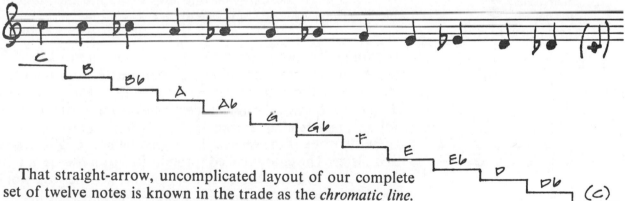

That straight-arrow, uncomplicated layout of our complete set of twelve notes is known in the trade as the *chromatic line*. And consequently, a step-by-step movement of chords up or down that line —no matter how few steps the progression takes along the line —is also known as *Chromatic harmony*.

Well, there is nothing involved or amazing about this linear kind of chord movement. It is certainly a lot more apparent to

This chord progression makes no pattern on the circle. But seen as a chromatic line it makes perfect sense.

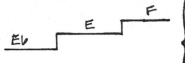

the naked eye than chord movement on the circle. So, at the risk of being obvious, here is an example of Chromatic harmony —of a linear progression on the move. It is the opening of *Close As Pages In A Book* by Sigmund Romberg. And as you can see, the chords move from root note to root note up three steps of the chromatic line: from Eb to E to F.

Try it on your piano and you will see (and feel and hear) that a line holds the progression together in Chromatic harmony the way a circle holds the progression together in Classical and Romantic chord movements.

THE BASIC SEVEN-TONE SCALE is also a line, coming along step-by-step up and down the keyboard. In fact, any scale taken from the full set of twelve is a line. So the 7th scale, the minor scale, the diminished scale and the rest can be used as linear paths for chord movement. And when the chords move along the line of any scale (no matter how short the progression) the movement goes by the name of a *Tonal* progession.

You can see a Tonal progression of two chords in the opening bars of *This Nearly Was Mine*. It moves from the home base of Eb up the basic Eb scale one stop to F, and then it comes back to the home base of Eb again.

The chords can also follow the line of a scale — basic scale, or any other scale. It's called a tonal line.

IT WOULD APPEAR FROM THE NAMES of the chords called for that linear progressions follow a path made by the root notes of the chords. For instance, in those opening bars of *Close As Pages In A Book,* the original sheet music shows that the chords follow the ascending chromatic line of bass notes.

But that is not the case in those opening bars of *This Nearly Was Mine*. The chords called for indicate an *up-and-back* tonal line. But if you looked at the original sheet music, you would see that the bass notes form *an ascending line only*. The first two bass notes in the line are the root notes of the chords called for. But the third bass note is the 3rd of the chord called for. And if you were to look farther —bars five through twelve— you would find a remarkable seven-bar chromatic bass line, made of a mixture of root notes and other chord notes of the chords

called for.

That is mentioned in some detail because it illustrates a very important fact concerning linear progressions. And that is, *the line is a very strong organizer* — so strong in holding progressions together that the chords do not necessarily have to move from root note to root note (as they move on the circle). In linear progressions, *any bottom note of the chord will do for transportation.*

In other words, you can play three-note and four-note chords in any position, with any component note on the bottom —root or 3rd or flatted 3rd or any of the other possibilities— *just as long as the bottom notes of the chords move stepwise* up or down along a chromatic or tonal line.

Well, you can see where that kind of transportation can take you.

For instance, you could take any melody and put under it a bass line —a line of notes in the bass which will be used as the bottom notes of chords. Try a sample on your own piano. Take the opening bars of *I Could Write a Book* and begin beneath it a descending chromatic bass line —a single-note melody in the right hand and a sort of single-note, step-by-step counter-melody in the left.

The line of the bass notes
— the bass line —
isn't always the root notes
of the chords called for.

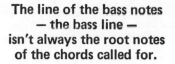

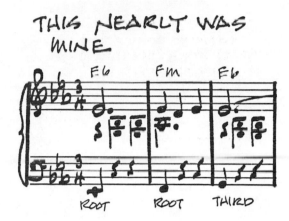

Line starts
on root

The bass line can
begin on any note
but frequently it
starts on the root
or on the 3rd
or on the 5th
of the home base chord.

Line starts
on 5th

This, of course, is only an illustration of what you *could* do. You *could* also have the bass line ascend instead. Moreover, it *could* begin on the 3rd or the 5th of the home bass chord rather than on the root —or on any other note— as long as it worked out well. Further, it *could* be a tonal line rather than a chromatic line or a mixture of both tonal and chromatic lines. And it *could* run only three steps in length or four or six . . .

The only requirement is that the bass line be used as the bottom notes of the chords in the progression. Which chords? Why, any chords that sound good beneath the melody and incorporate the bottom note as one of the notes of the chord. For example:

Next, make a chord which includes both the melody note and the bass note and sounds good to you. Abandon the bass line at your convenience and go back to the circle.

As you can hear, a linear chord progression isn't what you usually find with this melody. As you would see in the original sheet music, the chords move on the circle in an Elementary Classical progression around the home base. And in place of the bass line, you would see the familiar *alternating bass notes* which say very clearly that the chords move from root note to root note.

So, in this instance, a linear chord progression built on a bass line is a *re-harmonization* —a made-up, new chord setting for a melody. And that, in turn, illustrates three important facts about harmony.

First, it says that there is no wrong or right harmony, linear or circular. It's simply a matter of what sounds good to you at the time.

Second, it says that if you come across a progresssion which does not seem to conform either to the circle or to the line, take a look at the bass notes in the sheet music. If you see a bass line moving chromatically or tonally up or down, then you know how the land lies up above in the chord progression.

And third, this sample of re-harmonization of a melody says that you can do the same with any melody you are working with. You can take the harmony off the circle and put it on a line, and vice versa. (Whether it will always sound good is another matter.) But just keep a couple of things in mind. One: re-harmonization is a use of the unexpected, so a few bars of it go a long way. And two: a lot of different chords can be built on the same bass line. Only trial and error can winnow out the best progression.

As for how to play linear progressions, well, the bass line has to be heard clearly and distinctly because it holds the chord movement together. But at the same time, the individual notes in the bass must also be heard as the bottom notes of the chords. Under those circumstances, progressions on a line sound their best in 10th chord position or open voicing arrangement.

For those settings, the general idea is to play the melody where written and drop in the chord notes (except for the bottom notes) with your right hand. With your left, play the bass line notes —single notes or octaves —below the chord but well above the muddy, growling lower registers of the keyboard. Obviously, if only a few bars are linear, you have to play the entire part of the number where written to accommodate. You can't go around changing the melody stratum for three or four bars.

In the original sheet music, the chords move on the circle.

AS EVERYBODY WHO HAS EVER SEEN an axle in a wheel knows, a line and a circle can meet and work very effectively together. In fact, a line and a circle can make for very smooth harmony together, and —more important— very interesting and unexpected combinations as well.

After all, chords in most popular music move on the circle (and most of the time along quarter-circle Classical paths). Consequently, a bit of linear chord movement here and there adds something unexpected and thus interesting. So, most of the Chromatic and Tonal progressions in popular music last only a few bars —whereupon the chords return to their expected path on the circle.

How is the connection made so that the chords move from the line to the circle?

Simply by telling the chords to do so. Simply by halting a

linear progression at a convenient spot, declaring that the chord is now on the circle, and proving it by having the chords move in a clockwise rather than a lengthwise direction.

To be specific, take those first bars of *Close As Pages In A Book* once more. The first three chords move on a chromatic bass line. (In this instance, those bass or bottom notes in the line are the root notes of the chords.) So, the linear progression of chords ascends step-by-step from E♭ to E to F.

But with that F chord, the linear progression halts. The F is on the circle *simply because it says so.* And to prove it, the progression now moves clockwise from F to B♭ enroute home.

To get off the line and onto the circle, end the chromatic progression with a chord rooted on the circle.

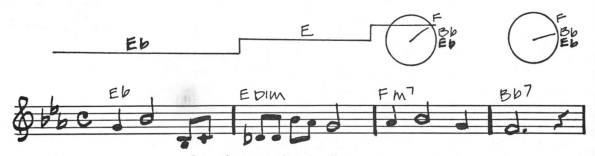

In other words, the linear progression is an *alternate path* from one place to another on the circle. In the opening bars of *Close As Pages In A Book,* the linear progression replaces a Classical backward jump from home base of E♭ to C7, and the next clockwise move to F.

Off the line and onto the circle in the original sheet music and in a re-harmonized treatment.

For another example of getting from line to circle, take a look at that re-harmonized version of *I Could Write A Book.* The bass line carries the progression through an odd selection of chords until it arrives at G7. By plain declaration and act of will, that G chord is suddenly on the circle. And to prove it, the progression next moves clockwise home to a pair of C chords.

Popular music is filled with this use of linear progressions as an alternate route from one place to another on the circle —a sort of now-and-then camouflage for the old, familiar Classical chord movements. To cite just a few instances, you can find it in that kind of employment in *Can't We Talk It Over, Stormy Weather, Deep Purple* and *You Made Me Love You*. You can find a linear progression used for itself rather than as camouflage in *Temptation*.

You'll also find it in a lot of numbers *you* make music with —now that you know how it works. There is something very tempting about trying a linear progression here and there to replace the circular progression called for in the original sheet music. It's like trying an overworked item on the menu with a new relish or seasoning.

One place to try a bit of linear seasoning is at the end of a number —replacing the expected circular progression for a bar or so, and bringing the number to a finish on a line.

In that event, you begin by an act of will, too. But in getting off the circle, you don't need a "convenient" chord. *Regardless of the chord just played,* you simply declare that the next will be on a line. And to prove it, you move onward from that point chromatically or tonally along the path of bass notes. In this example of re-harmonizing the tag of a number —of using a line instead of the expected circle —the bass line notes are root notes for the chords.

An effective re-harmonization: end a number with a brief linear progression taking you to the final home base. In this one, bass notes are all root notes of chords.

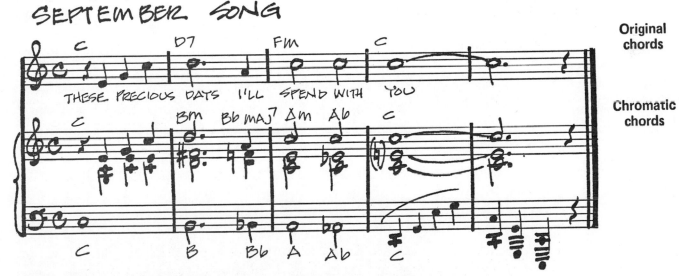

SEPTEMBER SONG

Original chords

Chromatic chords

SO IN A NUTSHELL: The circle isn't the only path on which to move chords. A line of bass notes is also a very compelling route. The listening ear will follow such a bass line and consequently accept the chords built on the notes in that line, whether or not they are used as the root notes of the chords in the progression.

If the notes in the bass line are used as root notes, the chord symbols will clearly follow a line up or down because chords are named by their root notes. But if the bass line notes are not necessarily root notes for the chords built on them, the chords called for may not fit a pattern you know. In that event, consult the sheet music if you can and look at the way the bass notes move.

A bass line can move up or down. It can move chromatically (note-by-note as on the keyboard) or tonally (as the notes appear in a scale) or in combination of both.

Most popular numbers use linear progressions sparingly, as a few bars of seasoning —as an alternate route from place to place on the circle. A linear progression usually ends on a convenient chord, a chord which is also on the homeward path on the circle. From there, the progression moves in a clockwise rather than stepwise direction. A linear progression can begin without reference to any chord played before.

You can re-harmonize a number by taking the progression off the circle and having the chords move on a bass line. But a little re-harmonizing goes a long way. Three or four chords' worth is a good helping.

Linear progessions sound best played as a sequence of 10th chords because the bass notes are separated a bit from the rest of the chord. For the same reason, linear progressions work very effectively in open voicing arrangements. Don't let the bass notes run into the lower, muddy, growling register of the keyboard or the line will blur.

How to play the piano despite years of lessons

THE MYTH: Like second sight, the ability to make music is an inborn knowledge. Either you've got it or you don't.

THE FACT: Like speech, the ability to make music is a part of being human. But you had to *learn* how to speak . . .

Part ten

How to play by ear (or, what this book has been about all along). The major difficulties diagnosed and remedies prescribed. How to recreate a melody and find the bare minimum chord progression. How to expand the harmonic setting. How to find the downbeat and the timing. Increasing the tension of a chord, including 9ths, 11ths, 13ths, etc. How to end a number.

How to play by ear

35

OF ALL THE DISABLING half-truths and full-color illusions about making music at the keyboard, the most misguided have to do with playing by ear.

On the one hand, there is the widespread belief that music made by ear is somehow shoddy, or at least vastly inferior merchandise to music played exactly as the composer wrote it in the sheet music.

But why that should be believed is hard to figure out when the sheet music may well have been written by committee —and, moreover, written as an after-thought (after having been put together originally as a score for stage, screen or recording studio). And besides, whatever the original purpose of the music, none of it was written down until the composer and/or arranger and the rest of the committee had played it by ear quite a few times.

On the other hand, there is the equally widespread hallucination that playing by ear is the only way, or certainly the very best way, to play the piano. According to this notion, the most desirable music is made by people who can sit down at the keyboard and —without having memorized any sheet music (or even having seen any)—can turn out one recognizable number after another all evening.

But by that undemanding definition of making music, a lot of people are said to be playing by ear when, in reality, they are only playing *by pinky*. All evening long they sit at the piano and turn out the same piece of music over and over, with nothing ever changing except the name of the tune. It is no accident that such performers are always pictured with a group of open-mouthed spectators surrounding them — some horrified, no doubt, some yawning, and others trying to drown out the piano by loud singing.

In real life, there is nothing either awful or magical about playing by ear. The term simply means that you have *recreated a melody* from memory, and have put *some sort of harmony* under it in a *rhythmic way*.

In other words, playing by ear is only a matter of taking a tune you have in mind (either a composer's tune or your own) and making music with it. And that ought to be well within the range of possibility, now that you have come through this book. After all, that's what the whole thing has been about: the basic facts with which most of our music is made —how to take a melody and make a lot of music with it.

IT MAY SEEM A BIT IDIOTIC to be saying this, but the first order of business in playing by ear is to have a tune in mind —a single-note melody line —to begin with. But that requirement isn't so ridiculous as it sounds because many people do not know even one simple song all the way through. In fact, many people cannot even sing, whistle or hum eight complete bars of the A part of a melody. (No, that is not a matter of being able to carry a tune. It has to do with *knowing* a tune —with *remembering* it well enough to pick it out on the keyboard, no matter how haltingly, no matter how many mistakes in the rendition. Many people simply do not know enough of any song to be able to put together even a *wrong version* of it with one finger.)

Consequently, the top priority in playing by ear is to get a few melodies in mind so that you have something to recreate and thus to make music with. How you get those melodies in mind is up to you. But trial and error is a good way. And that means you need printed copies of the melodies on hand so that you can check your trial and error version against them.

No doubt you will make mistakes. The distance from one note to another on the keyboard is a different order of things from the distances among notes in your mind. But the more melodies you work with and can recreate, the easier it will be to think in keyboard distances. In other words, you can *learn* to play melodies by ear. And after that, the rest of playing by ear —putting some sort of harmony under the tune in a rhythmic way —will fall into place, as you will see.

Now, for the melodies to work with at the outset, they should be of the simpler kind —folk songs, campfire songs, Christmas carols, old fashioned numbers and the like. There are several compelling reasons for beginning there:

1. Such songs are probably better fixed in your memory than the more sophisticated, complicated tunes.

It will be a whole lot easier to pick out *Home On the Range* —even with a lot of mistakes to correct —than to recreate *Stardust* or *Laura.* But ear-and-keyboard distance training with the simpler songs will give you the experience necessary to pick out the harder ones.

2. The words of the older, simpler songs are probably better fixed in your mind, too— a great help in recreating a melody and playing by ear.

The lyrics are a mirror of both the melody and the rhythm patterns. Consequently, you can make very fast progress in learning to play by ear by working with such songs for about ten minutes per day.

3. The social value of these melodies is also quite high.

These are the songs you will be playing most often at parties and special occasions: birthdays, Christmas festivities, engagements, weddings, divorces, etc. So. it's more than plain ear training and feel for distance. Knowing these kinds of songs is actually part of your responsibility to help keep our society, culture and the republic in good working order.

At the outset, it's easier and more instructive to work with the oldies such as these:

After The Ball Is Over
Drink To Me Only With Thine Eyes
Hark The Herald Angels Sing
Joy To The World
Long, Long Ago
Silent Night
Good Night Ladies
Swanee River
Here Comes The Bride
School Days
America
Auld Lang Syne
Home On The Range
My Old Kentucky Home
There Is A Tavern In The Town
Red River Valley
For He's A Jolly Good Fellow
The Band Played On
In My Merry Oldsmobile
When You Were Sweet Sixteen
In Old New York

These simpler oldies almost always begin on one of the 3 notes of the basic home base chord — root, 3 or 5...

...and usually work very well with Elementary Classical chord progressions.

AND ONE MORE THING about most of these simpler tunes — they usually begin on one of the three notes of the basic chord: on the root, on the 3rd or on the 5th of the home base chord. And that is of great value not only in learning how to pick out a melody by ear but also in learning how to put the harmony under the melody by ear.

So, when it comes to starting the melody, you begin by playing a three-note basic chord with your left hand —a basic C chord, say. And with your right hand, you proceed by trial and error to start the tune on one of those three chordal notes of C, E and G. And thus, in one move you have found a starting note for the song and a home base for the chord progression.

If you can't get the melody to start on one of the three notes of the basic chord, or if you find that the melody starts on some other note, forget the enterprise. The chances will be that the number is too complex for learning with. (*Stardust,* for instance, starts on the Major 7th; *Laura* on the 9th —neither of them the best fare for learning to feel distances or hear progressions on the piano. Wait until you are a bit more competent before tackling the more complicated melodies.)

Starting out with a known home base chord is a great advantage in putting the harmony under the melody.

If you've got the circle of root notes framed and facing you on your piano, then you are more than half-way to putting the chords together with the tune. That is because most of these simpler songs work quite well with Elementary Classical chord progressions —those which move no farther away from the home base than the neighboring root notes on either side. With a melody starting on a home base chord of C, it's quite likely that you will need in addition only the G chord and the F chord to have the minimum, essential chords necessary for the entire number.

AFTER THAT, IT REMAINS ONLY to know when to use each chord —when to change chords. And the answer to that is, simply, that your ear will tell you. When the melody notes begin to sound uncomfortable in the chord setting, it is time to change the chord. (Chord changes usually reinforce the rhythm. In 4/4 time, chords usually change on the first and/or third beat of a measure. In 3/4 time, usually on the first only.)

Trial and error —your ear— will tell you when to change chords. And so will the melody itself. After all, tunes are made of comfortable chordal notes and restless non-chordal notes. In these older standard melodies, there are far more comfortable chordals than unresolved non-chordals. Moreover, the comfortable chordals tend to be not only the vast majority of notes but also the longer-lasting tones on which the melody lingers. You have only to consult the melody to see the *comfortable chordals*

—and they will literally *spell out the chord* which makes them comfortable.

Take a look at the opening bars of *Home On The Range*. You will see in this example that the home base chord is G (with the melody starting on the 5th of that basic chord).

Further, the brackets beneath the melody will indicate how long each chord lasts before changing. Within each bracket, the chordals —the notes-of-the-chord —are in the vast majority as well as being the longest-lasting in duration, and they tell you in plain language the chord to which they belong.

The notes of
the melody
will tell you
which chord makes
most of them
most comfortable.
Read the names
of the notes
in the brackets.
You'll hear yourself
reciting chordals.

HOME ON THE RANGE

But that doesn't mean every note is a member of the chord. Some notes are non-chordals, and being so, they add some restlessness, some spice, to the melody. That points up a very important piece of advice about playing by ear —to wit: *don't try to harmonize every note in the melody.*

Some notes are best left as non-chordals. Changing chords to make each and every note in the melody a comfortable chordal will rob your music of interest. Besides, a chord should usually last at least two quarter notes' duration, giving it a chance to establish itself and sink into consciousness.

THERE'S ONE MORE CAUTION to be mentioned about putting the harmony under the melody when you play by ear. And that advice is: *there's no right or wrong chord progression to choose.*

Elementary Classical movement on the circle may work well. But so also may a Classical jump backward and a clockwise homecoming. And in that regard, a quarter-circle jump may work well —but so also may a longer jump backward. And so, too, a linear progression, either chromatic or tonal, may work with the very same melody.

It's all a matter of what sounds good to you. Just because a number sounds all right to you with one harmonic setting, that doesn't rule out any others. The important thing in learning to play by ear is to work out a bare, essential, minimum chord progression before experimenting with more far-ranging progressions. What you will find most of the time is that the Elementary Classical progressions around home base will serve as the essential minimum.

Take, for example, the opening eight bars of *Jingle Bells*. As you can see, the whole affair can be harmonized with two

First step: put the
minimum harmony
under the melody.

chords —or three — in an Elementary Classical progression,
which moves no farther away from the home base than the
neighboring root notes on either side.

JINGLE BELLS

Having put the minimum harmonization beneath the
melody, you may want to experiment with some additional
chord changes. So, you could add a bit more Elementary
Classical chord movement. In fact, you might try a Classical
jump backward over one intervening stop and then start for
home in the usual clockwise way.

JINGLE BELLS

Next step: en**lar**ge
the progression.
Add the **other** neighbor.
Then **try** a Classical
backward jump and its
clockwise homecoming.

That brief and timid Classical expedition on the circle,
however, is enough to add spice to the over-all sound by
providing the *unexpected*. After that, it becomes an easy experiment to try a Classical quarter-circle jump backward — to hear
whether it sounds good. That's the only test.

JINGLE BELLS

**Until, finally, you
go as far as you
can on the circle.
The only rule is·
how it sounds to you.**

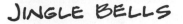

With the gates of experimentation open, you can try a jump
backward longer than a quarter-circle —over three intervening
stops. (After all, it's your piano and your ear, and you are doing no damage to either by trying this or that progression of
chords).

JINGLE BELLS

For the very same reasons, you might want to take your
chord progressions off the circle and move them instead along a
linear path for experiment's sake. (Linear progressions, you
may recall, follow ascending or descending *lines formed by the
bottom notes* of the chords. Those bottom notes are not
necessarily the root notes of the chords. What matters is that

the line move from note to note chromatically along the keyboard, or stepwise tonally along the path of one scale or another, or as a combination of chromatic and tonal steps.)

JINGLE BELLS

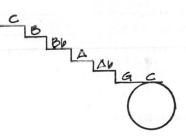

Or you can take the harmony off the circle and try it on a line, making chords which incorporate both the melody notes and the bass notes.

Now, none of these experiments is set out here to suggest that *Jingle Bells* would sound better if its traditional Elementary Classical progressions were replaced by a more sophisticated harmonic setting. The fact is that it's very hard to move traditional tunes away from their expected chord movements. It's a whole lot easier to try new and different progressions with popular songs and show tunes.

But the older, simpler, traditional tunes have the easiest minimum chord progressions to find. For that reason, they are the best material to use for learning how to experiment and elaborate on the bare essential harmony. Such experimentation and elaboration is part and parcel of playing by ear, and people who don't experiment are in jeopardy of playing by pinky.

AND THE SAME IS TRUE when it comes to playing the more sophisticated numbers by ear.

Most popular songs and show tunes will sit on a minimum, Elementary Classical chord movement around the home base. The sound may be a bit inappropriate, of course, just as *Jingle Bells* with a chromatic chord progression would sound somewhat outlandish. But in learning to play by ear it is important to begin even the most up-to-the-minute tune in a rudimentary chord setting before elaborating on it.

So, establish a home base chord (remembering that more sophisticated melodies may start on a note other than the root or 3rd or 5th of that chord). And then, when the melody begins to sound uncomfortable —when the melody tells you to change chords —try the chords on either side of the home base on the circle.

That done, begin experimenting and elaborating on that basic harmonic setting. Try Classical chord progressions, jumping backward over an intervening stop on the circle when a chord change seems necessary; and then move clockwise

Some numbers whose chord progressions begin with a quarter-circle jump:

Heart And Soul
Blue Moon
Once In A While
I Believe
More
The Way You Look Tonight
Paper Doll
My Heart Stood Still

And some whose progressions begin with more than a quarter-circle jump:

Lover Come Back To Me
All Of Me
Five Foot Two, Eyes Of Blue
I Cried For You
Who's Sorry Now?
Someday My Prince Will Come
Sweetheart Of Sigma Chi
Love In Bloom

Mister Sandman
Memories Of You

Some numbers whose progressions begin with less than a quarter-circle jump backward.

Somebody Loves Me
That Old Black Magic
Love Walked In
It's The Talk Of The Town
A Million Dollar Baby
For All We Know
Bidin' My Time
I'm In The Mood For Love

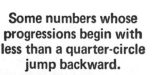

toward home when the next chord change appears obvious. Experiment with longer jumps backward over more intervening stops on the circle, coming home clockwise stop by stop as the melody asks for a change of chord.

That kind of experimentation can accomplish several things, particularly if you keep the sheet music handy for reference. (Checking what you do against what "they" did makes the sheet music a wonderful teacher.)

It will very likely lead you to a close approximation —if not a perfect recreation— of the chord progressions in the original sheet music. And in that way, you will start sorting out pieces of music in your mind according to how much of the circle each needs to sound acceptably good. That is a far cry from learning to play each number by rote. On the contrary, it is an invaluable logical device for building a vast repertoire because it gives you sensible categories for storing the pieces you will be playing.

"Ah yes, *Blue Moon,*" you can tell yourself. "That one jumps backward a quarter-circle on the first chord change; but *Somebody Loves Me* jumps back over only one intervening stop before coming back home."

Experimenting with longer and longer backward jumps can also take your arrangement of a number beyond the original chord progressions and into sounds you may also find very good and very interesting. That is also true of leaving the circle completely and experimenting with linear chord progressions —stepwise chromatic progressions or tonal progressions along the scale.

In any case, such experimentation is wonderful training for playing by ear. It makes you capable of hearing more music, of *growing musically.* It firms up your courage so that you are not intimidated by the tension of non-chordals and don't feel called upon to harmonize each and every tone in the melody. And, finally, such experimentation gives you the self-reliance necessary to playing by ear by proving again that there is no right or wrong harmony; there is only music that sounds either good or bad to you.

SO, THAT COVERS TWO of the components of playing by ear, namely recreating the melody from memory; and putting under it an essential minimum harmony on which to experiment and elaborate.

The final component needed to play by ear is the *timing* of the oncoming melody notes —stating the rhythm of the music. That means you have to know whether the number is in 3/4 time or in 4/4 time. (Most other timings you will need are either multiplications or divisions of those, such as 6/8 time and 2/4.)

There are a couple of simple ways to determine whether a

melody has to be played with three beats per measure or four.

One way is to hum, whistle or sing some of the tune and "conduct" it as a band leader might, using the standard figures in the air painted by a baton. (Those figures might not be obvious with every band leader you see, but they are the basis of the motions he makes as he keeps time for the group.) In most instances of the tunes you will be working with— old standards or new— one or the other figure will describe the beat you need.

Try it for yourself. Sing a few bars of a 3/4 number —*The Man On The Flying Trapeze,* say —and "conduct" it with the triangular figure which provides three beats per bar. You will see that the first stroke of the figure, *the downbeat,* matches the first beat of each measure and, consequently, the accented syllables of the lyrics —

ONCE *I was* HAP-*py but* NOW *I'm for-*LORN . . .

LIKE *an old* COAT *that is* TAT-*tered and* TORN

Those accents in the lyrics work just as well in 4/4 time to tell you that there are four beats per measure. Sing a few bars of *Good Night Ladies* and "conduct" it with the four-beat figure. Once again you will see that the first stroke of the figure, the downbeat, matches the first beat of each measure and coincides with the accented syllables of the lyrics—

GOOD *night ladies,* GOOD *night ladies*

GOOD *night ladies, we're* GOING *to leave you* NOW . . .

Another good way to get a feel for the proper beat is to hum, whistle or sing part of a number *and dance to it.* If you find youself doing a fox trot, you'll know that you have a number in 4/4 time. If you find yourself doing a waltz, then you are obviously working with a number in 3/4 time.

(Now, this is not to suggest that you get up and do a little fandango before playing each number by ear. It is only to say that you probably have a pretty good feel for the beat whether you know it or not. Otherwise you couldn't dance to a number. So, dancing to a few or conducting an imaginary orchestra's rendition will only serve to reassure you.)

There's one real hazard in determining the beat. You may begin counting on an *upbeat* —on the note or notes which precede the first accented downbeat in some numbers. (The upbeat precedes the double line.) Beginning to count beats per measure there, on an upbeat, may throw you off completely and lead you to make gibberish of the number by accenting the wrong notes. It would be like walking in on a cheering crowd at the wrong beat and thinking they were shouting, "Rayhoo! Rayhoo!"

How can you tell whether a number begins on an upbeat —on an incomplete bar —and where to start counting the beat? That's easy. Let the lyrics tell you. The first *accented* word or

How a conductor conducts a number in 3/4 time and a few numbers in it:

After The Ball Is Over (3)
Drink To Me Only With Thine Eyes (3)
Home On The Range (5)
Silent Night (5)
The Band Played On (5)
Happy Birthday To You (5)
A Bicycle Built For Two (5)
In My Merry Oldsmobile (5)
The Man On The Flying Trapeze (5)
In Old New York (5)
School Days (3)
Take Me Out To The Ballgame (root)
East Side, West Side (5)

The baton's movements for numbers in 4/4 time and a few to try it on:

America (5)
Auld Lang Syne (5)
Dixie (5)
Hark The Herald Angels Sing (5)
Joy To The World (root)
Long, Long Ago (root)
My Old Kentucky Home (3)
There Is A Tavern In The Town (5)
For He's A Jolly Good Fellow (3)
Jingle Bells (3)
Here Comes The Bride (5)

DRINK TO ME ONLY WITH THINE EYES

DRINK TO ME ON-LY WITH THINE

First accented syllable
falls on the first note,
so this one begins on the
downbeat. And so do these:

After The Ball Is Over
Drink To Me Only With Thine Eyes
Hark The Herald Angels Sing
Joy To The World
Long, Long Ago
Silent Night
Good Night Ladies
Swanee River
Here Comes The Bride
School Days

OH-H SAY CAN YOU SEE

The first accent in lyrics
comes after the double line.
So, this one begins on
the upbeat.
And so do these listed here:

America
Auld Lang Syne
Home On The Range
My Old Kentucky Home
There Is A Tavern In The Town
Red River Valley
For He's A Jolly Good Fellow
The Band Played On
In My Merry Oldsmobile
When You Were Sweet Sixteen
In Old New York

---

syllable in the lyrics is the first downbeat, and consequently the place to start counting the beat. But that first accented word or syllable may not be the first word of the song, or even the second word . . . .

"In the GOOD old summertime" clearly begins with an upbeat of two notes. So you start counting the 3/4 beat on the third word, "good."

"Oh COME all ye faithful" has the downbeat on the second word. That's where the 4/4 time begins. That's where the double line is.

But in *Jingle Bells,* the downbeat coincides with the first word of the lyrics —"DASH-*ing through the* SNOW" —so you begin the 4/4 count right from the jump.

On the other hand, *The Star Spangled Banner* begins with a two-note upbeat. The downbeat falls on the third note of the melody, and so the 3/4 time begins there. It sings this way: "O-oh SAY can you SEE . . ."

ONCE YOU HAVE THE PROPER RHYTHM for the number, it remains only to arrange it —to treat it with a skeleton arrangement, or an arpeggio or open voicing or full block or other setting. Which one you use depends, naturally, on what sounds good to you *at the time.*

It would be surprising if you arranged a number the same way each time you worked with it. It would also be surprising if you liked every treatment you tried on a number —or if you continued to prefer one treatment to all others all the time.

There are really only two generalities you can make when it comes to putting an arrangement together.

First, an arrangement should make a pattern —just as a melody makes a pattern. And that means a *repetition* of arrangement devices. So don't use too many of them, and put them together *with the melody,* arranging in full parts or half parts. (For a reminder on this matter of patterned arranging, take another look at CHAPTER 19.)

And second, preserve the *style* of a song when you arrange it. *Jingle Bells* will probably work out much better with some sort of skeleton treatment than played as a bolero. But few popular songs have any traditional style to preserve. *Blue Moon,* for instance, might work out quite well as a bolero.

SO, PUT IN A NUTSHELL: Playing by ear means recreating a melody from memory and putting some sort of harmony under it in a rhythmic way.

Recreating a melody requires that you have a melody in mind to recreate, and that you develop a feel for distances among the notes on the keyboard by picking out single-note melodies. Most older, simpler tunes begin on one of

the three notes of the home base chord.

Finding the harmony means putting together the barest minimum chord progressions from the home base chord. Usually, Elementary Classical movement will suffice. In simpler tunes, too, the melody notes will spell out the chords required. Once you have a minimum harmony, experiment with farther-ranging chord movement —on the circle and/or on a chromatic or tonal line. But don't harmonize every note. Some restless non-chordals are necessary spice.

Finding the rhythm is easier if you sing and either "conduct" the rendition or dance to it. But make sure you begin counting on the downbeat only. The lyrics will help you find the downbeat.

The arrangement you put together is not irrevocable. Most numbers can be played with many, many different treatments. Just make sure your arrangement is patterned and appropriate.

Expect to make mistakes as you learn to play by ear.

Higher chord tension— b5, sus4, 9th, 11th, 13th, &c

36

IN A SENSE, ANY ALTERATION of the basic three-note chord makes for an uncomfortable, unresolved sound —or at least it once felt that way.

There might well have been a time when even the solid minor chord had considerable tension compared with the basic chord. And even now there is still an unsettled quality to both the diminished and augmented chords. The melody seldom rests atop those two, and a number almost never ends with them. Or not yet, anyway.

The same has been true of additions to the basic three-note chord (and to its alterations, of course). The added 6th is still relatively new as a *named* four-note chord. The Major 7th is even newer and, to many, it is still a fairly high tension chord, an uncomfortable —but pleasing— sound. The 7th chord, of course, is much older than either of those two, and there is seemingly nothing usettled about it anymore. But on the other hand, it is used mainly in progressions *enroute* home because it is basically an unresolved chord which wants to move onward, homeward, clockwise, on the circle.

In a sense, then, the development of chords in our music has

been the history of created tensions (and their resolutions). There may be a general principle to be found in that view: perhaps something about tension being the spice of life (contrary to what the tranquilizer makers would have us believe). Or maybe the general principle is: the bigger they are, the harder they fall and thus the more comfortable they finally feel . . .

But whatever the moral lesson about life in general, you can look at most chords-with-explanations and most chords-higher-than-a-7th as instructions for increasing tension in the sound. And as for following those instructions and making the chords called for, that's simply a matter of using your knowledge about how chords are made.

Take the chord symbol C7b5. Now, that's a chord with an explanation just as older sheet music called for *CaddA* when it was explaining how to play a C6 chord. In this instance, C7b5 explains clearly that it wants a C7 chord with an alteration in one of the basic three notes, namely the 5th lowered one interval. The reason for the explanation is that there is as yet *no name* for an alteration of the basic chord which flats only the 5th —just as once upon a time there was no name for the C6 chord.

(Actually, a C chord with only its 5th flatted is a *half-way* C diminished chord —a *C nished,* so to speak. But it will probably be years before the world is ready for that name. If ever.)

Take another chord-with-explanation: *C7sus4* —or, as it is sometimes explained in the chord symbol, *C457.*

That is another C7 chord, and once again it calls for an alteration within the basic three notes of the chord. But this alteration has a name: the "sus" or *suspension.* And what it tells you is: play a C7 chord *but raise the 3rd one interval.*

By doing so, you are making a chord by combining the root, the *4th* and the 5th. If you try it on your piano, you will hear that it is not only unexpected but also rather discordant.

That will explain why you will usually find suspensions followed almost immediately by the expected and comfortable chord. A *C7sus4* is usually followed by a chord in which the suspended 4th is resolved into the expected 3rd, thus reducing the discomfort. That will also explain why this device is named a suspension. It creates its tension by means of suspense, making you wait through discord for resolution.

Locating the 4th in order to play these suspensions is simple. You have only to look at the circle again, and you will find the 4th named *one stop clockwise ahead* of the chord you are working with. The 4th note of the basic C scale is F. It is the note needed to replace the 3rd, (the E), and turn the basic C chord into a *Csus4* chord. You will find that 4th, that F, named on the circle just forward of C, the *root note* of the chord you are

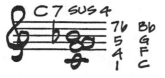

working with.

Similarly, a basic A chord becomes an *Asus4* when you raise the 3rd one interval and play the 4th. That needed 4th is D. It is named one stop clockwise ahead of A (which is the root note of the *Asus4* chord). But whatever the chord, the suspended 4th will usually be resolved into the 3rd at the next attack. For an excellent example of *sus4* chords in use, see *Lover* by Richard Rodgers.

WHEN IT COMES TO CHORDS higher than a 7th or Maj7 —9th chords, 11th chords, 13th chords —their tension is created by *adding notes onto the four-note 7th or Maj7 chords.*

Which notes are added? Exactly those you expect to find added to the four-note string of 1 + 3 + 5 + 7.

That, of course, exhausts the available notes for the chord in that octave. So, any chord longer than four notes has to take its tone or tones from the next octave up the keyboard. And that, in turn, means looking on the next octave up the keyboard *as a continuation of the one below.*

In that event, that next octave does not begin with note No. 1. Instead, it begins with note No. 8. What was the 2nd in the basic scale an octave below now carries the number 9 up here. The 3rd down there, as you recall from the 10th chord, is note No. 10 up here. And so on, with the 6th below becoming the 13th above.

Under the circumstances, it is elementary arithmetic to construct a C9 chord. You begin with a C7 chord and add onto it the D above. If you want the general formula for finding the 9th —it is the note *two intervals above the root* of whatever chord you're working with. (But usually with 9th chords, the added 9th note is the melody note.)

Under those circumstances, it's the same, plain addition to construct a *CMaj9* chord. You begin with a CMaj7 chord and add onto it the D above as usual.

A *C11* chord? Easy. You begin with a C7 chord and add onto it the 9th and 11th — the D and the F above. The 11th above is the 4th in the octave below. If you need its name in a hurry, just look at the circle for the note named one stop clockwise ahead of the root note of the chord you're working with.

A *C13* chord, as you would expect, is the C11 with the A added onto it. The 13th, obviously, is the upstairs name for the 6th.

The suspended 4th alters the basic 3-note chord by sharping the 3rd, making it the 4th.

The "sus4" tension is resolved by the next chord.

The 4th is found 1 stop clockwise ahead of the root.

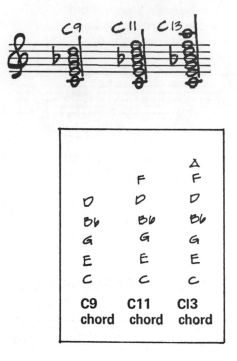

C9   C11   C13

		A
	F	F
D	D	D
B♭	B♭	B♭
G	G	G
E	E	E
C	C	C
C9 **chord**	**C11** **chord**	**C13** **chord**

The 11th is merely the 4th
an octave up. It is found
1 stop clockwise ahead
of the root.

As for any additional instructions which might be affixed to such longer, drawn out chords higher than a 7th —*C Maj13,* say, or *C 11b9* —well, use your head. A *C Maj13* begins with a C Maj7 chord. A *C 11b9* is merely a C11 chord with the D lowered one interval, and consequently played as D*b.*

In principle, the longer a chord and the more strung out, the higher its tension. So, in theory, the highest tension chord of this lot is the seven-note 13th chord. But despite its high tension name, number and appearance, it is really an 11th chord with the old, standard, familiar added 6th note on top —thus robbing the 13th of its punch and leaving the 11th chord with the highest tension of all.

The 11th chord, obviously, is a six-note chord. It is made by adding onto the 7th or Maj7 chord the 9th and the 11th. (The 9th is the 2nd one octave up. And the 11th is the 4th up in that octave.) You already know how to locate them: The 9th is two intervals above the root; the 11th is one stop clockwise ahead of the root on the circle.

The *raised* 11th chord —the 4th raised an interval in that next octave up— has a *lower* tension than the unaltered 11th chord. That is because the raised 11th chord has been widely heard for more than a century in the works of the Impressionist composers.

But if sheet music calls for a raised 11th chord —an F11♯, say— you can find the necessary tone easily by looking at the circle. The raised 11th is named directly opposite the *root note of the chord* you are working with. In the case of an F chord, its raised 11th tone is B —named diametrically across the circle. So, you add B to the F9 chord to make an F11♯ chord. (And vice versa. To make a B11♯ chord, you add an F to a B9 chord.) And so on around the circle, with the raised 11th tone named directly across the circle from the chord to which it belongs.

NATURALLY, THE RAISED 11TH, like the unaltered 11th, is added to a 9th chord —thus making a six-note chord in total. As for the 9th chord, that is a five-note chord inasmuch as the 9th is added to the four-note 7th or Maj7 chord. In the same way, the 13th chord is a seven-note chord —the 13th tone being added to the 11th and 9th tones.

To play only the highest note of the structure on top of the basic three-note chord or three-note altered chord is to drain the tension out of the long, drawn out structure. A basic C chord with an added F is not an 11th chord. It is simply a C chord with a 4th added. It does not provide its real tension and excitement until you insert the 7th tone and the 9th tone under the 11th — that is, until you use the supporting members of the structure.

Very few readers, even the most faithful, will be able to play a six-note or seven-note chord with one hand. And there's no real advantage in playing a five-note chord with one hand, either. You can much more easily spread these long chords out over two hands, dividing the notes between the chord and the block, and thus build the entire structure beneath the melody notes.

In fact, these high-tension chords sound their best with plenty of ventilation to let the overtones escape. So, these chords are excellent material for use in 10th chord position and open voicing arrangements. For a refresher on them, take another look at CHAPTERS 22 and 23.

One further item to keep in mind about these tall, brittle chords: The root note of the chord has to be clearly stated at the *bottom of the structure*. If you play the root note as a bass note, there can be no doubt about it. And having done that, you may not need to state the root in the chord itself. (In fact, once the root has been stated, you can play the upper several notes of the chord in just about any order.)

But without the root clearly mentioned at the bottom, the chord will sound unmoored, rootless, free-floating. (That effect was sought after by the Impressionist composers, and captured unmistakably by Debussy in *Reverie*. If it's the effect you want, then don't mention the root.) But without the root definitely stated, the chord is in jeopardy of losing its identity on the circle or line. In that case, the sense of *chord progression* may be lost when you change chords from tension to resolution. Consequently, the tension may not be resolved —which is no way to treat a listening ear.

IN A NUTSHELL, THEN: More and more you will see chord symbols calling for chords-with-explanations, suspensions, and numbers higher than 7 attached to them. For the most part, your knowledge of how chords are made will tell you what to do about playing these higher-tension chords.

Generally, they fall into two categories: those which *alter* the basic three-note chord (such as the ♭5 chord and the *sus4* chord); and those which *add notes* onto the four-note 7th or Maj7 chord.

Those higher-than-a-7 chords are the 9th, 11th and 13th chords (and their alterations such as ♭9th and raised 11th chords). They are five, six and seven-note chords. Spread their notes out over two hands, using chord and block notes to produce the sound. The root should be stated clearly. If it is stated as a bass note, it's not needed in the chord. But the supporting members of the chord are needed— the 7th (for a 9th chord), the 7th and 9th (for an 11th cord), etc.

The 9th, like the 2nd, is named two intervals above the

The raised 11th sits directly across the circle from the root, making each the other's raised 11th.

REVERIE (DEBUSSY)

The root note isn't at the bottom of the chord. That makes for a free-floating sound.

root. The 11th, like the 4th, is one stop ahead of the root on the circle. The raised 11th is directly opposite the root on the circle. The 13th is the 6th an octave up.

How to end a number

37

ONE TROUBLE WITH A LOT OF BOOKS about how to play the piano is that they never tell you how to *stop* playing the piano. That is, you don't find out how to end a number until it is too late and you are removed bodily from the piano bench and wrapped in cool, wet sheets. So this book will make amends for the rest of the library.

When it comes to hymns, there is no difficulty about ending. It is *Amen* — two long chords or three.

But in the case of standard numbers, there is only an indication of how to treat a goodbye. And that hint is to be found in the *number of beats* in the final two bars.

In waltzes, usually, there are four beats to finish with. And they are played with separate, single-note attacks of the chord tones. While the final chord is sounded and dies away (your foot is on the sustaining pedal), you play the individual notes of the chord in a down-the-keyboard arpeggio — hitting the root, the 5th, the 3rd and the root again— to account for those final four beats. As a variation, you can use root, 3rd, 5th and root.

Hymns usually end with 2 or 3 chords for the Amen.

A waltz ends with 4 octave basses and a curtsy.

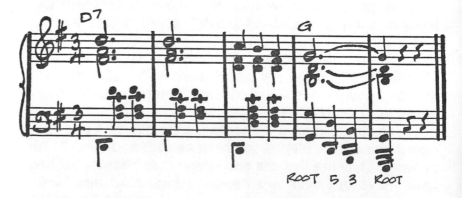

In the case of 4/4 time, the final two bars usually provide seven beats. So, the first four (the next-to-last bar) gets a skeleton bass-&-chord treatment. And the last bar, with its three beats, gets three attacks —the root, then the 5th and finally the root again— dropping down the keyboard.

190

GOOD NIGHT READERS*

GOOD NIGHT READERS WE'RE GOING TO LEAVE YOU NOW

End a 4/4 number in 2 bars:
a bar of straight skeleton
followed by a bar of
root-5th-root octave basses.
Applause is optional.

*IN A NUTSHELL: The end.

How to play the piano despite years of lessons

Contents *

Try it on your own piano

By Ward Cannel and Fred Marx

Part eleven

A bonus. A supplement. A folio for making music and expressing yourself at the keyboard. For amazing your friends, your relatives and yourself. For use on holidays, birthdays, weddings, divorces and other important occasions. With suggestions, explanations and diagrams for both arranging these numbers and learning to play by ear, using all the techniques you now know.

Read this first

You can get picture of arranger's setting without reading it note-by-note.

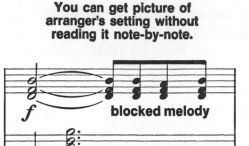

bass-&-chord

blocked melody

Skeleton variation

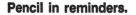

Pencil in reminders.

Guitar and uke fingering diagrams beneath chord name.

AS THE ROOSTER SAID, CALLING THE HENS TOGETHER to look at a big goose egg: "It might help you in your work to see what others are doing."

Consequently, the music in this folio contains the full piano arrangements supplied by the sheet music publisher. Even though you'll be working with only the vocalist's melody line and chord symbols above it, it might be helpful to see what others are doing and what they consider appropriate arranging.

Not that you have to follow their advice. On the contrary. Just about any tune can sit atop just about any arrangement — skeleton or variation of it, arpeggio, open voicing, locked hands, bolero and the rest. But in real life, some settings may not sound suitable. *I Love You Truly* might be a bit insincere in shuffle rhythm. Too many arrangement devices could turn *Joy To The World* into chaos. The Major 7th chord, well-established for a generation, may stick out like too modern a thumb in a number written in the gay 90s. Higher tension chords such as the raised 11th and suspended 4th might sound out of place in hymns, which are songs of comfort and affirmation.

So, it could be beneficial to see what's going on in these arrangements, if only to observe what professional propriety says about how to do things —and then to disregard it and do what sounds good to you. (No, you don't have to know how to read the notes of these piano settings to get the picture and see what sort of attacks are used to break the silence. And anyway, everything will be spelled out in detailed captions and diagrams throughout this folio.)

All of that said, it remains only to mention:

1. Feel free to deface this supplement with graffiti. Write in the names of chord notes if you need them, and devices to try here and there. But use a pencil so that you can erase when you change your mind. And don't arrange a number until you are familiar with its raw material —the path of the melody and the chords called for.

2. Enlarge three-note chords and play them as four-note chords. Play basic chords as 6th chords or as Major 7th chords (depending on which sounds better to you). Play minor chords as minor 7th chords. Naturally, this advice applies only to chords without numbers. If a *Cm6* is printed, don't play it as a Cm7.

3. Some sheet music carries diagrams for guitar and ukulele. The black dots in the diagrams indicate finger placement. The circles above indicate a string left open, unfingered. The name of the chord itself is printed **above** the diagram along with symbols for altering or adding to it.

4. If you find a four-bar introduction to a number (no lyrics, no chord symbols) you can try it if you like. But it's not essential to the number or to your arrangement.

5. Most popular songs have two endings indicated. Often the first ending leads you into mid-air, forcing you to go back to the beginning of the chorus (the double line, usually) and play the whole thing again and finish with the resolved, final second ending. So, if you want to play the chorus once only, by-pass the first ending and play the second ending only.

Sometimes the second ending comes a lot earlier than the last bar or two of the number. (See *Ida! Sweet as apple cider!* on page 223.) Such a chorus isn't complete unless you play through the first ending, go back and play through the chorus again, and finish with the second ending.

6. Composers often give instructions for the proper feeling. *Moderato,* they may demand. Or *allegretto.* Or *with expression.* In everyday language, such terms mean *play what sounds good to you.*

7. In newer sheet music you may find very small notes printed at the very bottom of the bass or left-hand piano part. These notes are for organists and refer to the pedals. Piano players, please disregard.

8. In newer sheet music, too, chord symbols may be two letters divided by a slash. For example: G/A. The first letter is the chord name. The second, beyond the slash, is the bass note to use with that chord. So, G/A means a basic *G* chord with an *A* bass note.

Why? Because the arranger wants a particular sequence of single notes heard in the bass —a particular bass line— to make for an interesting sound. Look at the piano bass part and see for yourself.

9. The old songs of bygone days make excellent material for learning to play by ear. The tunes are so well-known that you can get them in mind readily. They usually start on one of the three notes of the home base chord. Usually, too, the minimum necessary chords are few. If more than that minimum are called for in the printed sheet music, you can often delete the extras without any jeopardy. You will see that done in this folio. Try these numbers both ways —with and without the crossed-out chords —to hear the difference for yourself.

On the other hand, you can often brighten up a tired number by enlarging the chord progression beyond what the sheet music calls for. So, insert a chord farther back on the circle and make a longer stepwise, clockwise homecoming of the harmony. Consequently, here and there in this folio you'll see chords added and inserted by hand in the printed arrangements

But nobody says you have to follow that advice. All anybody said was: *if it sounds good to you, then it is good.* In other words, as ye fool around, so shall ye find.

1st and 2nd endings.

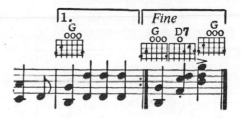

Play it both ways to hear the difference.

In the good old summer time

Lyrics by REN SHIELDS
Music by GEORGE EVANS

THE PRINTED BASS PIANO PART reveals pattern of attacks you can translate easily into a variation of skeleton setting —bass-ch-ch-chord. It's shown beneath the first bar of the tune. The inserted chords are optional. They enlarge the harmony with a longer jump backward on the circle. Try it.

Introductions are optional. You can begin with the chorus. That's where the words start.

Skeleton variation

Oom-p-p-pah. Also known as Bass-ch-ch-chord.

A longer jump backward on circle.

lanes with your ba - by mine, _____ You hold her

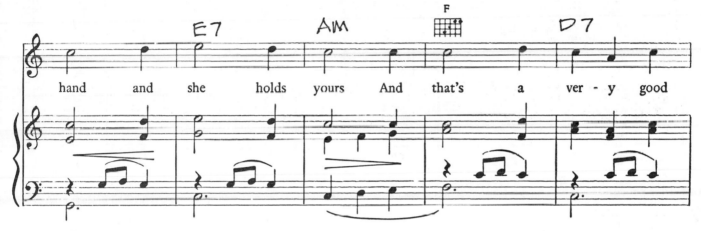

hand and she holds yours And that's a ver - y good

sign _____ That she's your toot - sey woot - sey

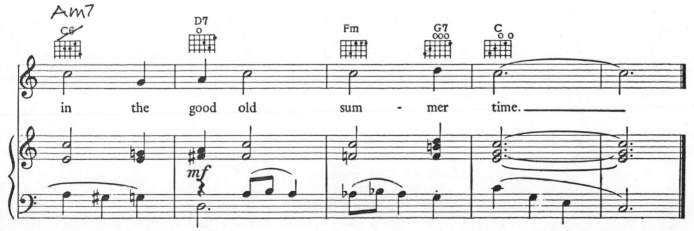

in the good old sum - mer time. _____

Work, for the night is coming

Lyrics by A.L. COGHILL
Music by L. MASON

Tiny bass notes for organ pedals. Pianists, disregard!

Work, for the night is coming, Work thru the morning hours;

Work when the dew is sparkling, Work 'mid springing flowers;

Work when the day grows brighter; Work in the glowing sun;

Work, for the night is coming, When man's work is done. A - men.

Basically, it's Elementary Classical harmony, with home base on G and movement to its neighbors D and C.

Amazing grace

Lyrics by JOHN NEWTON
Music: ANONYMOUS

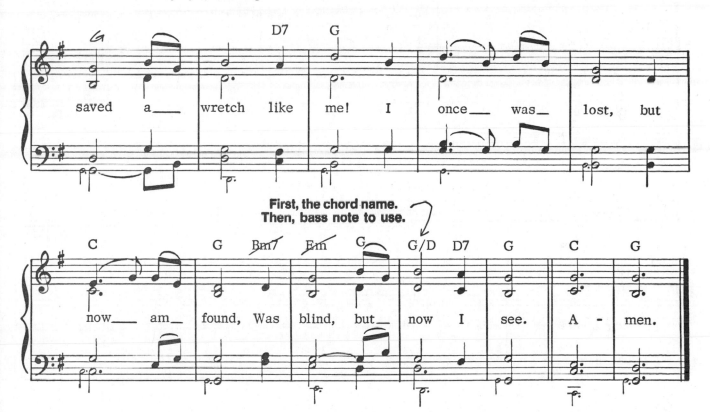

Try open voicing

First, the chord name.
Then, bass note to use.

A - maz - ing grace! How sweet the sound, That saved a wretch like me! I once was lost, but now am found, Was blind, but now I see. A - men.

A BRIEF REMINDER. Our harmony follows this route in most of our songs. The key signature names the home base chord. Elementary Classical progressions move no farther from home base than the neighbor on either side. But much more often, progressions are Classical. Chords begin with a backward jump from the home base over intervening stops on the circle. Then they come back home clockwise, touching each stop along the way. Once home, they jump backward again . . .

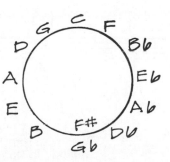

O little town of Bethlehem

**Lyrics and music by
LEWIS H. REDNER and
PHILLIPS BROOKS**

CHRISTMAS CAROLS, LIKE HYMNS, often sound their best arranged as blocked melody supported by 10th chords. In that arrangement, as in open voicing, the melody is played where printed. If you change to an arpeggio setting, the melody stratum changes to an octave higher. Make that jump logically—after the silent stars go by (bar 8).

Part begins here.

Try arpeggio

* Melody in bar 2 requires Gm chord. So. Elementary Classical harmony won't work. A backward jump on circle is needed.

We wish you a merry Christmas

TRADITIONAL

A VERY SIMPLE SONG, so treat it very simply. Try a skeleton arrangement with blocked melody played an octave higher than printed. Mix it with variation of skeleton attacks. But if you do so, be sure the mix makes a pattern. Too many variations and settings create chaos.

Falling in love with love

Lyrics by LORENZ HART
Music by RICHARD RODGERS

STRIPPED OF THE PRINTED piano parts is a version of a number known in the trade as a lead sheet— melody line, chord symbols and lyrics only. With this information, you have all you need to create your own arrangement. Just keep one thing in mind. This waltz is too fast for anything more than skeleton and its variations. Here, ingenuity works in altering the traditional chords and progressions.

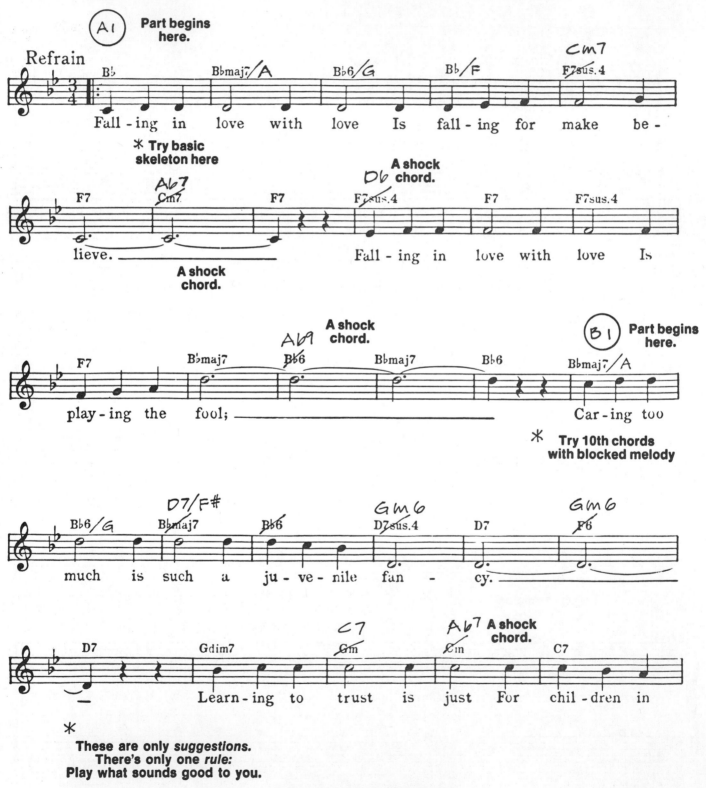

* Try basic skeleton here

A shock chord.

A shock chord.

* Try 10th chords with blocked melody

*
These are only *suggestions*.
There's only one *rule*:
Play what sounds good to you.

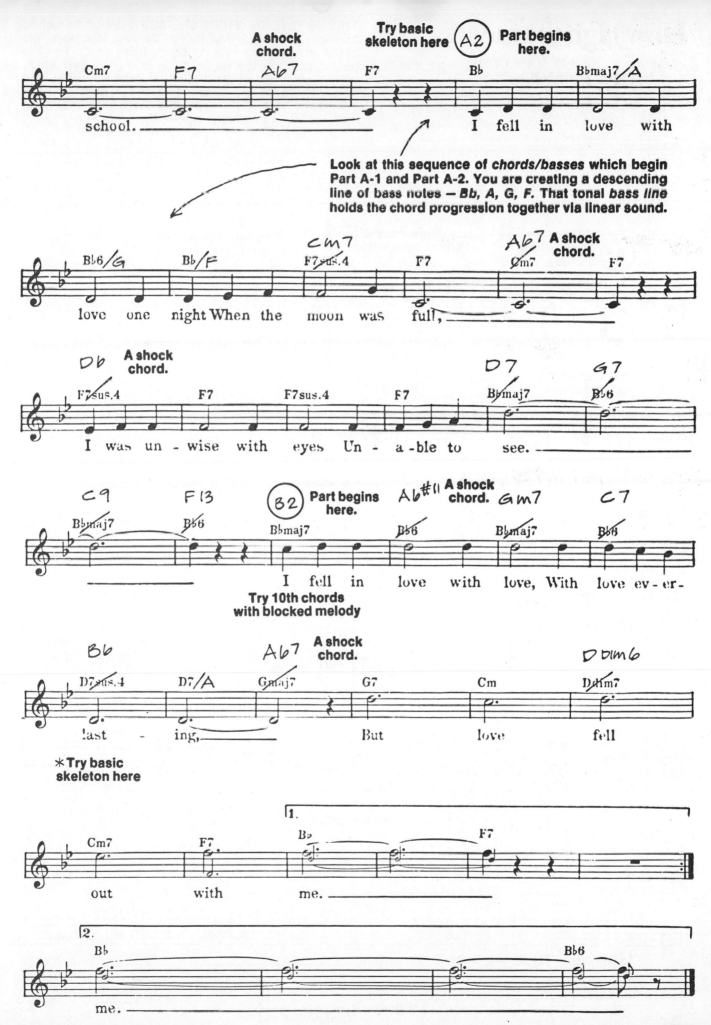

Look at this sequence of *chords/basses* which begin Part A-1 and Part A-2. You are creating a descending line of bass notes — *Bb, A, G, F*. That tonal *bass line* holds the chord progression together via linear sound.

Try 10th chords with blocked melody

*Try basic skeleton here

203

How high the moon

Lyrics by NANCY HAMILTON
Music by MORGAN LEWIS

THIS IS ONE OF THE EARLIEST uses of Romantic harmony in popular music. For the first four bars, the chord progression has its home base on G. For the next four bars, the home base is on F —two stops *clockwise ahead* of the first home base. And that shift of home bases is repeated in the second A part. (Romantic harmony is explained more fully beginning on page 161.) The form is ABAC.

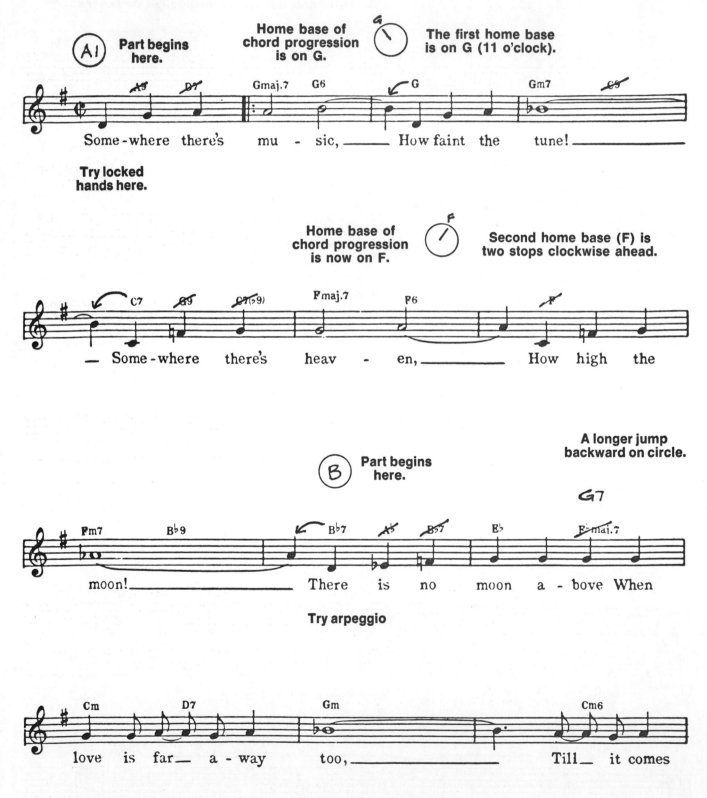

Bill Bailey, won't you please come home

Lyrics and music by
HUGHIE CANNON

A STANDARD FROM DIXIELAND to Dayton. So, no expected setting. It's free for use as... well, try a tango, bolero, skeleton, shuffle, etc. B chord in next-to-last line enlarges progression on circle. Look at the bass line called for in bars 5,6 and 8. Read up on linear harmony (page 167) and try it for yourself.

Allegretto

"Won't you come home, Bill Bai - ley? Won't you come home?"

Skeleton variation

She moans de whole day long. _____ "I'll do de

Stepwise bass notes & tune notes form outer shape of chords _you_ choose.

cook - ing, dar - ling; I'll pay de rent; I knows I've done you

wrong. _____ 'Mem - ber dat rain - y eve Dat I drove you

out Wid noth - ing but a fine tooth comb? _____ I

It's also a
Cdim6 chord.

know I'se to blame, Well, ain't dat a shame? Bill

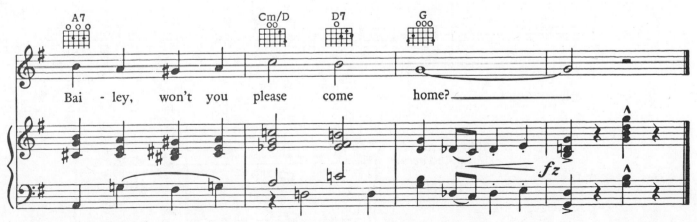

Bai - ley, won't you please come home? _____

Come, ye thankful people, come

Lyrics by H. ALFORD
Music by G.J. ELVEY

WHY SO MANY CHORD CHANGES in simple hymns? Because hymns are often sung in unison by untrained voices, making it likely that non-chordal notes in the tune will stand out as uncomfortable sounds. The solution: harmonize most of the notes, making each a member of a chord. Crossing out some of the chords, restores non-chordal notes to the tune and makes it more interesting. Try it both ways on your piano to prove it.

* 10th chords are indicated here.

Try this variation.

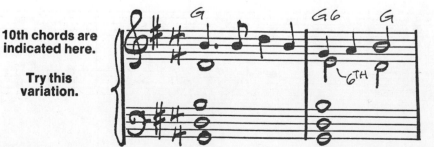

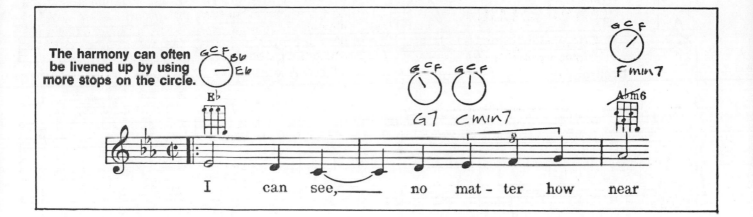

I can dream, can't I?

Lyrics by IRVING KAHAL
Music by SAMMY FAIN

THIS NUMBER COMES in the form A-B-A-C. If you arrange it in parts, it's a good idea to treat both A parts the same way so as to make a pattern. B and C can be treated differently. For instance—play A-1 in locked-hands style; play B in skeleton; A-2 locked-hands again; and finally C as arpeggio. Or you could use a bolero throughout the entire number.

P.S. Whatever settings you use, save the fullest treatment for the end of the number so as to finish big.

211

The old-time religion

Lyrics and music:
ANONYMOUS

THE MATTER OF STYLE and suitability is clearly revealed in this song. The lush arpeggio obviously sounds much too fancy. And open voicing may be too sedate. That's because this tune is reminiscent of camp meetings. So, you might try a skeleton setting and a variation or two of that oom-pah-oom-pah.

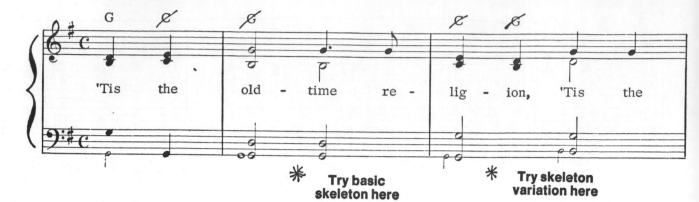

'Tis the old - time re - lig - ion, 'Tis the

Try basic skeleton here

Try skeleton variation here

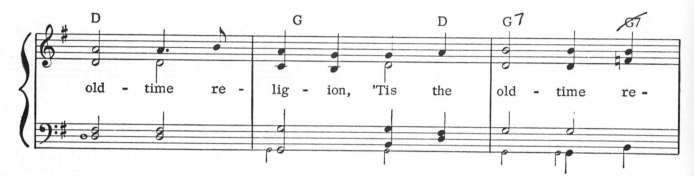

old - time re - lig - ion, 'Tis the old - time re -

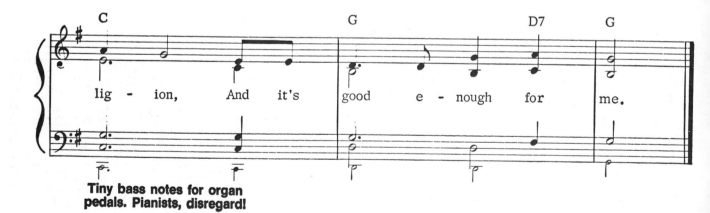

lig - ion, And it's good e - nough for me.

Tiny bass notes for organ pedals. Pianists, disregard!

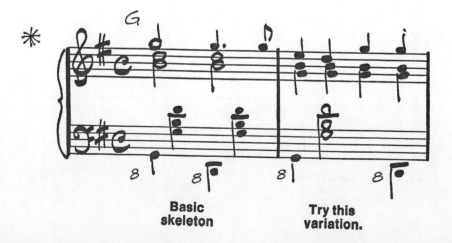

Basic skeleton

Try this variation.

Nearer, my God, to Thee

Lyrics by S.F. ADAMS
Music by L. MASON

THE TOPIC OF SUITABILTY (cont'd.)
This hymn has the more traditional and slow-moving style. So, there's plenty of time for each chord to sink in and make itself felt. A four-note, well-ventilated, overall chordal sound of open voicing will lend the necessary, expected decorum. But look at the printed arrangement. Many notes of the tune are part of thin two-note or three-note over-all sounds.

10th chords are *
indicated here.

Near-er, my God, to Thee, Near-er to Thee! E'en though it be a cross That rais-eth me; Still all my song shall be, Near-er, my God, to Thee; Near-er, my God, to Thee, Near-er to Thee. A-men.

* **10th chord indicated.**

213

A foggy day

Lyrics by IRA GERSHWIN
Music by GEORGE GERSHWIN

ANOTHER LEAD SHEET. But it's all you need to be your own arranger. Just watch the activity of the melody. Are the bars sparse or busy? That will determine how busy or sparse you make your setting. Something — but not *everything*—should be going on all the time. For a slow version, you might alternate one part shuffle rhythm with one part open-voicing. A faster version can be made with skeleton-and-variation. Arpeggio may not work because of syncopation in the melody.

The form is ABAC.

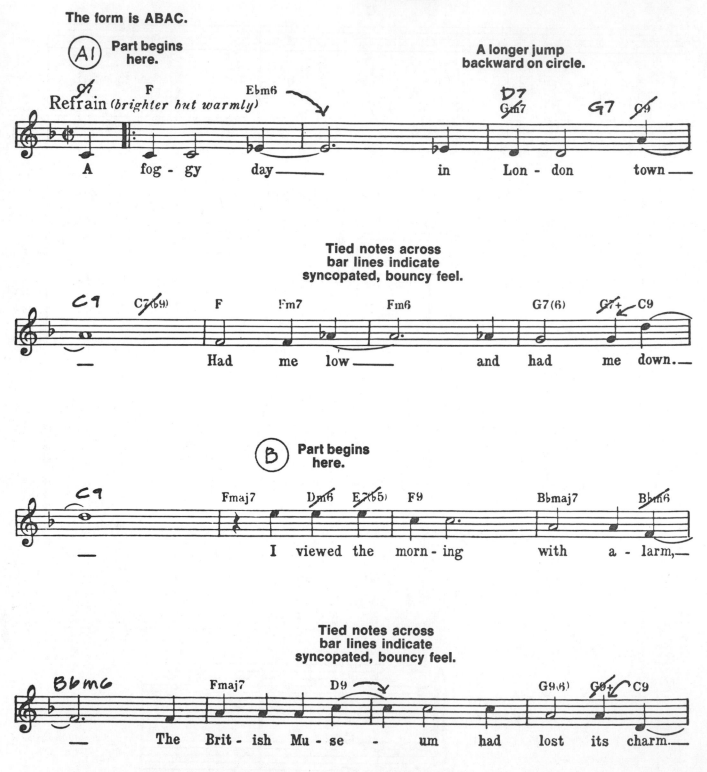

A1 Part begins here.

A longer jump backward on circle.

Refrain *(brighter but warmly)*

A fog - gy day ———— in Lon - don town ———

Tied notes across bar lines indicate syncopated, bouncy feel.

— Had me low ——— and had me down.

B Part begins here.

— I viewed the morn - ing with a - larm,—

Tied notes across bar lines indicate syncopated, bouncy feel.

— The Brit - ish Mu - se - um had lost its charm.——

215

O come, all ye faithful

Translation by F. OAKLEY
Music: WARD'S "CANTUS DIVERSI"

LOOK AT IT THIS WAY. A congregation has to hit an A and a C in the tune while the organ plays a G chord (see footnote).* Result: the voices sing two non-chordals, potentially sour sounds. Much safer to harmonize most non-chordals, even if the final sound is bland. That explains in part why so many hymns and Christmas carols are often crammed with needless chords.

Try open voicing

Remember: tiny lowest bass notes are for organ pedals.

Try arpeggio

216

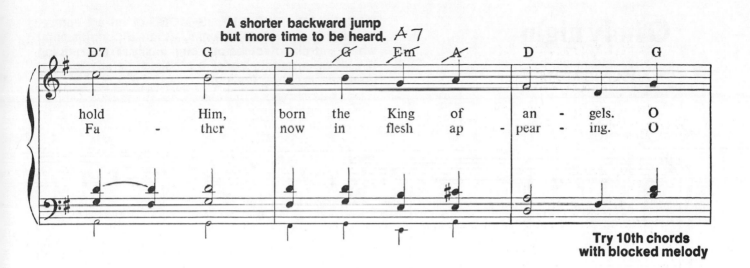

A shorter backward jump but more time to be heard. A7

D7		G		D	G	Em	A	D		G

hold   Him,   born   the   King   of   an - gels.   O

Fa - ther   now   in   flesh   ap - pear - ing.   O

Try 10th chords with blocked melody

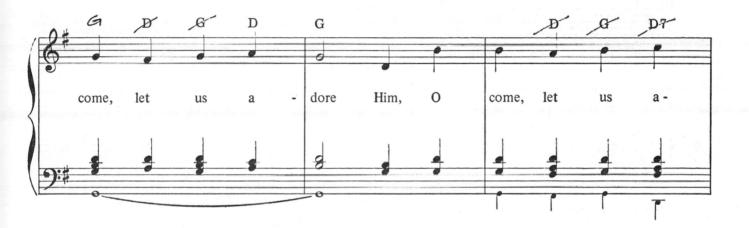

| G | D | G | D | G | | | D | G | D7 |

come,   let   us   a - dore   Him,   O   come,   let   us   a -

A longer backward jump than the sheet music uses. B7   Em Am

| G | D | G | D7 | G | D | Em | D | D7 | G | C | G | D7 | G |

dore   Him,   O   come,   let   us   a - dore   Him, ___   Christ, ___   the   Lord.

*Bar No. 3 with voices singing A and C as notes-not-of-the-chord. (×) Now see how the sheet music makes them chordals.

G $\binom{D}{B}{G}$

B   A   B   C
   ×   ×

217

O holy night

Lyrics and music by
ADOLPHE ADAM

BASICALLY, THIS ONE IS MORE of an art song—like *Because* and *At Dawning*—than a popular song which untrained voices can sing easily. Try arranging it with an arpeggio under a blocked melody for that good old art song feeling.

Moderately

1. O ho-ly night, the stars are bright-ly shin - ing, It is the
(2.) light of faith se - rene-ly beam - ing, With glow-ing
(3.) taught us to love one an - oth - er,

Try arpeggio *

night of the dear Sav-ior's birth. _____ Long lay the world in
hearts by His cra - dle we stand. _____ So, led by light of
love and His gos - pel is peace, _____ Chains shall He break, for the

C7 chord with 5th note flatted.

sin and er - ror pin - ing, Till He ap - pear'd and the soul felt its
star sweet-ly gleam - ing, Here come the wise men from the O - rient
slave is our broth - er, And in His name all op - pres - sion shall

worth. _____ A thrill of hope, the wea - ry world re -
land. _____ The King of kings lay thus in low - ly
cease. _____ Sweet hymns of joy in grate - ful cho - rus

218

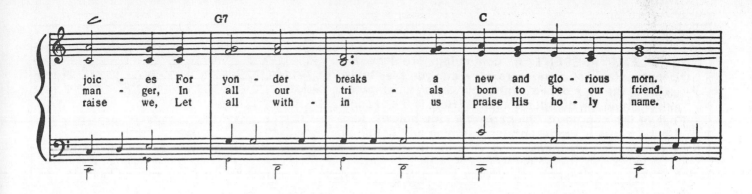

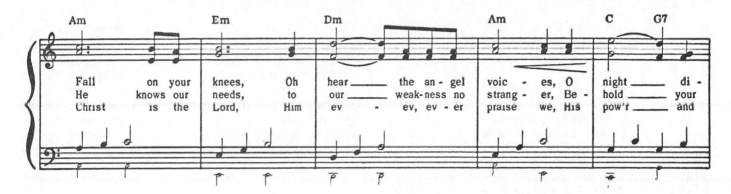

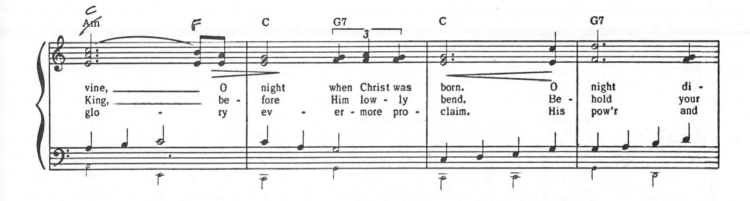

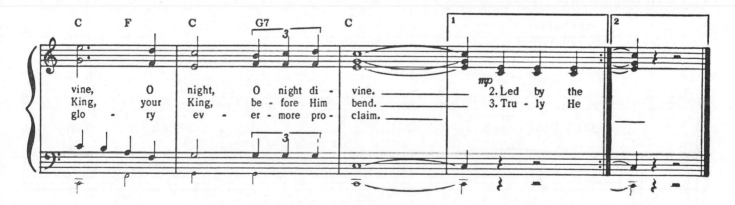

Non-chordal notes

✳ **Try this variation.**

219

TRIPLETS PRESENT A continuing problem for people in awe of composers. How can you play three notes in the time of two? Either by playing a computer or re-timing the composer's notes. Here is the second bar of the chorus of *Blueberry Hill* (see below). And beneath it is a suggestion for re-timing and counting the notes to play them.

Blueberry hill

Lyrics and music by
AL LEWIS, LARRY STOCK
and VINCENT ROSE

THIS ONE IS DELIVERED in A-A-B-A form. Beware of one treatment through A-1 and A-2 because that's sixteen unvaried bars. A few suggestions: A-1 in crossed-hands style; A-2 in locked-hands style; B as a single-line melody over an arpeggio; and the final A-3 as blocked melody over arpeggio. Other ideas: throw some non-chordals into the A-3 arpeggio; use shuffle rhythm for one part.

Part begins here.

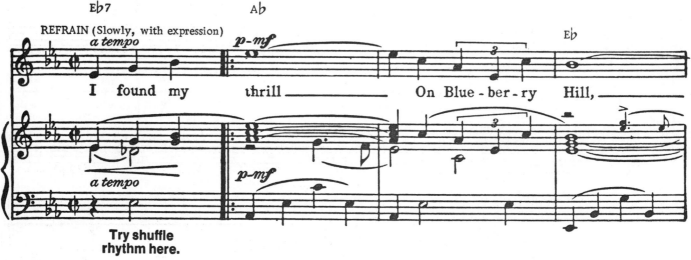

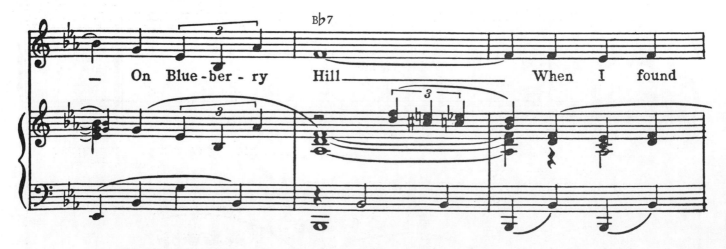

Ida! Sweet as apple cider!

Lyrics by EDDIE LEONARD
Music by EDDIE MUNSON

NOTE THE DISTANCE between the 1st and 2nd endings. If you stop after the 1st, you haven't played the full chorus. You must go back to the double line and play it again, Sam. This time skip the 1st and play the 2nd only. And that's how to fit 32 bars on one page.

You'd be so nice to come home to

Lyrics and music by
COLE PORTER

THE ARRANGEMENT —and not the tune—gives a song its feeling. The printed setting (not shown) calls for a skeleton treatment, thus creating a bouncy feeling. But put an arpeggio under the tune and the story changes. You can also play it as a bolero and produce an entirely different effect on listeners.

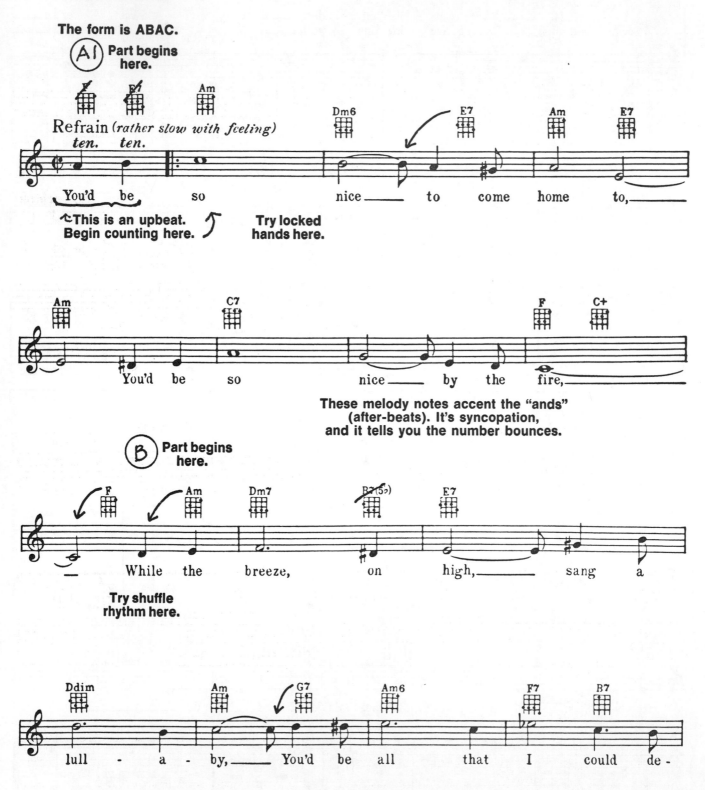

The form is ABAC.

A Part begins here.

Refrain *(rather slow with feeling)*

You'd be so nice to come home to,

↶ **This is an upbeat. Begin counting here.**

Try locked hands here.

You'd be so nice by the fire,

These melody notes accent the "ands" (after-beats). It's syncopation, and it tells you the number bounces.

B Part begins here.

While the breeze, on high, sang a

Try shuffle rhythm here.

lull - a - by, You'd be all that I could de-

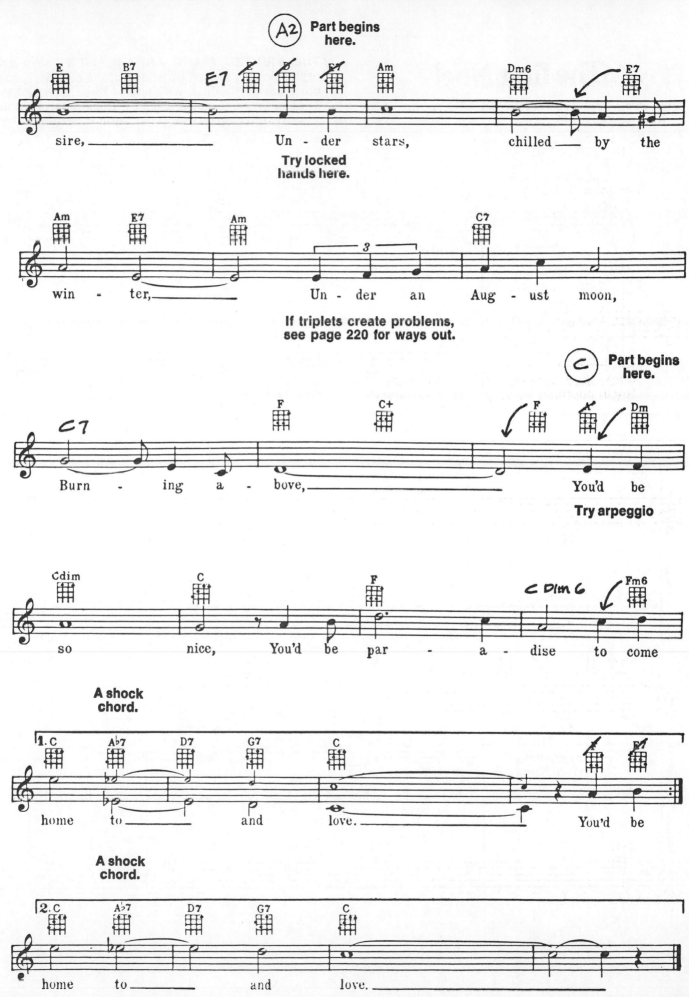

The first Noel

TRADITIONAL

THE PRINTED PIANO ARRANGEMENT lays out a professionally patterned attack of the chords. Two per bar most of the time, with one or three now and then. That suggests skeleton mixed with skeleton variations or with 10th chords. Heed the pattern or tempt chaos.

Moderately slow

1. The ___ first ___ No - el the ___ an - gel did

Basic skeleton — **Skeleton variation**

say, Was to cer - tain poor shep - herds in fields as they

lay; In ___ fields ___ where ___ they lay ___ keep - ing their

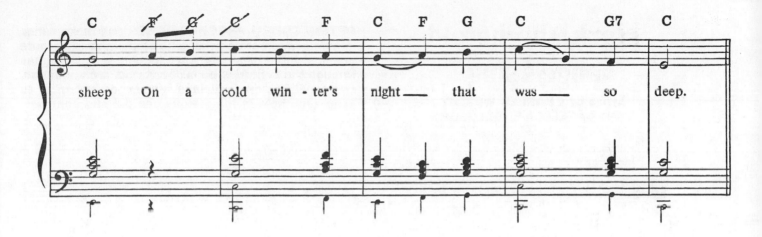

sheep On a cold win-ter's night___ that was___ so deep.

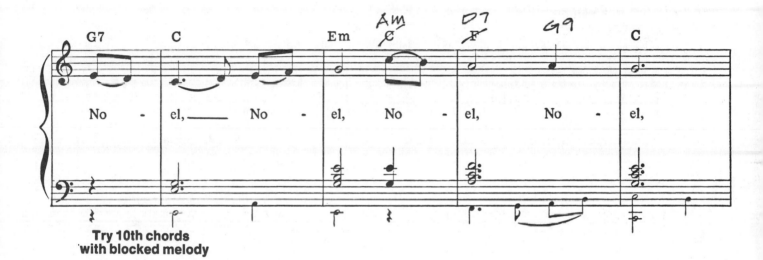

No - el,___ No - el, No - el, No - el,

Try 10th chords with blocked melody

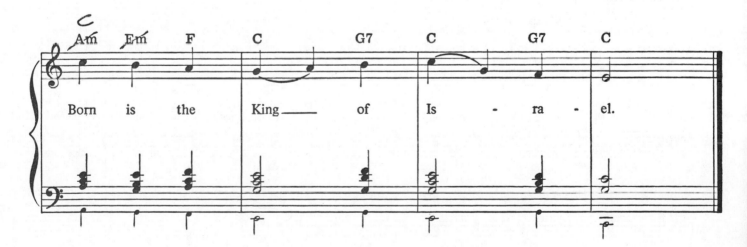

Born is the King___ of Is - ra - el.

Basic skeleton   Skeleton variation

Hark! the herald angels sing

Lyrics by CHARLES WESLEY
Music by FELIX MENDELSSOHN

Jingle bells

**Lyrics and music by
J.S. PIERPONT**

LOOK AT THE LEFT HAND piano part in this professionally-made arrangement. It's busy when the melody is sparse, and sparse when the melody is busy. Go thou and do likewise. By the way, the chorus is excellent material for play-by-ear training. Not so the verse as its chords use more of the circle.

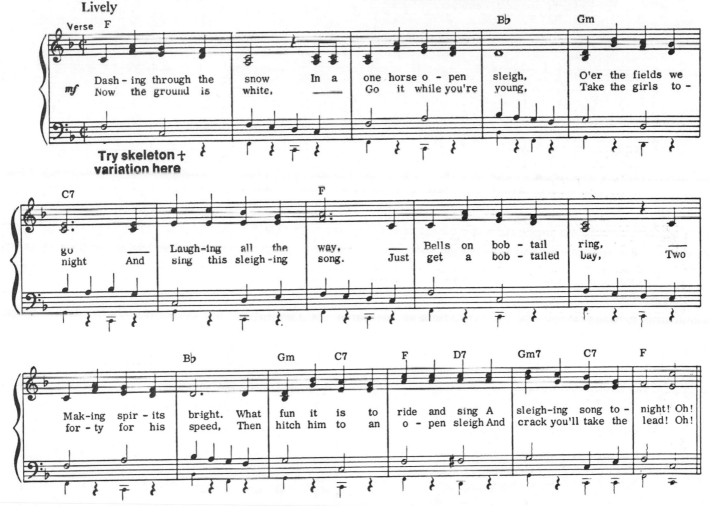

Try skeleton + variation here

Try 10th chords with blocked melody

Where or when

Lyrics by LORENZ HART
Music by RICHARD RODGERS

AVOID MONOTONY BY ARRANGING in parts. This one is an AABA. So, try locked hands for AI, crossed hands for A2, an arpeggio for B, etc. But save your fullest sound for the finish. The inserted chord in the second line is another way out of monotony. Ab6 and Fm7 contain the same notes. But the roots are different. Changing those bass notes gives the feeling of movement and variety.

Copyright © 1937 by Chappell & Co., Inc.
Copyright Renewed

230

231

My gal Sal

**Lyrics and music by
PAUL DRESSER**

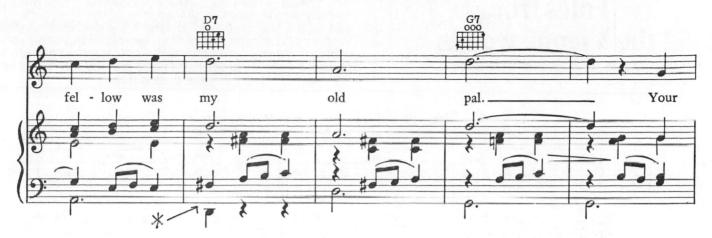

fel - low was my old pal._____ Your

trou - bles, sor - rows, and care _____ she was al - ways

10th chords are indicated here.

will - ing to share._____ A wild sort of dev - il, But

Try arpeggio + 10th chord

dead on the lev - el, was my gal Sal._____

dim. e rit.

＊**10th chords**

Tales from the Vienna woods

Music by JOHANN STRAUSS

AN "EASY-TO-PLAY" ARRANGEMENT, meaning "mostly single notes in the middle of the keyboard." But as the left-hand part shows, it's just a shorthand version of the oom-pah-pah so typical of the Strauss waltz, so clearly a skeleton setting. How to find chords when no symbols are printed? The melody will tell you (see page 178). So will the bass notes.

Use 6th chords if you like . . .

. . . but Maj7th are too modern for this antique.

O Christmas tree

TRADITIONAL

A VERY GOOD TUNE TO experiment with in enlarging the chord progression. As printed, it's the most basic of Elementary Classical—from home base F to one neighbor, C. But look at the inserted chords. A backward jump *four* stops and then clockwise home, naturally.

Joy to the world

**Lyrics and music by
GEORGE F. HANDEL and ISAAC WATTS**

THIS MELODY WAS WRITTEN by Handel, who doubtless had professional performers in mind—full orchestra and chorus. To match that history, the more orchestral the setting the better. Try a full-block treatment with nine or ten fingers at work together, stacking up as many chord notes below the melody as possible.

With spirit

Try full blocks here.

1. Joy to the world! The Lord is come; Let earth re- ceive her King; Let ev- 'ry heart pre- pare Him room And heav'n and na- ture sing, And heav'n and na- ture sing, And heav'n and heav'n and na- ture sing.

2. Joy to the world! The Sav- ior reigns; Let men their songs em- ploy, While fields and floods, Rocks, hills, and plains Re- peat the sound- ing joy, Re- peat the sound- ing joy, Re- peat, re- peat the sound- ing joy.

Try open voicing

Try full blocks here.

Deck the halls

TRADITIONAL

A VERY BUSY MELODY. Consequently you don't need all those chords printed in this arrangement. For the same reason, a skeleton treatment will probably do. But if you decide to mix it with any variations— well, there's a ready-made pattern in the two bars at the end of each line straight down the page.

Try basic skeleton here

Try 10th chords with blocked melody

1. Deck the halls with boughs of hol - ly,
2. See the blaz - ing yule be - fore us,
3. Fast a - way the old year pass - es,
Fa la la la la la la la la!

'Tis the sea - son to be jol - ly,
Strike the harp and join the chor - us,
Hail the new, ye lads and lass - es,
Fa la la la la la la la la!

Don we now our gay ap - par - el,
Fol - low me in mer - ry mea - sure,
Sing we joy - ous all to - geth - er,
Fa la la la la la la la la!

Troll the an - cient yule - tide car - ol,
While I tell of yule - tide trea - sure,
Heed - less of the wind and wea - ther,
Fa la la la la la la la la!

Good King Wenceslas

TRADITIONAL

ANOTHER INSTANCE of a too-busy chord background. Those crossed-out can be easily missed. If you want to do something much more effective with the harmony than pile chord on chord, look at the B and A chords inserted in the third line. They enlarge the progression to a longer backward jump on the circle.

* A longer jump backward on circle.

Silent night

Lyrics by JOSEPH MOHR
Music by FRANZ GRUBER

A VERY GOOD SONG TO practice playing by ear. Chord changes are few and the progression is Elementary Classical. But get the tune in mind first. Now, as to arranging it: try an arpeggio mixed with open voicing or with 10th chords. When to change the setting? The lyrics will give you a pattern that makes sense.

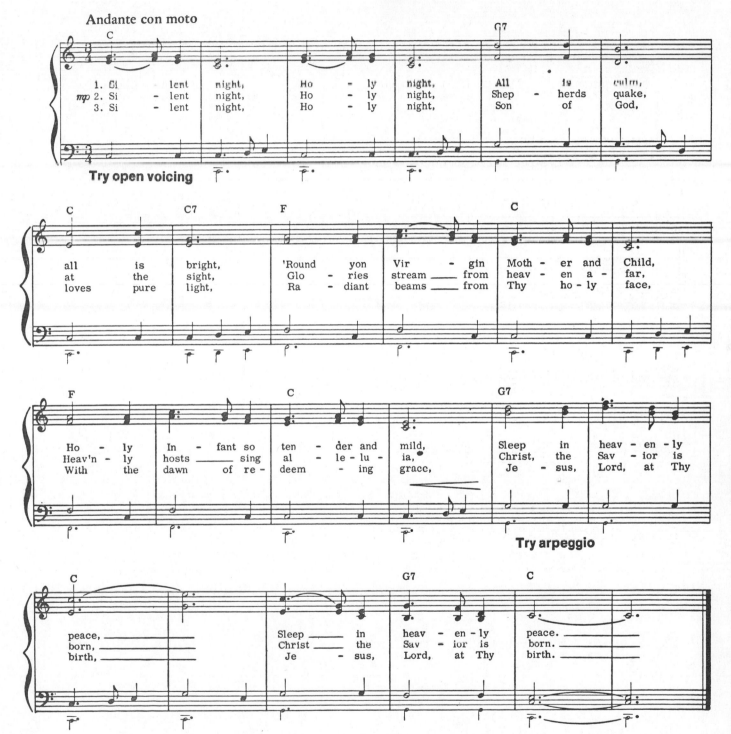

only a home base chord and its two neighbors.